Multimedia Information Storage and Retrieval:
Techniques and Technologies

Philip K.C. Tse
University of Hong Kong, China

IGI PUBLISHING

Hershey • New York

Acquisition Editor: Kristin Klinger
Development Editor: Kristin Roth
Senior Managing Editor: Jennifer Neidig
Managing Editor: Jamie Snavely
Assistant Managing Editor: Carole Coulson
Copy Editor: April Schmidt
Typesetter: Michael Brehm
Cover Design: Lisa Tosheff
Printed at: Yurchak Printing Inc.

Published in the United States of America by
        IGI Publishing (an imprint of IGI Global)
        701 E. Chocolate Avenue
        Hershey PA 17033
        Tel: 717-533-8845
        Fax: 717-533-8661
        E-mail: cust@igi-global.com
        Web site: http://www.igi-global.com

and in the United Kingdom by
        IGI Publishing (an imprint of IGI Global)
        3 Henrietta Street
        Covent Garden
        London WC2E 8LU
        Tel: 44 20 7240 0856
        Fax: 44 20 7379 0609
        Web site: http:/www.eurospanbookstore.com

Library of Congress Cataloging-in-Publication Data

Tse, Philip K. C.
  Multimedia information storage and retrieval : techniques and technologies / Philip K. C. Tse, author.
     p. cm.
  Summary: "This book offers solutions to the challenges of storage and manipulation of a variety of media types providing data placement techniques, scheduling methods, caching techniques and emerging character-istics of multimedia information. Academicians, students, professionals and practitioners in the multimedia industry will benefit from this ground-breaking publication"--Provided by publisher.
  Includes bibliographical references and index.
  ISBN-13: 978-1-59904-225-1 (hardcover)
  ISBN-13: 978-1-59904-227-5 (ebook)
  1. Multimedia systems. 2. Information storage and retrieval systems. 3. Information resources management. I. Title.
  QA76.575.T78 2008
  006.7--dc22
                         2007031978

British Cataloguing in Publication Data
A Cataloguing in Publication record for this book is available from the British Library.

All work contributed to this book is new, previously-unpublished material. The views expressed in this book are those of the authors, but not necessarily of the publisher.

Multimedia Information Storage and Retrieval:

Techniques and Technologies

Table of Contents

Section I:
Background

Section IIb:
Data Placement on Hierarchical Storage Systems

Section III:
Disk Scheduling Methods

Section IV:
Data Migration

Section V:
Cache Replacement Policy

Foreword

Most systems nowadays are designed with multimedia functionalities irrespective of the applications domain, and in many applications, the multimedia component is central to the operation of the system. A key requirement of many multimedia and visual information systems is the ability to locate and retrieve relevant data objects. Compared with conventional database processing, such as OLTP (Online Transaction Processing) and OLAP (Online Analytic Processing), the data intensity in such systems in terms of size and volume tends to be much greater. At the same time, performance constraints on multimedia data delivery are also more stringent, since failure to retrieve data in time may mean that the progress of a song or a movie has to be undesirably interrupted.

Although secondary and tertiary storage technologies have improved substantially in recent years, they are still several orders of magnitude slower than processor speed, and such a substantial performance gap is likely to persist for some time into the future. Therefore, it is vital that algorithms and strategies are developed and deployed to optimize storage performance and behavior. Such performance enhancement strategies generally take a number of forms, some of which are static and some dynamic.

First, data must be judiciously situated and positioned so that their location and retrieval may be carried out efficiently. This involves exploiting the characteristics of both the data objects and the storage structure. Without a sound data placement strategy, optimal processing will not be possible. Different methods of data placement for multimedia processing are systematically and exhaustively treated in Section IIa of this book. The extension of such techniques for hierarchical storage systems represents a different level of complexity and is carefully developed in Section IIb of the book.

While data placement corresponds to the relatively static aspect of processing, the dynamic operations invariably involve considerable choices and optimizations. These relate to the scheduling of data requests, the staging and migration of data, and cache management so as to meet the performance constraints. These topics as well as the underlying ideas are systematically built up and treated in Section III, Section IV, and Section V of the book, respectively.

Throughout this book, all relevant concepts and principles are systematically and lucidly explained, and the expositions are always accompanied by carefully designed diagrams and illustrations. In any serious performance analysis, the use of mathematical modeling is unavoidable. The mathematics in the book are presented in a lucid style, and the notations adopted are natural, making the mathematical developments easy to understand and follow.

Systems designers will find the wealth of techniques and analysis presented in the book an indispensable resource. Students of multimedia systems and advanced databases will find the treatment of topics and development of ideas in the book valuable to their understanding of efficient multimedia storage systems. Researchers of multimedia and database systems will find the book a vital source of reference. The unique and systematic coverage of topics in the book will make it an important and up-to-date resource for many types of readers.

Clement Leung
Foundation Chair in Computer Science
Victoria University, Australia

Clement Leung: Prior to taking up his present Foundation Chair in Computer Science at Victoria University, Australia, Clement Leung held an Established Chair in Computer Science at the University of London. His publications include two books and well over 100 research articles. His services to the research community include serving as program chair, program co-chair, keynote speaker, panel expert, and on the program committee and steering committee of major international conferences in the U.S., Europe, Australia, and Asia. In addition to contributing to the editorship of a number of international journals, he has also served as the Chairman of the International Association for Pattern Recognition Technical Committee on Multimedia and Visual Information Systems, as well as well as on the International Standards (ISO) MPEG-7 committee responsible for generating standards for digital multimedia, where he played an active role in shaping the influential MPEG-7 International Standard. He is listed in *Who's Who in Australia*, *Who's Who in the World*, *Great Minds of the 21st Century*, *Dictionary of International Biography*, and *Who's Who in Australasia & Pacific Nations*. He is a Fellow of the British Computer Society and a Fellow of the Royal Society of Arts, Manufactures and Commerce.

Preface

This book explains the techniques to store and retrieve multimedia information in multimedia storage systems. It describes the internal architecture of storage systems. Readers will be able to learn the internal architectures of multimedia storage systems. Many techniques are described with details. Examples are provided to help readers understand the techniques. By understanding these techniques, we hope that readers may also apply similar techniques in the problems that they encounter in their everyday life. In particular, this book would be helpful to managers who wish to improve the performance of their multimedia storage systems.

To the best of our knowledge, there are many books about multimedia information and only a few books discuss the storage systems in detail. Only one of them describes the storage and retrieval methods for multimedia information. However, none of them have discussed the storage and retrieval methods in hierarchical storage systems. Therefore, we consider it necessary to explain the storage techniques for multimedia information on storage systems and hierarchical storage systems in a new book. This book discusses the research on multimedia information storage and retrieval techniques.

This book focuses on the storage and retrieval methods. Some other techniques, though somewhat related, are however outside the scope of this book. Those topics include security of multimedia data in the storage systems, protocols to deliver multimedia information across the networks, and real time processing of multimedia information. Readers can easily find these topics from other books.

This book is divided into the following six sections:

1. Background information in Section I.
2. Data placement on disks in Section IIa.
3. Data placement on hierarchical storage systems in Section IIb.
4. Disk scheduling methods in Section III.
5. Data migration methods in Section IV.
6. Cache replacement policies in Section V.

We start this book with the background of multimedia storage technology in Section I. Multimedia applications process digital media that were only present in the entertainment industry. Multimedia information systems process digital media data according to the needs in these applications. Data compression is vital to the success of multimedia information systems and we explain two image and video compression standards. Traditional storage systems need to be enhanced or improved to support the data storage and retrieval operations. The characteristics of multimedia access patterns have significant impacts on the performance of the storage systems.

In Section IIa, "Data Placement on Disks," we describe the data placement methods that organize the storage locations of multimedia data on disks. Data placement methods organize the multimedia data according to the characteristics of multimedia data access patterns. New techniques have been designed to improve the performance of multimedia storage servers to an acceptable level. Data placement methods are grouped according to the strategies being applied, including statistical placement, striping, replication, and constraint allocation.

In Section IIb, "Data Placement on Hierarchical Storage Systems," we describe the storage organization of multimedia data on hierarchical storage systems. Data placement methods have been designed to achieve efficient retrievals of multimedia data. The data placements are categorized according to the strategy in use, including contiguous placement, statistical placement, striping, and constraint allocation.

In Section III, "Disk Scheduling Methods," the disk scheduling methods that rearrange the service sequences of the waiting requests are described. The methods that schedule normal disk requests are first described. The feasibility conditions to merge concurrent streams are then followed. After that, we describe the scheduling methods for streams of multimedia requests.

In Section IV, "Data Migration," we show the methods to migrate data across the storage levels of the hierarchical storage systems. Data residing on the hierarchical storage systems are migrated from high levels with high access latency to lower levels with low access latency. Staging methods move multimedia objects across the storage level via staging buffers. Time slicing method accesses objects in time slices in order to reduce the start-up latency of streams. Pipelining methods minimize the start-up latency and staging buffer size for multimedia streams.

In Section V, "Cache Replacement Policy," the cache replacement methods of multimedia servers are described. Efficient cache replacement policies on these servers keep the objects with high access probability on the cache. They improve the cache replacement methods of multimedia streams so that multimedia data can be delivered efficiently over the Internet. Memory caching methods replace objects with low cache value so that high cache value objects can be kept for efficient cache performance. Stream dependent caching methods assign cache values to object segments in order to improve the cache efficiency for multimedia objects. Cooperative proxy servers share their Web cache contents so that the cache performs efficiently when similar objects are accessed by their clients.

The organization of chapters in this book is as follows:

1. Background in Section I.
   a. Introduction in Chapter I.
   b. Multimedia information in Chapter II.
   c. Architectures of storage systems in Chapter III.
   d. Data compression techniques and standards in Chapter IV.
2. Data placement on disks in Section IIa.
   a. Statistical placement on disks in Chapter V.
   b. Striping on disks in Chapter VI.
   c. Replication placement on disks in Chapter VII.
   d. Constraint allocation on disks in Chapter VIII.
3. Data placement on hierarchical storage systems in Section IIb.

In Chapter I, "Introduction," we give an overview of the techniques that are covered in this book. The techniques are described briefly according to the division of parts in this book.

In Chapter II, "Multimedia Information," we start with describing the characteristics of multimedia data. Some applications that are involved in using and processing multimedia information are listed as examples. The representations of multimedia data show how the large and bulky multimedia data are represented and compressed. The multimedia data are also accessed in request streams. Readers who are familiar with multimedia processing may skip this chapter.

In Chapter III, "Storage System Architectures," the architectures of storage systems are explained. Multimedia systems are similar to traditional computers systems in term of their architectures. Multimedia computer systems are built with stringent processing time requirements. The components of the computer system, including the storage servers, need to process a large amount of data in parallel within a guaranteed time frame. The storage server needs to access data continuously to the clients according to the clients' requests. Multimedia objects are large and the magnetic hard disks need to access segments of the objects within a short time. These requirements lead to the emergence of constant recording density disks and zoned disks. Readers who have deep understandings of the computer storage architectures may skip some descriptions and go to the performance equations immediately.

In Chapter IV, "Data Compression Techniques and Standards," the data compression techniques and standards are described. We describe the general compression model, text compression, image compression and JPEG2000, and video compression and MPEG2. These data compression techniques are helpful to understand the multimedia data being stored and retrieved.

In Chapter V, "Statistical Placement on Disks," two statistical placement methods are described. The statistical placement strategy is based on the difference in access characteristics of the multimedia streams. The frequency based placement method optimizes the average request response time. It uses an algorithm to place the objects according to their access frequencies. The bandwidth based placement method places objects according to their data rates. The storage system maintains its optimal performance according to the object data transfer time without reorganizations. Readers may find this chapter useful in other situations which involve probabilities.

In Chapter VI, "Striping on Disks," three striping methods are explained in detail. Multimedia streams need continuous data supply. The aggregate data access requirement of many multimedia streams imposes very high demand on the access bandwidth of the storage servers. The disk striping or data striping methods spread data over multiple disks to provide high aggregate disk throughput. The simple striping methods increase the efficiency of serving concurrent multimedia streams. Multimedia streams access the data stripes according to their actual data consumption rates. The disk bandwidth and the memory buffer are used efficiently. The staggered striping method provides effective support for multiple streams accessing different objects from a group of striped disks, and it automatically balances the workload among disks. The pseudorandom placement method maintains that the data stripes are evenly distributed on disks and it reduces the number of data stripes being moved when the number of disks increases or decreases. It reduces the workload on data reorganization when disks are added or removed.

In Chapter VII, "Replication Placement on Disks," several replication placement methods on disks are shown. When extra storage space is available, the storage system may keep extra copies of the stored objects. Extra copies of objects may be able to increase the storage system performance. The recent trend of technology shows that storage capacity is increased at a faster pace than the access bandwidth. Storage capacity may not be a problem when compared to the access bandwidth. The replication strategy applies redundancy to increase reliability of the storage system and availability of the stored objects. It reduces network load, start-up latency. It avoids disk multitasking. It maintains the balance of space and workload.

In Chapter VIII, "Constraint Allocation on Disks," two constraint allocation methods are described. Constraint allocation methods limit the available locations to store the data stripes. They reduce the overheads of serving concurrent streams from the same storage device. The maximum overheads in accessing data from the storage devices are lowered. When many streams access the same hot object, the phase based constraint allocation supports more streams with less seek actions. The region based allocation limits the longest seek distance among requests.

In Chapter IX, "Tertiary Storage Devices," the tertiary storage devices are detailed. Several types of storage devices, including magnetic tapes, optical disks, and optical tapes, are available to be used at the tertiary storage level in hierarchical storage systems. These storage devices are composed of fixed storage drives and removable media units. The storage drives are fixed to the computer system. The removable media unit can be removed from the drives so that the storage capacity can be expanded with more media units. When data on a media are accessed, the media unit is accessed from their normal location. One of the storage drives on the computer system is chosen. If there is a media unit in the storage drive, the old media unit is unloaded and ejected. The new media unit is then loaded to the drive. Readers who are familiar with the robotic tape libraries may skip this chapter and directly move on to the placement methods.

In Chapter X, "Contiguous Placement on Hierarchical Storage Systems," two contiguous placement methods are described. The contiguous placement is the most common method to place traditional data files on tertiary storage devices. The storage space in the media units is checked. The data file is stored on a media unit with enough space to store the data file. When tertiary storage devices are used to store multimedia objects, the objects are stored and retrieved similar to traditional data files. Since the main application of the tertiary storage devices is to back up multimedia objects from computers, the objectives of the contiguous method are (1) to support back up of multimedia objects efficiently and (2) to reduce the number of separate media units that are used to store an object.

In Chapter XI, "Statistical Placement on Hierarchical Storage Systems," we describe the statistical strategy to place multimedia objects on hierarchical storage systems. The objective of the data placement methods is to minimize the time to access object from the hierarchical storage system. The statistical strategy changes the statistical time to access objects so that the mean access time is optimal. The frequency based placement method differentiates objects according to their access frequencies. The objects that are more frequently accessed are placed in the more convenient locations. The objects that are less frequently accessed are placed in the less convenient locations.

In Chapter XII, "Striping on Hierarchical Storage Systems," two striping techniques are explained with details. The data striping technique has been successfully applied on disks to reduce the time to access objects from the disks. Thus, the striping technique has been investigated to reduce the time to access objects from the tape libraries in a similar manner. Similar to the striping on disks, the objective of the parallel striping method is to reduce the time to access objects from the tape libraries. The parallel tape striping directly applies the striping technique to place data stripes on tapes. The triangular placement method changes the order in which data stripes are stored on tapes to further enhance the performance.

In Chapter XIII, "Constraint Allocation on Hierarchical Storage Systems," two approaches to provide constraint allocations on different types of media units are described. Multimedia objects are large in size, but the access latency of hierarchical storage systems is high. The hierarchical storage systems need to provide high throughput in delivering data. Multimedia streams should be displayed with continuity. Depending on the data migration method, the whole object or only partial object is retrieved prior to the beginning of consumption. The constraint allocation methods limit the freedom to place data on media units so that the worst case would never happen. They reduce the longest exchange time and/or the longest reposition time in accessing the objects. The interleaved contiguous placement limits the storage locations of data stripes on optical disks. The concurrent striping method limits the storage locations of data stripes on tapes.

In Chapter XIV, "Scheduling Methods for Disk Requests," two common disk scheduling methods are explained. Disk scheduling changes the sequence order to serve the requests that are waiting in the queue. While data placement reduces the access time of a disk request, scheduling reduces the waiting time of a request. The longer the waiting queue, the more useful is the scheduling method. When there are not any requests in the waiting queue, any scheduling methods perform the same. A disk scheduling policy changes the service order of waiting requests. It accepts the waiting requests and serves them in the new service sequence. The first-in-first-out policy serves requests in the same order as the incoming order of the waiting requests. The SCAN scheduling method serves the waiting requests in the order of their accessing physical track locations to serve the requests efficiently.

In Chapter XV, "Feasibility Conditions of Concurrent Streams," we prove the feasibility conditions to accept homogeneous and heterogeneous streams to a storage system. Multimedia storage systems store data objects and receive streams of requests from the multimedia server. When a client wishes to display an object, it sends a new object request for the multimedia object to the multimedia server. The multimedia server checks to see if this new stream can be accepted. The server encapsulates the data stripe of the accepted streams as data packets and sends them to the client. The server sends data requests periodically to the storage system. Each of these data requests has a deadline associated with it. Every request of a stream, except the first one, must be served within the deadline to ensure continuity of the stream. We prove that heterogeneous streams can be accepted when their streams accessing patterns satisfy the feasibility conditions. Readers may skip the proofs of the equations in this chapter in the first reading.

In Chapter XVI, "Scheduling Methods for Request Streams," we describe three scheduling methods for multimedia streams of requests. These scheduling methods use either serve requests according to their deadline or serve the stream in round robin cycle in order to provide real-time continuity guarantee. They all use the SCAN scheduling method to improve the efficiency in serving requests. The earliest deadline first scheduling method serves requests according to their deadlines so that the requests would not wait too long and miss their deadlines. The SCAN-EDF scheduling method serves requests with the same deadline in the SCAN order. It improves the efficiency of the storage system using the EDF scheduling method. The group sweeping scheduling method serves groups of streams in round-robin cycles. It improves the efficiency of the storage system and provides real-time continuity guarantees to the streams. It is also fair to all the streams by serving one request of every stream in each cycle.

In Chapter XVII, "Staging Methods," we describe one of the data migration methods. Data migration is the process of moving data from tertiary storage devices to secondary storage devices in hierarchical storage systems. The three approaches to migrate multimedia data objects across the storage levels are staging, time slicing, and pipelining. The staging method accesses an object using two stages. The staging method is simple and flexible. It is suitable for any type of data on any tertiary storage systems. Some readers may find the staging method is simple and just browse through this chapter.

In Chapter XVIII, "Time Slicing Method," the time slicing method is described. Tertiary storage devices provide huge storage capacity at low cost. Multimedia objects stored on the tertiary storage devices are accessed with high latency. The time slicing method is designed to reduce the start up latency in accessing multimedia objects from tertiary storage devices. The start-up latency is lowered by reducing the amount of data being migrated before consumption begins. The time slicing method accesses objects at the unit of slices instead of objects. Streams can start to respond at an earlier time.

In Chapter XIX, "Normal Pipelining," the first pipelining method is introduced. Three pipelining methods, including normal pipelining, space efficient pipelining, and segmented pipelining, can be used to access multimedia objects with minimal start-up latency. Apart from reducing the start up latency, the pipelining methods also reduce the usage of the staging buffers. The normal pipelining method finds the minimum fraction of the object before the stream can start to display it. The formula to find minimum size of the first slices is explained. The pipelining method minimizes the start-up latency for the tertiary storage devices whose data transfer rate is lower than the data consumption rate of the objects.

In Chapter XX, "Space Efficient Pipelining," the space efficient pipelining method is explained. The space efficient pipelining method is designed for pipelining objects from low bandwidth storage devices for display. It retrieves data at a rate lower than the data consumption rate. It keeps the front part of objects resident on disk cache to start a new stream at disk latency. It uses the disk space efficiently to handle more streams. The basic policy reuses the circular buffer to store the later slices of the objects. The shrinking buffer policy reduces the circular buffer size after a slice is displayed. It is particularly useful when the circular disk buffer constraint is tight. The space stealing policy reuses the storage space containing the head of the object as part of the circular buffer.

In Chapter XXI, "Segmented Pipelining," the segmented pipelining method to reduce the latency in serving interactive requests is presented and analyzed.

The segmented pipelining method divides objects into segments and slices so that the object can be pipelined from the hierarchical storage system. The segmented pipelining method is analyzed in terms of disk space requirement and the reposition latency. It uses small extra disk space to support object previews and efficient interactive functions. It can offer extra flexibility in controlling the amount of disk space usage by adjusting the storage location of the preload data. The segmented pipelining is an efficient and flexible data migration method for the multimedia objects on hierarchical storage systems.

Multimedia objects can be stored in the content servers on the Internet. When clients access multimedia objects from a content server, the content server must have sufficient disk and network to deliver the objects to the clients. Otherwise, it rejects the requests from the new clients. The server and network workloads are important concerns in designing multimedia storage systems over the Internet. The Internet caching technique helps to reduce the number of repeated requests for the same objects from popular content servers. As caching consumes myriad storage space, the cache performance is significantly affected by the cache size. Cache admission policies determine whether a newly accessed object should be stored onto the cache devices. Cache replacement policies decide which objects should be removed to release space. The cache replacement policy can be divided into memory caching and stream dependent caching.

In Chapter XXII, "Memory Caching Methods," we describe several replacement policies in memory caching. Memory cache replacement policies assign a cache value to each object in the cache. This cache value decides the priority of keeping the object in the cache. When space is needed to store a new object in cache, the cache replacement function will choose the object with the lowest cache value and delete it to release space. The objects with high cache values will remain in the cache. Different cache replacement policies assign different cache values to the objects. The traditional LRU method keeps the objects that are accessed most recently. It is simple and easy to implement and the time complexity is very low. The LFU, LUV, and mix methods keep track of the object temperature and remove the coldest objects from the cache first. The LRU-min, GD-size, LUV, and mix methods keep the small and recently accessed objects in the cache. The GD-size, LUV, and mix methods also include latency cost of objects in the cache to lower the priority of objects that can be easily replaced.

In Chapter XXIII, "Stream Dependent Caching," the stream dependent caching methods that guarantee continuous delivery for multimedia streams are described. The storage techniques on stream dependent caching include resident leader, variable length segmentation, video staging, hotspot caching, and interval caching. They will divide each multimedia object into smaller segments and store selected segments on the cache level. The resident leader method trades off the average response time of requests to reduce the maximum response time of streams. The variable length segmentation method divides the objects into segments of increasing length so that large segments may be deleted to release space more efficiently. The video staging method retrieves high bandwidth segments to reduce the necessary WAN bandwidth for streaming. The hotspot caching method creates the hotspot segments of objects to provide fast object previews from local cache. The interval caching method keeps the shortest intervals of video to maintain the continuity of streams from the local cache content. The layer based caching method adapts the quality of streams to the cache efficiency. It uses the continuity and completeness as metrics to measure the suitability of the caching method for multimedia streams. The cost based method for wireless clients reduces the quality distortion over the error-prone wireless networks with the help of the cache content. The cache values of the segments are composed of the network cost, the start-up latency cost, and the quality distortion cost.

In Chapter XXIV, "Cooperative Web Caching," we describe how Web caches cooperate to raise the overall cache performance on the Internet. Hierarchical Web caching reduces network latency on requests. Front and rear partitioning reduces the start-up latency of streams. Directory based cooperation avoids the contention on parent proxy server. Hash based cooperation achieves low storage overheads and update overheads. Multiple hotspot caching keeps the hotspot blocks to provide fast local previews. The performances of various object partitioning methods in cooperative multimedia proxy servers are analyzed.

Acknowledgment

It is my pleasure to acknowledge the help of all involved in the writing, editing, and review of this book. Without their support, this book could not have been satisfactorily completed.

My first note of thanks goes to all the staff at IGI Global for their valuable contributions in the process. In particular, I would like to thank Kristin Roth and Corrina Chandler for their timely e-mails in keeping the schedule of this project. My special thanks go to Dr. Mehdi Khosrow-Pour whose invitation gave me a chance to write this book.

I would like to thank Professor Clement Leung for writing the foreword of this book. It is also his early invitation to write a book on multimedia storage that gave me motivation and courage to write this book.

I would like to thank my colleagues in the University of Hong Kong for being supportive and cooperative. My special thanks go to Professor Victor Li whose support and trust let me finish this book.

I owe my appreciation to my wife, Peky, for her consistent support with trust and love during the nights I was writing. I miss the time that I could spend with Joshua and Jonah who are growing up to understand the world.

Last but not least, I praise God for leading my life, answering my prayers, and fulfilling my needs during this work.

Section I

Background

We shall provide the background of multimedia storage techniques and technology in this part. The first chapter gives an introduction to the book. Multimedia information is described in Chapter II. The architectures of storage systems are described in Chapter III. The data compression techniques and standards are explained in Chapter IV.

Chapter I

Introduction

This book explains the techniques to store and retrieve multimedia information in multimedia storage systems. It describes the internal architecture of storage systems. Readers will be able to learn the internal architectures of multimedia storage systems. Many techniques are described with details. Examples are provided to help readers understand the techniques. By understanding these techniques, we hope that readers may also apply similar techniques in the problems that they encounter in their everyday life.

This book focuses on storage and retrieval methods. Some other techniques, though somewhat related, are outside the scope of this book. These topics may include security of multimedia data in the storage systems, streaming protocols to deliver multimedia information across the networks, recognition of information from multimedia data, and real time processing of multimedia information. Readers may find information on these techniques in many other books. To our understanding, the data placement techniques, disk scheduling methods, and data migration methods are three areas which are not sufficiently covered in the books on the market.

This book is divided into the following six sections:

1. Background information in Section I.
2. Data placement on disks in Section IIa.
3. Data placement on hierarchical storage systems in Section IIb.
4. Disk scheduling methods in Section III.
5. Data migration methods in Section IV.
6. Cache replacement policies in Section V.

The data placement methods are divided into Section IIa and Section IIb because they are similar but different techniques applied in different storage levels.

We start this book with the background multimedia information. Multimedia applications process digital media that were only present in the entertainment industry. Multimedia information systems process digital media data according to the needs in these applications. Traditional storage systems need to be enhanced or improved to support the data storage and retrieval operations. The characteristics of multimedia access patterns have significant impacts on the performance of the storage systems. New techniques have been designed to improve their performance to an acceptable level. Data placement methods organize the multimedia data according to the characteristics of multimedia data access patterns in disk and hierarchical storage systems. Disk scheduling methods rearrange the service sequences of the waiting requests. Data residing on the hierarchical storage systems are migrated from high levels with high access latency to lower levels with low access latency. Cache replacement policies improve the replacement methods of multimedia data for efficient cache performance over the Internet.

In the next chapter, we start with describing the characteristics of multimedia data. Some applications are involved in using and processing multimedia information. Several examples are shown to provide the basic understanding on the processing environment of multimedia information. The representations of multimedia data show how the large and bulky multimedia data are represented and compressed. The multimedia data are also accessed in request streams. Readers who are familiar with the multimedia information may skip this chapter and jump to the next chapter.

In Chapter III, the architectures of storage systems are explained with details. In order to process continuous multimedia streams, multimedia computer systems are built with stringent processing time requirements. When storage servers are designed to handle multimedia streams, the architecture of the storage servers also needs to handle the processing time requirements. The storage server needs to access data continuously for the clients according to the clients' requests. Multimedia objects are large and the magnetic hard disks needed to access segments of the objects within a short time. These requirements lead to the emergence of constant recording density disks and zoned disks. Readers who are familiar with the architectures of storage devices may skip this chapter.

In Chapter IV, the data compression techniques and standards are described. Because the performance of a computer system depends on the amount of data retrieved and the multimedia objects are large, the performance of the computer system can be enhanced by reducing the object sizes. Therefore, multimedia objects are always kept in their compressed form when they are stored, retrieved, and processed. We shall describe the commonly used compression techniques and compression standards in this chapter. We describe the general compression model, text compression, image compression and JPEG2000, and video compression and MPEG2. These data compression techniques are helpful to understand the multimedia data stored and retrieved.

The organization of chapters in this book includes:

1. Background in Section I.
    a. Introduction in Chapter I.
    b. Multimedia Information in Chapter II.
    c. Architectures of Storage Systems in Chapter III.
    d. Data Compression Techniques and Standards in Chapter IV.
2. Data placement on disks in Section IIa.
    a. Statistical Placement on disks in Chapter V.
    b. Striping on disks in Chapter VI.
    c. Replication Placement on disks in Chapter VII.
    d. Constraint Allocation in Chapter VIII.
3. Data placement on hierarchical storage systems in Section IIb.
    a. Tertiary Storage Devices in Chapter IX.

Chapter II

Multimedia Information

Introduction

To start this book, I shall first describe the characteristics of multimedia data. Then, some multimedia applications are listed. After these, I shall explain the representations of multimedia data. Lastly, the multimedia requests are presented as streams.

Multimedia Data

What is Multimedia Information?

Traditional data represent the logical meaning only of real world entities in computers. We use numbers such as 1, 2, 3, 4, and so on to represent values. Textual information is described by words. These words are built up by alphabets such as A, B, C, and D. We use drawings to represent spatial information graphically.

In order to capture the records of real world entities, images are recorded on films and handled by photographic equipment; sound is recorded on cassette tapes and CD-ROMs. Sound is also transmitted by telephones. Moving images (video) is recorded on tapes and transported physically. Everything is fine except that these are analog signals. Computers can only process and handle digital signals. As a result, all these real world entities could not be directly processed in computers.

The word "multimedia" is created by joining the two words "multiple" and "media" together. Multimedia data provide a direct representation of the physical world in the digital format. The multimedia data that we encounter everyday include photographs, X-ray images, sound, and video. Other multimedia data include drawings, charts, and animations. Any visible images and audible sound are multimedia data.

Digital Multimedia Data

Multimedia data are stored and processed in the digital format. Multimedia data are handled in the digital format with several benefits.

Digital data are 100% reproducible. Digital data are precise. Any difference can be compared and found out. It is inadvertent to making copies. Many exact copies can be produced that are the same as the digital original. Digital data are also independent of the storage media. New storage media may come out in the future. The same digital data can be copied or transferred to the new media when necessary.

In addition, digital data can be processed by computers to produce new software effects. For example, a digital photo can be blurred or sharpened. The colour of any part of the photo can be changed. The orientation of the photo can be rotated. Some image processing software, such are Microsoft imaging and Photoshop can easily perform these changes.

Digital data can be transmitted over the networks. Computers can transfer digital data from one end to another end of the networks. The ease of transmitting digital data brings the possibility of building new types of applications for multimedia information.

Multimedia Objects

A multimedia object is a separate unit of multimedia data that can be displayed independently. Many of these objects appear in daily life. Still images such as photographs and X-ray images are multimedia objects. Graphic charts are multimedia objects that are generated by reporting programs. Speech and voice are multimedia objects that are recorded. Music is one type of multimedia object that is composed. Animation graphics are artificial multimedia objects. Video and movies are multimedia objects recorded and edited by specialized producers.

In summary, multimedia data can directly represent real world entities in the digital format. Digital multimedia data can be processed by computer programs to produce software effects that were never before possible. Many multimedia objects can be found in daily life, and these objects can now be processed by computers.

Multimedia Applications

Many applications can make use of multimedia information to enhance the quality of their products.

The broadcast companies create and broadcast television programmes to the viewers. Cable television companies such as iCable® and OptusVision® in Australia transmit their encrypted audio and video programmes via dedicated network cables to the set-top box. The set-top box then decrypts and transmits these television signals to the television. The viewer can thus watch them on the television.

Television can also be provided via the Internet. Some Web sites containing live radio and live television programmes are available for listeners and viewers. Audience members who have missed some programmes may select to watch them again via browsers.

Movie producers create digital movies using computers and allow paid viewers to watch them. They may allow everyone to watch the advertising materials to attract more viewers. The music companies may produce song albums for artists. Amateur artists may directly produce their songs and publish them to increase their personal fame.

Video on-demand, or Interactive TV, systems show video to the viewers who have subscribed to watch the videos. They transmit selected video and audio objects according to user's choice. Education on-demand systems provide video of course lectures to students enrolled in the course. They help students in learning at their own pace. News-on-demand and sports-on-demand systems can provide instantaneous news and sports information to interesting viewers.

Remote communication and cooperation can be achieved by transmitting video and audio information. Video telephones transmit telephone and small video image over broadband networks. Microsoft Netmeeting® and CUSeeme® provide video conference over computers connected over the network. Collaborative computing can be achieved by synchronizing the working task over remote communications. Video e-mails may also enhance desynchronized communications. Voice over IP software reduces international telephone calls charges by using the Internet.

Commercial companies may install security monitoring systems that provide around-the-clock monitoring for the office and factory areas. Advanced systems may provide automatic alerts when too many video cameras are being watched by a few security officers. Multimedia information can also provide automatic quality control to enhance production. Video cameras can take images of products. Products with significant defects will be filtered and removed from the production line.

Visual information systems interactively search the multimedia databases using image and audio information. Many libraries have digitized their books and journals. With the support of government, many digital libraries have been built, and they are available to visitors around the world. Some museums have created an online version of some of their collections. These virtual museums allow virtual visitors to watch their collections online.

Hospitals install patient monitoring systems to monitor patients who are staying in intensive care units. The Earth Observatory System records and stores video information from satellites. The system produces petabytes (10^{15} bytes) of scientific data per year.

Multimedia information has always been used in the entertainment industry. Interactive video games can be enriched by high resolution graphics. Interactive stories can become a reality for story readers who may make their choice on how a story proceeds and ends.

Major System Configuration

A multimedia application system has to consider the data storage and distribution system, the data delivery network, and the delivery scheduling algorithms.

Data Storage and Distribution

Several data storage and distribution systems have been researched. These include the centralized system, the storage area network (SAN), the content distribution network (CDN), and the serverless or peer-to-peer (P2P) network.

The centralized system stores all the multimedia objects in one location. The storage area network stores the multimedia objects on several servers. These storage servers are connected over a local area network using optical fibres. The content distribution network distributes the multimedia objects on servers that are spread over a wide area network. Client requests are sent to the nearest server that contains the object to serve the request.

The serverless systems or peer-to-peer networks do not permanently store the objects on the servers. The server containing the object will only serve the first few requests for the object. Afterwards, the nodes that have the object will become the seed and serve other clients (Jeon & Nahrstedt, 2002). Thus, the server can become free, and it can be disconnected from the network.

Delivery Network and Scheduling

The data delivery network can be built by laying dedicated cables or by the Internet. The multimedia objects can be delivered via broadcasting or video-on-demand (VOD) systems. Depending on the delivery scheduling and the delivery network, at least four types of system architectures can be built.

The interactive television (ITV) companies build their systems by broadcasting over dedicated cables (Figure 2.1). In the systems, the users subscribe to an ITV company. The ITV company broadcasts a number of channels of

Figure 2.1. Broadcasting over dedicated cables

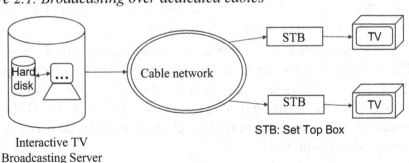

Figure 2.2. Video-on-demand over dedicated cables

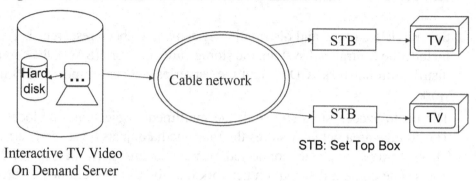

Figure 2.3. Broadcasting over the Internet

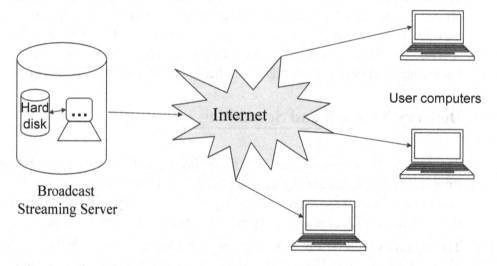

video content via a cable to a dedicated set-top box (STB). The STB is then connected to the television set. The user selects a channel to watch via a remote control unit of the STB (Furht, 1996).

The ITV companies may provide video-on-demand via dedicated cables (Figure 2.2). In the systems, the users subscribe to an ITV company. The ITV Company downloads a movie list to the Set Top box. User then selects a movie from the list using remote control of set top box. The ITV Company broadcasts the movie in a new channel to the user. Some user may join an existing channel to watch.

Figure 2.4. Video-on-demand over the Internet

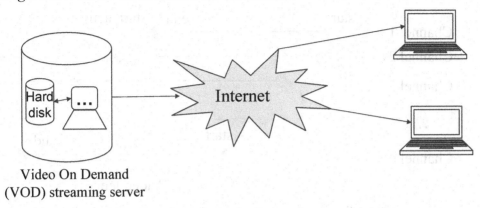

Video On Demand
(VOD) streaming server

The content providers may deliver multimedia objects by broadcasting over the Internet (Figure 2.3). Users first subscribe to a content provider on the Internet. They are then allowed to join a live video/audio channel. The content provider then delivers the live multimedia objects from the streaming servers to all users. Users then use their browser to receive and play streams.

The content providers may also provide video-on-demand services over the Internet (Figure 2.4). Users first subscribe to a content provider on the Internet, and the user may select a multimedia object from the content provider's Web site. The content provider then tests the streaming ability to the user's computer. The streaming server delivers the low or high resolution object suitable for delivery to the user. The browser on the user's computer receives and plays the streaming object.

Video-on-Demand Systems

Four different types of video-on-demand systems have been investigated (Furht, 1996). These include the near video-on-demand (NVOD) systems, true video-on-demand (TVOD) systems, partitioned video-on-demand (PVOD) systems, and dynamically allocated video-on-demand (DAVOD) systems.

In the true video-on-demand systems, the user has complete control of a multimedia program. The user can perform normal play, reverse play, fast forward, random positioning, pause, and resume. In this system, each user is allocated a unique channel during the total duration. It allows complete user interactivity. The number of concurrent users is however limited by the

Figure 2.5. Near video-on-demand system

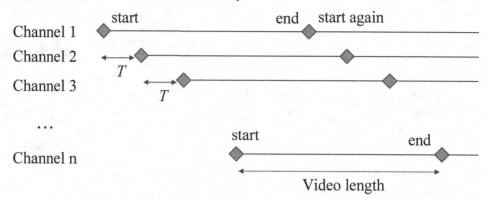

Consecutive channels start the same video with a time difference of *T* sec. User waits for a time period up to *T* seconds to watch a video from the beginning.

Figure 2.6. Partitioned video-on-demand systems

50 broadcast channels	450 interactive channels	
	Near VOD 250 channels	True VOD 200 channels

All channels are divided into broadcast channels and interactive channels. The interactive channels are subdivided into Near Video On Demand channels and True Video On Demand channels.

number of available channels. As a result, many potential viewers may not be able to access the system during the busy period of time.

The near video-on-demand system (Figure 2.5) provides video distribution at relatively low cost. This system however provides only limited user interactivity. A popular video is broadcast using several streams or channels. Each channel is separated from the previous channel at a fixed interval. When the user requests for this video, the user's access will be delayed until the start of the next stream.

The partitioned video-on-demand system (Figure 2.6) combines the advantages of both NVOD and TVOD systems. User interactivity is provided at the capacity of the system. Digital channels are partitioned into two groups: NVOD and TVOD services. NVOD channels broadcast the most popular video with limited user control. TVOD channels will provide complete user control functions. For example, the digital channels are divided into 50 broadcast channels and 450 interactive channels.

The dynamically allocated video-on-demand system is an extension of the PVOD scheme. The user, watching a video from the NVOD list of most popular videos, can request the interactivity with the video at any time. If a channel is available, the user will be switched to the TVOD group of channels which allows complete control. The split-and-merge (SAM) protocol provides a mechanism to split user streams for interactive functions and merge streams when possible (Liao & Li, 1997).

Video Conference System

In video conference systems (Figure 2.7), computers are each installed with a video camera, microphone, and connected to the network. A user initiates and hosts a conference meeting. Other users then join the meeting. All of them send their own video and audio signals to all the other users. Users may speak, type, or draw on whiteboard.

In these systems, the network needs to deliver the video capture stream from every user to all other users. The number of video streams is equal to $n(n-1)$ for n concurrent users. Thus, the network needs to support a very large number of streams.

Data Representations

Multimedia data types include numbers, text, graphics, animations, image, audio, and video. However, a computer can only handle digital data that

Figure 2.7. Video conference system

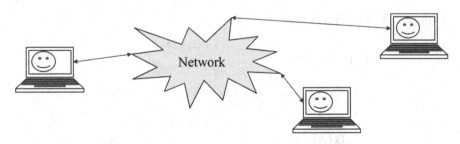

represents either 0 or 1. In this section, we shall describe how the computer represents multimedia data.

Numbers and Text

In computers, positive integers are represented as a number with the base of 2 instead of a base of 10. Negative integers are represented in the 2s complement form. Real numbers are divided into mantissa and exponent such that the significant digits are represented in the mantissa (Hennessy & Patterson, 1996).

Each text character is represented by eight bits called a byte in the computer. For ASCII representation, the binary byte of "0100 0001" represents an A, and "0100 0010" means B, and so on. An English word is thus represented by a string of bytes.

Graphics

Each position on the screen is specified as a coordinate (x, y), x-axis from left to right and y-axis from top to bottom. For example, in an 800 x 600 screen, the top left corner is (0, 0), the top right corner is (800, 0), the bottom right corner is (800, 600), and the bottom left corner is (0 ,600).

A line is represented by a pair of coordinates. A curve is represented by a list of coordinates of the starting point, several turning points, and the end point. A circle can be represented by the coordinate of the centre and the length of the radius (Figure 2.8).

Figure 2.8. Simple graphics

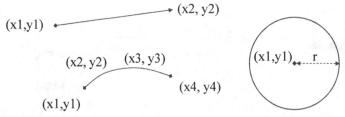

Animations

Computers use graphic tools to provide visual effects in a frame buffer (Figure 2.9). The frame buffer is changed continuously by the animation program. It scans, converts, erases, and redraws the graphic image (Figure 2.10). These changes are repeatedly drawn on the display to appear like continuous motions.

Normally, the animation program should make 15-20 changes per second. That is, the program has around 50 milliseconds to update the frame buffer. If the animation updates are running too fast, the viewer may not be able to see the changes clearly. If the animation updates are running too slowly, the display may become jerky.

Figure 2.9. Animation

Figure 2.10. The animation programs scan, convert, erase, and redraw the frame within 50 msec

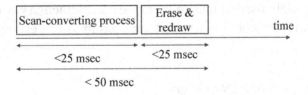

Figure 2.11. Double buffering

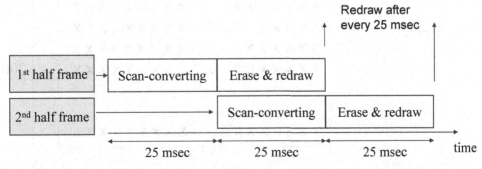

When the processes of scan, convert, erase, and redraw operations take longer than 50 msec, the program may use the double buffering technique. The frame buffer is divided into two parts. Each part is used to store half the bits per pixel of the overall frame buffer. In this way, the erase and redraw process of the first half frame buffer overlaps with the scan and convert process of the second half frame. Each process may then have more time to modify the frame buffer.

Images

An image is represented as a two-dimensional array of sample points called pixels. Different from the coordinates used in mathematics, the Y coordinate increases in the downward direction. For example, Figure 2.12 shows a 320 x 200 image that has 320 pixels on each horizontal line and 200 pixels on each vertical line. The coordinates of the top left corner are (1, 1). The coordinates of the top right corner are (320, 1). The coordinates of the bottom left corner are (1, 200). The coordinates of the top left corner are (320, 200).

Image Bits Per Pixel

Different images may use a different number of bits per pixel. The black and white image (B&W) format uses only one bit per pixel. This B&W image format is widely used in facsimile images. In elementary computer graphics with 16 different colours, four bits are required to describe in each pixel.

Figure 2.12. A 320 x 200 image

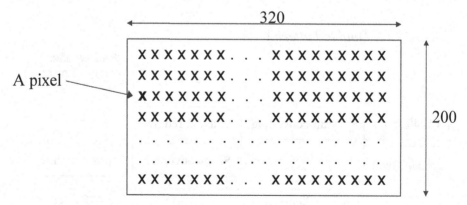

Figure 2.13. RGB representation

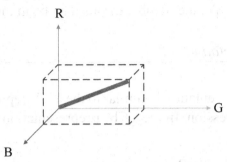

The grey-scale image format uses 8 bits per pixel, and it can describe 256 different levels of colour intensity in each pixel. This image format can be used in black and white photos.

Full colour images are described using 16 to 24 bits per pixel. They can be represented using three different representations: RGB, YUV, and YCbCr format (Rao, Bojkovic, & Milovanovic, 2002; Witten, Moffat, & Bell, 1999). These representations are described in more details in the paragraphs below.

RGB Representation

Our eyes have three classes of receptors called rods. Each type of rod has a different sensitivity to three colours: red, green, and blue. The trichromatic theory states that the sensation of colour is produced by selectively exciting the different types of rods. Thus, each pixel is represented by the intensity of red, green, and blue. Each intensity value is usually coded with eight bits to the grey-scale range of [0,255].

YUV Representation

The cones in our eyes are very sensitive to brightness in a dark environment. Human perception is more sensitive to brightness than any colour information. YUV separates brightness information (luminance Y) from the colour information (chrominance U and V) using:

$$Y = 0.3R + 0.6G + 0.1B$$
$$V = R - Y$$
$$U = B - Y$$

The luminance value can be coded with more bits than the chrominance values; for example, the number of bits may be in the ratio of (4: 2: 2).

YCbCr Representation

The YCbCr representation is similar to the YUV representation. It is used in the JPEG compression. In the YCbCr representation:

$Y = 0.3R + 0.6G + 0.1B$
$Cb = U/2 + 0.5$
$Cr = V/1.6 + 0.5$

Each of these values is scaled and zero shifted to the range [0, 1].

Representation for Printing CMYK

When images are being printed, the CMYK representation is used to print the images in colours. The four colours are Cyan, Magenta, Yellow, and Black. Each dot is printed as the combination of these four colours at different intensities.

Sound and Audio

In this section, we first describe the concept of sound waves. Then, we briefly explain how sound waves are processed by computers. We then present a few standard sound and audio formats.

Figure 2.14. Sound is a longitudinal wave of air pressure

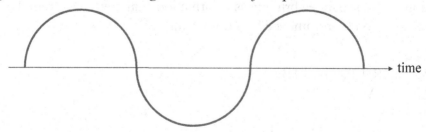

Sound Concept

Sound is a longitudinal wave of air pressure (Figure 2.14). Sound is characterized by the pitch and loudness. Like other waveforms, sound can be represented by a combination of waves with frequency and amplitude. Frequency
of the wave measures the pitch of the sound, and the amplitude of the wave
measures the loudness of the sound.

Wavelength is the distance between repeating units of a waveform. Frequency is the number of occurrences of a repeating event per unit time, and
it is inversely related to the wavelength. While wavelengths are measured in
units of metres, frequency is measured in units of Hertz (Hz), where 1Hz =
1/second. The frequencies of some common ranges of sound waves are:

- Infra sound: 0-20 Hz
- Human hearing: 20Hz -20KHz
- Ultrasound: 20KHz – 1 GHz
- Hypersound: 1GHz – 10 THz

The amplitude of a sound wave (Figure 2.15) measures the loudness of the
sound. Amplitude is measured in units of bell or decibel (dB). Different sound
amplitudes have different effects on us:

- The background noise usually has low sound amplitude. It is difficult
  to hear clearly, and we ignore these low amplitude sounds.
- The speaking level is normal amplitude sound.
- When the sound amplitude is too high, it is uncomfortable to our ears.

Figure 2.15. Amplitude of sound wave

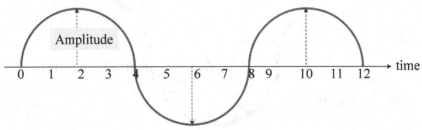

Figure 2.16. Computer processing of sound

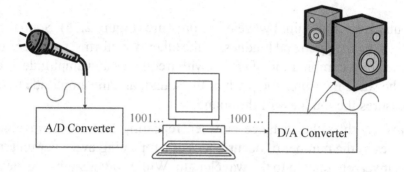

Computer Processing of Sound

Computers cannot process sound waves without converting the sound waves into digital signals (Figure 2.16). In order to process sound, the sound needs to be processed. Sound waves are accepted from the microphone as analog electronic signals. An analog-to-digital (A/D) converter converts the analog electronic signals to digital signals in binary representation. The computer can thus store and process the binary data.

After processing, the computer may output binary data as digital signals. A digital-to-analog (D/A) converter does the reverse operation of changing the digital signals back to analog electronic signals. The speakers can then output the signals as sound waves to be heard.

Figure 2.17. Digitization of sound wave

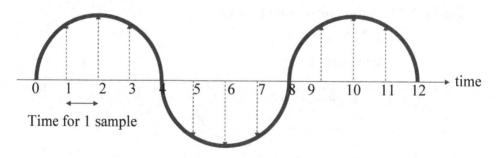

Digitization of Sound Wave

A digitization process is used to convert the analog signals into digital signals. The A/D converter takes sample values at different times of the analog wave according to a sampling rate. The sampling rate in number of samples per second is usually fixed. The amplitude values of the analog signal of a cycle are then taken as the digital data.

When the digitized sound (Figure 2.17) is output, the analog wave is generated at the same sampling rate. The amplitude of the analog wave is adjusted according to the values of the digital data. The reproduced analog wave resembles the original analog wave before digitization.

The reproduced analog wave may not be the same as the original analog wave before digitization. In order to reproduce the analog wave, the sampling rate must be at least more than or equal to twice of the frequency of the analog wave. If the sampling rate is lower than twice of the frequency, then some data would be lost.

Sample Values

The sample values can be encoded with more or less bits. If more bits are used to describe each sample value, the amplitude of the analog wave is described in finer details. If the sample values are encoded in 8 bits, then 256 different amplitude values can be described. If the sample values are encoded in 16 bits, then 65,536 different amplitude values can be described. When more bits are used to describe the sample values, the sound quality would be higher. However, more data would need to be stored and processed.

Standard Audio/Sound Formats

Different sound needs to be represented in different quality levels. The high sound quality level needs to be described with more sample values at high sampling rate. Thus, high quality sound is described with more bits per second. For example, telephone quality is sufficient for normal speech, and CD quality is required for audio music and songs:

Figure 2.18. MIDI format

- Telephone quality speech takes 8,000 samples/second and 8 bits/sample.
- CD-quality audio has 2 channels, a left channel and a right channel, taking 44,100 samples/second and 16 bits /sample.
- DVD quality audio has 6 channels, including a front-left channel, a front-right channel, a front-centre channel, a back-left channel, a back-right channel, and a subwoofer channel.

MIDI Format

Apart from the encoding of nature and recorded sound, audio may be encoded using music scores. The musical instrument digital interface (MIDI) is a digital encoding format of musical information. In the MIDI format (Figure 2.18), the sound data are not necessary. Only the commands, that is, music scores, that describe how the music should be played are encoded.

The MIDI format uses the smallest number of bits/second to describe the music. If recorded audio can be compressed into the MIDI format, it would have achieved the highest compression ratio. Since the music score describes how the music is played, a music score file in MIDI format can be edited easily. However, the MIDI format only describes the music score that can be easily understood by human beings. It requires a music synthesizer to generate music.

Video

In the following paragraphs, we shall describe the representations of video data. The concept of video leads us to the data representation of video. The video frame rates and the aspect ratio determine the quality of the video. The viewer should watch video at the most suitable viewing distance. Lastly, the video formats that are used in computers are described.

Figure 2.19. Video format

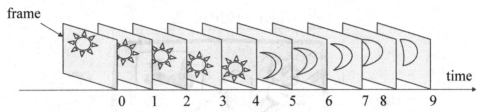

Video Concept

Since the creation of movies, a video (Figure 2.19) is represented as a list of images called frames. Each image frame is separated from the previous frame by a time interval. Each frame may have an image that has some difference from the image in the previous frame. The images of consecutive frames are usually slightly different. The video would then exhibit some continuous motion over time.

At camera cuts, the images of two consecutive frames may be completely different. Before and after a camera cut, the consecutive frames should only be different slightly again. If all consecutive frames have completely different images, the video exhibits a chaotic scene which can be unpleasant to view.

Video Frame Rates

The video frame rate is the number of frames that are displayed per unit time (Wang, Ostermann, & Zhang, 2002). It is usually described in number of frames per second. The video frame rate has an important impact on the video quality.

Our human eyes hold the captured vision for a very short period of time. If the frame rate is high enough, the viewer would observe a continuous motion. If the frame rate is too low, the viewer would observe freeze in the video. In order to show continuous motion, the video frame rate should have at least 15 frames per second. For full motion video, 30 frames per second are necessary.

Some video frame rates have been standardized. For movies in the cinema, 24 frames are displayed per second. The PAL TV standard in the UK, Australia,

Figure 2.20. Aspect ratio

Width = 1920 pixels

Height =
1080 pixels

and Hong Kong displays 25 frames per second. The NTSC TV standard in Japan and the U.S. uses 29.97 frames per second. The High Definition Television (HDTV) displays 59.94 frames per second.

Aspect Ratio

Aspect ratio (Figure 2.20) is the ratio of number of pixels in the horizontal direction to the number of pixels in the vertical direction. Thus, the aspect ratio is the ratio of the width to the height of the image. When the displaying aspect ratio is different from the recording aspect ratio, the image may become distorted. If the aspect ratio value is increased, more pixels are displayed in the horizontal direction, and the image would appear to be fatter. If the aspect ratio is decreased, fewer pixels are displayed in the horizontal direction, and the image would appear to be thinner.

Figure 2.21. Viewing distance

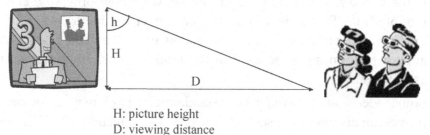

H: picture height
D: viewing distance

The conventional aspect ratio in television is 4:3. Thus, the width of the image is 1.33 times of the height of the image. The wide screen of HDTV uses the 16:9 ratio, and the movies in cinema use an even wider aspect ratio.

Viewing Distance

The viewer watches the video at a viewing distance (Figure 2.21). The optimal viewing distance depends on the size of the displaying video. In Figure 2.21, the picture height and the angle (h) determine the viewing distance (D). We can easily see that the viewing distance, D, can be found using:

tan(h) = (D/H),
⇔   D = H tan(h).

For traditional cathode ray tube (CRT) televisions, the radiation of television is high. tan(h) should = 6. Thus, the optimal viewing distance is 6 times the picture height. For LCD and plasma televisions, the radiation is low. The tan(h) can be as low as 3.

Computer Video Formats

Computers display their output to the screen. The graphic cards inside the computer control the video format of the display screen. Some common standard computer video formats are CGA, EGA, VGA, XGA, and SVGA.

The colour graphics array (CGA) format uses the resolution of 320 x 200 pixels. Each pixel has 4 colours and it is described with 2 bits. Thus, each image is described with (320x200) pixels x 2 bits/pixel = 15.625 kilobytes (KB).

The enhanced graphics array (EGA) format uses the resolution of 640 x 350 pixels per image. Each pixel uses 4 bits to describe the 16 colours. Thus, each image is described with (640x350) pixels x 4 bits/pixel = 109.375 KB.

The video graphics array (VGA) format uses the resolution of 640 x 480 pixels. Each pixel requires 8 bits to show 256 different colours. Thus, each image is described with (640x480) pixels x 8 bits/pixel = 300 KB.

The extended graphics array (XGA) format uses the two different resolutions with different numbers of colour. It may use the resolution of 640 x 480 pixels with 65,536 colours, and each pixel is described in 16 bits. Thus, each image is described with (640x480) pixels x 16 bits/pixel = 600 KB. Alternatively, it may use the resolution of 1024 x 768 pixels with 256 colours, and each pixel is described with 8 bits. Each image is then described using (1024x768) pixels x 8 bits/pixel = 768 KB.

The super video graphic array (SVGA) format also uses two different resolutions. It may use the resolution of 800 x 600 pixels with 16,777,216 colours, and each pixel is described in 24 bits. Thus, each image is described with (800x600) pixels x 24 bits/pixel = 1.37 megabytes (MB). Alternatively, it may use the resolution of 1024 x 768 pixels with 65,536 colours, and each pixel is described with 16 bits. Each image is then described using (1024x768) pixels x 16 bits/pixel = 1.5 MB.

Summary to Data Representation

Computer graphics are represented using the coordinates on the displaying screen. Computer animations are performed by updating changes to the frame buffers and these changes are then drawn on the displaying screen. Images are represented as two-dimensional pixels of colours. Each colour pixel can be described using colour representations RGB, YUV, YCbCr, or CMYK.

Sound waves need to be accepted and digitized into digital signals for computer processing. The digitization of analog waves is done by taking sample values at a fixed sampling rate. The quality of the digitized sound is mainly determined by the number of sample values and the sampling rate.

Video are represented as an array of image frames. 24 to 30 frames should be displayed per second to show full continuous motions. High definition televisions use a very high frame rate of around 60 frames per second.

Multimedia Access Streams

In traditional client/server computer systems, the types of data being accessed are usually textual and binary data. Binary data are often stored in database files, and textual data are stored in document files. In multimedia systems, multimedia data such as video, audio, and images are stored in data files. These data may be accessed in a pull-based manner or a push-based manner.

Figure 2.22. Request streams

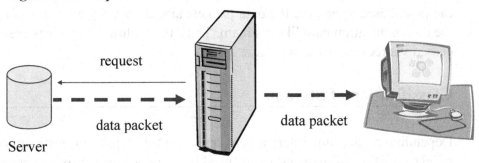

Traditional data are usually accessed in a pull-based approach. The client programs send discrete requests to load data from the server. The request may look like this to human beings: "Give me the 10th block of data in file A." Upon receiving this request, the server accesses the block of data, encloses it in a data packet, and passes it to the client. The client then opens the data packet and accesses the data inside the packet. After serving this request, the server program would wait for another request from the client.

Multimedia data are often accessed in a push-based approach. The client program sends a request to the server asking for the multimedia file starting at a particular block. The request may look like this to human beings: "Give me the file M starting from the 10th block." Upon receiving this request, the server accesses the 10th block of data in file M, encloses it in a data packet, and passes it to the client. The server then accesses the 11th block of data in file M and passes it to the client, and so on. The server would continue to access the next block of data in file M and pass it to the client until it receives another request from the client. When the client receives a data packet, it opens the packet and accesses the data inside.

Due to the continuous nature of the multimedia data, many data requests would be sent to the server in the pull-based approach. All the requests and

Figure 2.23. Strongly periodic stream

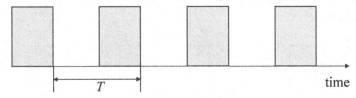

Each packet is separated from the
previous packet at a constant time T.

the returned data packets flow continuously like water in a river stream. In the push-based approach, the data packets also flow continuously through the communication path like a stream. Thus, the multimedia objects are accessed via request streams (Figure 2.22).

Classification of Streams

Depending on the time interval between consecutive packets, a stream can be classified as strongly periodic, weakly periodic, or aperiodic streams.

Figure 2.24. Weakly periodic stream

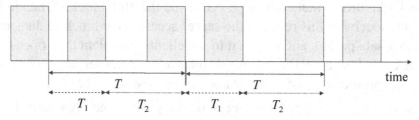

Each group of packets is separated from the previous group at a constant time T. The packets are separated at different time periods T_1 and T_2.

Figure 2.25. Aperiodic stream

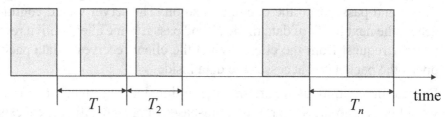

Figure 2.26. Strongly regular stream

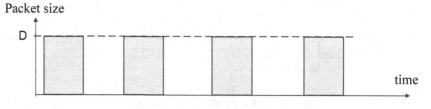

All packets of a strongly regular stream are of the same size.

Depending on the variation of data size between consecutive packets, a stream can be strongly regular, weakly regular, or irregular. Depending on the continuity of consecutive packets, a stream can be continuous or discrete (Furht, 1996).

- **Strongly Periodic Stream:** If the time interval between any two consecutive packets is constant, then the stream is called a strongly periodic stream. In the ideal case, the jitter is zero. Figure 2.23 shows a strongly periodic stream that has a fixed time interval between consecutive data packets. For example, the pulse code modulation (PCM) coded speech is a strongly periodic stream.

Figure 2.27. Weakly regular stream

Packet size

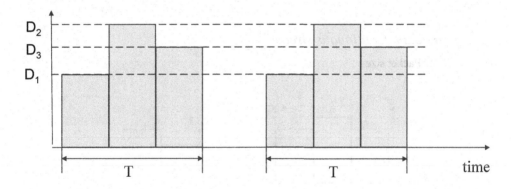

Figure 2.28. Irregular stream

Packet size

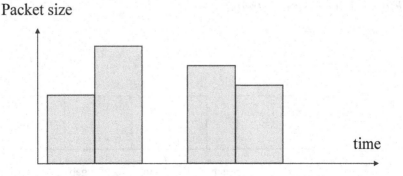

- **Weakly Periodic Stream:** If the time intervals between two consecutive packets are not constant but only periodic, then the stream is called a weakly periodic stream. Figure 2.24 shows a weakly periodic stream in which the time interval between consecutive packets oscillates between T1 and T2. When we merge two strongly periodic streams with different periods, the resultant stream is a weakly periodic stream.

- **Aperiodic Stream:** Aperiodic streams are streams such that the time intervals between consecutive packets are neither constant nor periodic. An aperiodic stream with different time intervals between consecutive packets is shown in Figure 2.25.

- **Strongly Regular Stream:** If all data packets are of the same constant size, then the stream is called a strongly regular stream (Figure 2.26). An uncompressed video stream created from a capturing video camera is usually a strongly regular stream.

- **Weakly Regular Stream:** If the data size of packets changes periodically, then the stream is called a weakly regular stream (Figure 2.27).

Figure 2.29. Continuous stream

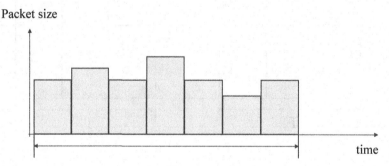

Figure 2.30. Discrete stream

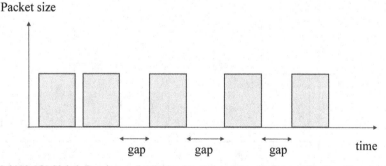

- **Irregular Stream:** When the data sizes of packets are not constant and they are not periodic, the stream is called an irregular stream. Since the data sizes of packets change, it complicates the transmission and processing of the data packets. When temporary buffers are allocated, their size should be large enough to accommodate the largest data packet. Thus, the buffers cannot be utilized to their full capacity. Therefore, some efficiency is lost in handling irregular streams.

- **Continuous Stream:** When the large objects are accessed and the multimedia data need to be returned in small data packets, the data packets would be sent continuously over a long time. The data stream is called a continuous stream. Video and audio objects are usually accessed by continuous streams.

  When the data packets are transmitted over the communication path, the data packets occupy some capacity of the communication path for a long period of time. If the data packets are transmitted without any intermediate gaps, they may fully occupy the communication path (Figure 2.29). The system resources may not be able to serve other users of the resources.

- **Discrete stream:** Some multimedia objects such as images are not continuous in nature. These objects may be large, but they can be accessed with discrete requests. A packet is not connected to its preceding and following packets. The data stream is thus discrete. For example, a large image object may be accessed by a request, and the object is returned via a discrete stream.

Request Streams Summary

We have described the three classifications of request streams. First, a stream may be classified according to the time interval between consecutive packets. Second, a stream may be classified according to the data size of the packets. Third, a stream may be classified according to the continuity of the packets.

Chapter Summary

Multimedia data can be used in many types of applications. These applications include broadcasting, video-on-demand, communications, monitoring and control, and even information systems. The design of multimedia systems should consider the storage system, delivery network, and the scheduling algorithms. Most of these systems store large multimedia objects in their storage system for future retrievals. Inside the storage system, multimedia objects are stored as large binary data files, and they are accessed and delivered using streams. Multimedia streams can be classified by their periodicity, regularity, and continuity.

References

Furht, B. (1996). Multimedia technologies, systems, tools, and applications.

Hennessy, J., & Patterson, D. A. (1996). *Computer architecture: A quantitative approach* (2nd ed.). Morgan Kaufmann.

Rao, K. R., Bojkovic, Z. S., & Milovanovic, D. A. (2002). *Multimedia communication systems: Techniques, standards, and networks*. Prentice Hall.

Tse, P. K. C. (1999). *Efficient storage and retrieval methods for multimedia information*. Doctoral dissertation, Victoria University, Melbourne, Australia.

Wang, Y., Ostermann, J., & Zhang, Y. Q. (2002). *Video processing and communications*. Prentice Hall.

Witten, I., Moffat, A., & Bell, T. (1999). *Managing gigabytes: Compressing and indexing documents and images* (2nd ed.). Morgan Kaufmann.

Chapter III

Storage System Architectures

Introduction

Multimedia systems are similar to traditional computer systems in terms of their architectures. Both types of systems have central processing unit (CPU), random access memory, hard disks, and so forth. The CPU connects to the memory and other components via the memory bus, and it connects to the peripherals via the input/output (I/O) bus.

In order to process continuous multimedia streams, multimedia computer systems are built with stringent processing time requirements. Each component of the computer system needs to be able to process large amounts of data, process data in parallel, and finish the processing within a guaranteed time frame. Otherwise, undesirable effects would appear to lower the quality of the multimedia streams.

When storage servers are designed to handle multimedia streams, the architecture of the storage servers also needs to handle the processing time requirements. The storage server needs to access data continuously to the clients according to the clients' requests.

Multimedia objects are large, and the magnetic hard disks need to access segments of the objects within a short time. These requirements lead to the emergence of constant recording density disks and zoned disks.

We shall describe the architecture of storage servers in the next section. After that, we shall describe the zoned disks performance model.

Server Architectures

Multimedia servers need to provide continuous delivery of multimedia objects to the clients. The remote clients are usually connected through a local area network or several networks. The Internet today is a best effort network, and it does not provide any service guarantees to multimedia streams. Thus, the present technology uses dedicated networks to deliver the streams. The dedicated networks, such as cable TV, are able to deliver multimedia streams in a controllable environment.

Multimedia servers store many objects in their storage. They need to access the objects and deliver the objects according to the requests from many clients. The storage server should access and deliver the objects efficiently in order to maintain the quality of the streams.

Simple Multimedia Server System

An example of a simple multimedia server system is shown in Figure 3.1. The storage server or storage system is composed of a storage subsystem and a processor subsystem. The processor subsystem serves requests from the clients via the network. It maintains the quality of streams that are delivered to the clients. When data are required, it sends requests to the storage subsystem.

The main responsibility of the storage subsystem is to store the multimedia objects. All the multimedia objects are stored on the storage devices in the storage subsystem. The storage subsystem serves data requests from the processor subsystem. The main reason to separate the storage subsystem from the processor subsystem is because of the workload. Since the object

Figure 3.1. A simple multimedia server system

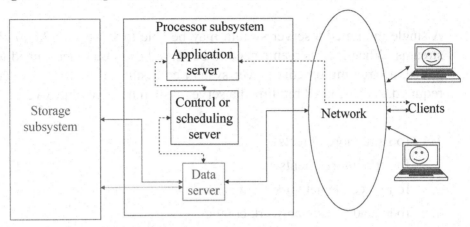

is large and the stream is long, it takes a long time to deliver the object to the clients. The workload on the storage subsystem is thus heavy. If the storage subsystem and the processor subsystem are running on the same server, the application server's ability to respond interactively to the users will be adversely affected. The user may need to wait a long time for a very simple mouse click.

The processor subsystem is composed of three servers: the application server, the scheduling server, and the data server. The application server receives requests from the clients and provides a response back to them. The scheduling server divides a request stream into a number of requests. It then schedules the requests in a timely manner. It sends the requests to the data server. The data server searches for the location of the requested object and forwards the requests to the storage subsystem.

When the storage subsystem serves a read request from the data server, reads the object from the storage device, and passes the accessed data to the data server. When the storage subsystem serves a write request, it writes the object to the storage devices. Most multimedia clients only access the objects for viewing purposes only. Since multimedia objects are often read and played to users, most requests would only read the object from the server. Thus, the main concern on the storage subsystem is on the read operations only even though the storage subsystem provides both read and write operations.

When the data server receives data from the storage subsystem, it directly passes the data to the clients via the network. It will then send another data request to the storage subsystem at the time controlled by the scheduling server.

Distributed Multimedia Server System

A single multimedia server system may be able to serve 1 to 2,000 client streams. When more streams need to be served or more objects need to be stored, a large multimedia server system consisting of multiple servers is required. A distributed multimedia server system has five objectives:

1. To store more objects
2. To serve more clients
3. To reduce the network contention
4. To spread out the network contention
5. To balance the server workloads

A multimedia server that has the accessed object may not be able to serve a client stream for two reasons. First, if the server is overloaded, the server does not have disk bandwidth to access the object from the storage subsystems. Second, if the network around the server is already congested, the server does not have network bandwidth to deliver the object to the client. In either situation, the server shall reject the client stream even though it has the object on its storage devices.

The first objective is to store more objects. Several servers in the distributed multimedia server system have more disks to store more objects than a simple multimedia server. To store the most number of objects, the storage space on the servers should be used carefully. Extra copies of objects may be created according to their access popularity. When a new object is stored, the extra copies of objects may be deleted to release storage space for the new object.

The second objective is to serve more client streams. Unless all the requests are served by only one server, a distributed server system can serve more client streams than a single server. In order to serve the most number of streams, the objects should be distributed so that the requests are evenly spread to the servers. Therefore, the workloads on the servers should be well balanced.

The third objective is to reduce the network workload. The workload on the network also depends on the distance from the servers to their requesting clients. If the server is far from a requesting client, the data need to be transmitted over a long distance from the server to the client. The workload imposed on the network is then heavy. If the server is close to the requesting client, the data can be transmitted over the smallest number of hops from the server to the client. The workload imposed on the network is then light. In distributed systems, the server that is closest to the requesting client may be chosen to deliver the request stream. Thus, the imposed workload on the network would be reduced.

The fourth objective is to spread out the network contention. If the servers are close to each other, they would send packets from nearby routers on the network. When the servers are busily serving clients, the workload on the network around these routers becomes heavy. If the servers are far from each other, then the routes from these servers to their serving clients may not overlap. Thus, the workload on the network can be spread out to more routes.

The fifth objective is to balance the server workloads. While a server is busily serving some streams, it may not have sufficient resources, such as disk load, to serve any additional new stream. New streams will then need to wait. If other servers are available to serve this stream, the new stream can be served immediately. The workload on the busy server is then transferred to the other servers. Thus, the server workloads can thus be balanced.

In general, a distributed multimedia server system is composed of multimedia servers, clients, and the network as shown in Figure 3.2. Multimedia objects are stored on the simple multimedia servers. The servers are connected to the network. Clients send requests to the multimedia servers over the network.

Figure 3.2. A distributed multimedia server system

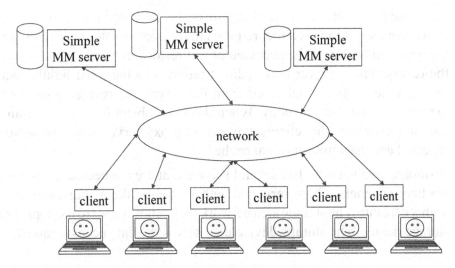

The multimedia servers then serve the client requests and deliver object streams to the clients.

Several options are available to build a distributed multimedia server system. Here are some choices in building the system architecture:

1. Multiple independent servers share their storage to store the objects
2. A depot system to direct request to appropriate server
3. A reverse proxy server in front to balance the workload
4. A storage area network to spread the workload
5. A distributed server system to balance the server workload and spread out the network workload
6. A content distribution system to balance server and network workload

If the server system is simply a list of independent multimedia servers, then the clients need to know which server a particular object resides in. In addition, some servers containing hot objects may be overloaded while other servers containing cold objects are idle. Thus, some mechanisms need to be applied so that these servers operate like a single server system to the users.

A depot system may be placed in front of the servers to direct the client requests to the appropriate server. Such a depot server may deliver a new client request to an idle server or the less busy server. The servers would then serve the requests directly.

A reverse proxy server is placed in front of the multimedia servers to receive client requests. It may redirect requests to the appropriate server containing the accessed object. If the accessed object resides in more than one server, the reverse proxy server may redirect requests to the most lightly loaded server. When data are delivered from the server, the reverse proxy server may create a local cache copy. When the same object is accessed again by the same client or other clients, the reverse proxy server may then serve the repeated accesses from its local cache.

A storage area network has several servers that are connected to each other via fibre channels. These servers together operate like a single server with higher capacity. The storage area network redirects requests to the appropriate storage device. The storage device then serves the data access request.

A distributed servers system has several storage servers and these servers reside at different geographical locations. The objects divided into segments and these segments are distributed over several servers. It operates like a single multimedia server system to the users. A client may send requests to the application server. The application server would then identify the segments and the server containing the segments of the object. The appropriate server then delivers data segments directly to the requesting clients. Each segment of the server may be delivered from a different server. The distributed server system thus balances the workload among servers and spreads out the workload on the network.

A content distribution system is composed of several storage servers. A client may send requests to one of the servers. The server system then chooses the server that is closest to the client to deliver the object to the client. If this closest server does not have the required object, it will access the object from other servers and keep a copy in its storage. After some time, each storage server will store the objects that are recently or frequently accessed by its neighbouring clients.

In multimedia database systems, a client who is connected to the network sends queries to the database system (Figure 3.3). The database system then looks up the index tables and finds the objects that can satisfy the query. The data server then sends a few most relevant objects to the user for preview. The user may then select the most relevant objects for display. The multimedia server or multimedia server system then delivers the chosen object to the user.

Figure 3.3. Multimedia database server system

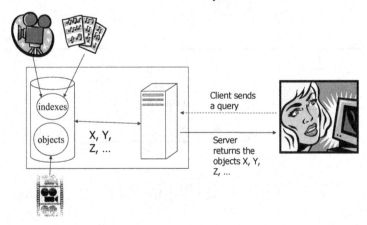

Input/Output Processors

Inside the computer system, data are stored on different storage devices depending on their usage requirements. Permanent data are stored on the hard magnetic disks. Temporary data are stored on the random access memory (RAM) or memory. Frequently accessed data are temporarily stored on the cache memory for quick accesses. Data are either read or written to these storage devices by the running user programs or operating system programs.

Traditional computer systems run programs when they are invoked by users or timer events. A job task is a fragment of codes belonging to a running program and it is executed by the CPU. A program may invoke one or more job tasks. Many tasks belonging to different programs are concurrently executed by the CPU. Since the CPU can serve only one job task at any one particular moment, the tasks are served on a time-slice manner. After the CPU serves a task for one unit of time, it switches to another task. The order of service is determined by the job scheduling policy.

When a task arrives at a code to receive input from the keyboard, output to the screen, read from hard disk, or other input/output operations, the running task will be suspended and put into the waiting queue until the I/O instruction is finished. The CPU then resumes the suspended task and continues the task after the I/O operation.

Inside the computer system, the memory bus connects all the main components, including the CPU and memory (Figure 3.4). Other peripheral devices

Figure 3.4. I/O processor

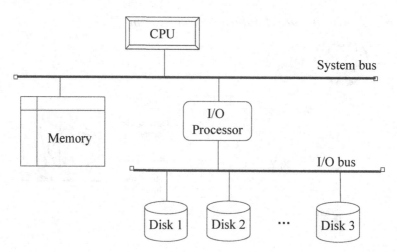

and the hard disks are connected to the I/O bus. An input/output processor (IOP) connects the I/O bus to the memory bus. Since the input and output devices are very slow devices when compared to the memory and CPU. The memory bus would be very slow if the I/O devices are directly connected. With the help of the I/O processor, the I/O devices can communicate with the CPU and memory without slowing them down.

When the CPU executes a line of code that performs an I/O instruction, it works with the I/O processor to execute the I/O instruction in four steps:

1. The CPU issues an I/O instruction to the I/O processor.
2. The I/O processor reads a command from memory.
3. The I/O processor transfers data to/from memory directly.
4. The I/O processor sends an interrupt to CPU when done.

In the first step, the CPU issues an I/O instruction to the I/O processor as shown in Figure 3.5. The I/O instruction is composed of the operation code (OP), the target device number (device), and the command address (address). The operation code specifies which command to execute. The device specifies the target device number. The address contains the address location of the I/O command inside the memory.

Figure 3.5. Step 1: CPU issues I/O instruction to I/O processor

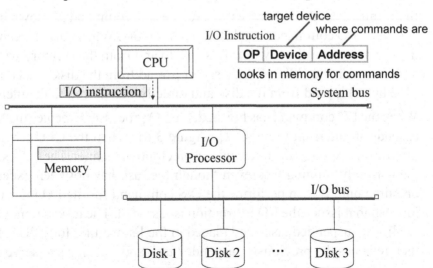

Figure 3.6. Step 2: IOP reads command from memory

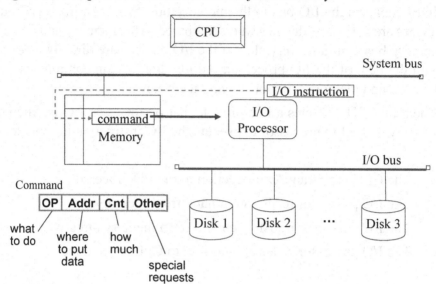

Command

what to do / where to put data / how much / special requests

In the second step, the I/O processor looks in the memory for the command as shown in Figure 3.6. The command is composed of four fields: the OP field, the Addr field, the Cnt field, and Other field. The OP field specifies what to do. The Addr field specifies where to put data. The Cnt field specifies the count of how much data can be accessed by the command. The Other field only specifies details of the command. The I/O processor then reads the command from memory and executes the command.

In the third step, the I/O processor executes the command as shown in Figure 3.7. Most I/O commands need to access memory. When data are transferred, the I/O processor directly transfers data to and from the memory without interfering with the CPU. When a sector is read from the disk, a sector of data (512 bytes) is read from the disk and directly transferred to the memory.

When the I/O command has finished, the I/O processor executes the last step. It sends an interrupt to the CPU (Figure 3.8). When the CPU receives this interrupt, it executes the interrupt in a preemptive manner. The CPU suspends the currently running task even though the task has not been executed for one time unit. It then performs the O/S command for the I/O interrupt. The job task that issues the I/O instruction is resumed. The task is removed from the list of suspended tasks and placed in the list waiting for CPU. The CPU then resumes the previously suspended task and continues to serve it.

Figure 3.7. Step 3: IOP transfers data to/from memory directly

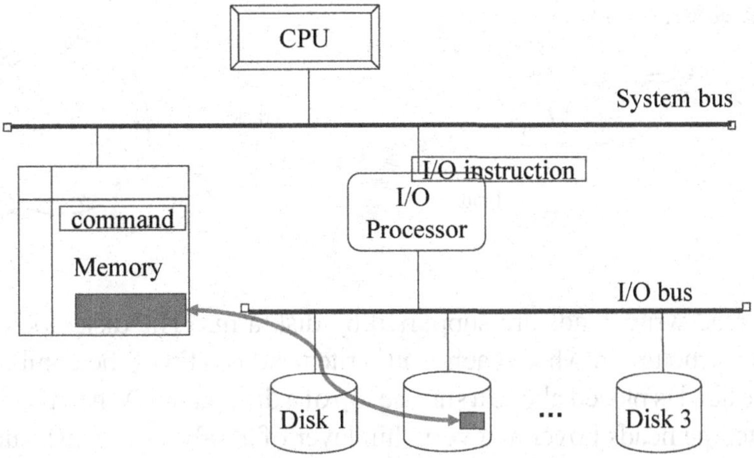

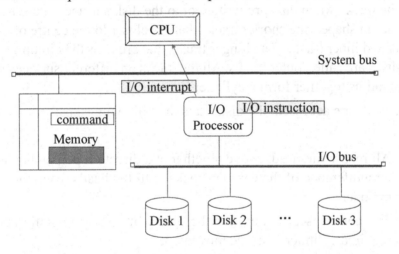

Figure 3.8. Step 4: IOP sends interrupt to CPU when done

Storage Devices

Magnetic disks are inexpensive disks. The storage device is inexpensive because it stores data using two-dimensional circular disk platter and the disk platters are stacked up on the third dimension. Magnetic disks are composed of disk platters and read/write heads as shown in Figure 3.9. The disk platters are connected together at the centre on a spindle. When the spindle rotates, all the disk platters move at the same speed.

Figure 3.9. Magnetic disks

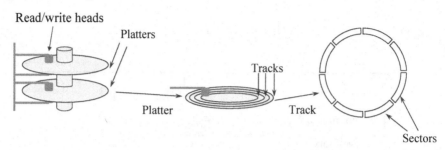

The read/write heads are supported by disk arms. The disks look like a hair comb structure in which each read/write head is a tip of the comb. Each read/write head is placed above a surface top of a disk platter. When the disk platters rotate, the heads hover at a very thin layer of air above the disk surface.

While the read/write heads are fixed and the disk platters are rotating, each head forms a circle on the corresponding disk platter surface. These circles are the tracks when data are written onto the disk surface. These tracks are circular in shape. The shorter tracks that are closer to the centre of the disks are called inner tracks. The longer tracks that are near the circumference of the disks are called outer tracks. All the tracks on different surfaces with the same radius together form a cylinder.

When data are accessed, the disk takes the following steps:

1. All read/write heads move together at a direction perpendicular to the circumference of the circular tracks until the heads reach the required cylinder.

2. The control servo waits for the read/write heads to settle above the required cylinder after the movement.

3. The head above the required tracks within the cylinder is chosen.

4. The heads then wait for the rotation of the disk until the beginning of the required data on the track come under the head.

5. The I/O path from the disk controller to the memory is established.

6. When the beginning of the required data comes under the head, data are immediately transferred between the disk and the memory.

Data are written in units of 512 bytes. Each unit of 512 bytes is called a sector. When the read/write head is above a track, it can access all the data on this track by waiting for the disk to rotate. At any moment, only one of the read/write heads can transfer data. When the read/write head is fixed, it can access all the data on the cylinder by choosing the appropriate read/write heads.

Traditionally, the magnetic disks rotate at a fixed angular speed and the read/write heads transfer data at a fixed speed. All the tracks store the same number of bytes. When the heads are close to the disk centre, the length of the circular tracks is short and data bits on the tracks are densely written. When the heads are far from the disk centre, the tracks are longer in length and data bits on the tracks are sparsely written. Thus, the recording density varies when the heads are close to or far from the centre of disks. Thus, the traditional disk recording format is called variable density recording.

In these traditional magnetic disks, the disk platters simply rotate at fixed speed. However, it does not fully utilize the storage capacity of the long outer tracks. In order to store more data on the outer tracks, the constant recoding density method is widely accepted in recent years. The constant density recording format stores more data on the longer outer tracks and less data on the shorter inner tracks. This constant density recording is applied in two layouts: the zoned disk layout and the spiral track layout. These two layouts are described in the paragraphs below.

After that, we shall describe the millipede disks and the nanodisks. For mobile devices, the storage devices need to be small, compact, and light. The millipede disks and the nanodisks are products that address these requirements.

Zoned Disks

Magnetic disks use the zoned disk format to increase their storage capacities. The disk surface of magnetic zoned disks is divided into zones as shown in Figure 3.10. Each zone is a group of neighbouring tracks within a range of radii. Thus, each zone is a ring-shaped region on the disk surface.

Within a zone, the disks operate like a variable density recording disk. The disks rotate at a fixed angular speed. Thus, all the tracks within a zone store the same number of sectors and the number of sectors per track is fixed within a zone. To store the maximum number of sectors within a zone, the innermost track within the zone should store the most sectors. Other tracks in the same zone then store the same number of sectors.

Since the innermost track of the inner zones are shorter than the innermost track of the outer zones, tracks of the inner zones store less data than the

Figure 3.10. Zoned disk format

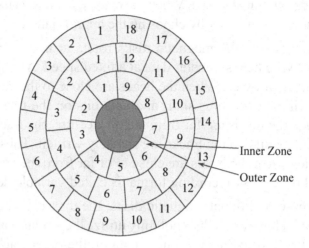

tracks of the outer zones. Although the number of sectors per track is fixed within a zone, each zone may have a different number of tracks. The storage capacity of a zone is found as the product of the storage capacity of a track and the number of tracks within the zone.

In addition, the I/O path transfers data at a fixed number of bits per second and the disks rotate at a fixed speed. All the data on one track can be accessed by one disk revolution. Thus, the data transfer rate within a zone is fixed. Since the track capacity of outer zones is larger than the track capacity of the inner zones, data are transferred faster when the heads are above the outer zones. Thus, the outer zones have higher data transfer rate than the inner zones.

Magnetic zoned disks have two main advantages over traditional magnetic disks. First, they have higher storage capacity than traditional magnetic disks of the same size. Second, data on the outer tracks of zoned disks can be accessed more quickly. In traditional magnetic disks, the motor speed is fixed. Whereas in zoned disks, the motor speed changes when the heads change from one zone to another. Since changing the motor speed is very simple, it is not difficult to be implemented.

Spiral Track Layout

Optical disks, such as compact disk (CD) and digital versatile disks (DVD) use the spiral track to increase their storage capacities. The optical disks can

Figure 3.11. CD and DVD layout

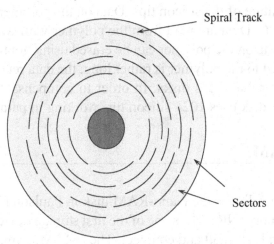

Spiral Track

Sectors

record data at a fixed speed continuously for a very long time.

On the surface of the optical disks, data are recorded on a long spiral track in sectors. The spiral track runs continuously from the inside near the centre of the disk to outside near the rim. Dual layer DVD may have a second spiral track at the second layer that runs in the same or opposite direction.

The motor changes the disk rotation speed according to the position of the optical read/write head. The servo controls the motor speed and changes it automatically. While the optical head is near the centre of the disk, the optical disk speeds up. While the optical head is near the rim of the disk, the disk slows down. The motor speed is maintained so that the data on the track pass the optical head at a fixed linear speed.

Millipede Project

The millipede project creates a new type of disk (Paulson, 2002). The size and shape of the millipede disk looks like a postage stamp. The disk is composed of silicon tips above a polymer. Data are written on the polymer by punching holes on the polymer with a silicon tip. The holes are separated at a distance of around 10 nanometres or 50 atoms. The disk can record data at a density of 1 trillion bits per square inch. It records data at 20 times denser than the magnetic disks.

The disk is rewritable. Data on the polymer can be read or written by changing the temperature of the silicon tips. Data on the polymer are written with hot tips at 400°C. Data are read from the polymer with warm tips at 300°C. In addition, data on the polymer can be erased using hot tips. Since the time to conduct heat to the polymer is rather long, the data recording speed is 1,000 times slower than hard disks. In order to compensate for the long access latency, the disk uses 1024 silicon tips working in parallel.

Nano RAM

Another new disk is the Nano-RAM disk in Paulson (2003). Nano random access memory (NRAM) is one of the first storage devices that use the nano-technology. It is small and compact. The NRAM is small and compact. The NRAM is composed of carbon nanotubes that are a billionth of a metre in size. The disk head sends differing electrical charges into the nanotube and swings the tubes into one of the two positions. One of the two positions represents a binary digit 0 while the other position represents a binary digit 1.

Inside the NRAM, the nanotubes only move a very short distance, and it takes a very short time to finish this movement. Thus, the read/write operations can be finished very quickly. This short latency feature makes the NRAM suitable for high performance systems.

The position of the nanotubes is nonvolatile. The nanotubes do not need power to maintain their current positions as in random access memory. Thus, the NRAM is suitable for permanent storage of information. In addition, the NRAM does not need to maintain continuous rotations like magnetic disks and optical disks. It saves power, and the NRAM can be used in mobile devices.

The NRAM is 50 times stronger than steel. The nanotubes can swing into positions many times in order to support a large number of write cycles. Recent developments on quality control help to select only nanotubes that are growing properly.

In summary, the nanotube is a durable, compact, low power, compact, high capacity, and low latency storage device. The NRAM can be used in mobile and high performance systems in which the system requirements are stringent.

Disk Performance

Individual Disk Access Operation

When data are accessed from the disks, the disks access data in sector size of 512, 1024, or 2048 bytes. The disk executes the following steps to read or write data:

1. Obtain I/O channel to memory
2. Seek the required cylinder
3. Switch to the selected head within the cylinder
4. Wait for the start of the required sector to meet the head
5. Transfer the sector via I/O channel to memory
6. Send interrupt to the CPU for I/O completion

Most of these steps involve mechanical and electronic operations. The mechanical steps are much slower than the electronic steps. The mechanical steps occupy more than 95% of access time. Thus, the time spent in the mechanical steps is considered with significance when the performance of the disks is investigated.

The major mechanical steps are:

1. **Seek time:** Move the read/write heads to the track.
2. **Rotational latency:** Wait for the start of the required sector to come under the head.
3. **Optional RPS miss:** Additional cycle if I/O path fails to establish before transfer dependent on the duration between consecutive seeks.
4. **Transfer time:** Transfer the sector via I/O path to memory

Other steps are electronic and contribute to less than 5% of the disk access time.

The seek time and rotational latency are overheads that should be reduced as much as possible. The data transfer time increases linearly with the motor rotation speed.

Performance of Zoned Disks

We may use a discrete or continuous model to investigate the zoned disk performance. The discrete model may provide accurate formulae for the disk access time with more parameters. The continuous model can be used to find disk access time using some approximations.

The continuous model makes three approximations to calculate the zoned disk performance. First, the disks are divided into the maximum number of zones so that each zone has the smallest number of tracks. Second, the inter-track gaps are very small. Third, the maximum number of sectors is stored on each track. These approximations allow us to find the optimal performance of zoning. The access time formulae can also be found using integrations.

In the continuous model, a track is modeled as a ring-shaped area on the disk surface. Data are recorded on the track. Consider a circular track at a distance x from the centre of the disk; the length of the track is $2\pi x$. Thus, the area of the track is $2\pi x dx$.

The total area of the disk surface is the integration of the ring area from the innermost radius a to the outermost radius b. Thus, the disk area can be found as:

$$= \int_a^b 2\pi x dx$$

$$= \pi(b^2 - a^2) \tag{3.1}$$

Assume that each sector has the same probability of being accessed. After data on the track of radius x are accessed, the read/write head stays within the ring area of radius x and width dx. The probability that the previous request accesses data on the track of radius x, $P_x dx$, is equal to the ratio of the ring area of radius x to the total disk area.

Thus, the probability that the previous request accesses data on the track of radius x, $P_x dx$, is found as

$$P_x dx = \frac{2x dx}{(b^2 - a^2)} \tag{3.2}$$

Figure 3.12. Disk performance model

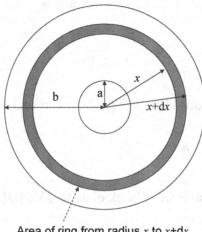

Area of ring from radius x to $x+dx$

In the following sections, we shall use this probability to find the seek distance, rotational latency, and data transfer time.

Seek Time

The first mechanical step is the seek action. The seek action consists of the following components:

1. The disk arm is accelerated until it reaches the maximum speed.
2. The disk arm is traveling at the maximum speed.
3. The disk arm is decelerated until it stops.
4. The read/write heads are settled on the required track.

The seek distance is the number of tracks being traveled by the read/write heads in performing a seek action. When the disk heads are positioned on a track of radius x and the accessed data on another track of radius y, they travel from track of radius x to the track of radius y. The seek distance is thus equal to the difference in number of tracks. That is the seek distance, D, is

$$= |y - x| \tag{3.3}$$

For completely random seeks, the mean seek distance can be found by integrating all possible absolute seek distances:

$$\overline{D} = \int_a^b \int_a^b \frac{2x}{(b^2 - a^2)} \frac{2y}{(b^2 - a^2)} |y - x| dy dx$$

After simplifications (Tse, 1999), the mean seek distance, $\overline{D}$, is found as

$$\overline{D} = \frac{4(b-a)(a^2 + 3ab + b^2)}{15(a+b)^2} \tag{3.4}$$

In addition, the variance of seek distance, Var[D], is found in Tse (1999) to be

$$
\begin{aligned}
&= \int_a^b \int_a^b \frac{2x}{(b^2 - a^2)} \frac{2y}{(b^2 - a^2)} (y - x)^2 \, dy dx - \left(\overline{D}\right)^2 \\
&= \frac{(b-a)^2 (3a^2 + 14ab + 3b^2)(3a^2 + 4ab + 3b^2)}{225(a+b)^4}
\end{aligned}
\tag{3.5}
$$

Seek time is the time required for the seek action, and it consists of the following time components:

1. The time spent in accelerating the arm until it reaches the maximum speed.
2. The time spent in moving the arm at the maximum speed.
3. The time spent in slowing down the arm until it stops.
4. The time spent in settling the read/write heads on the required tracks.

During the acceleration and deceleration period, the seek time increases with the square root of the seek distance. During the maximum traveling period, the seek time increases linearly with the seek distance. In addition, the settling time is a fixed value. Therefore, the seek time, s, relates to the seek distance, D, below.

$$s = \begin{cases} a_1 + a_2 D, & D > a_5 \\ a_3 + a_4 \sqrt{D}, & D \le a_5 \end{cases} \tag{3.6}$$

Figure 3.13. Seek time is almost linearly proportional to the seek distance

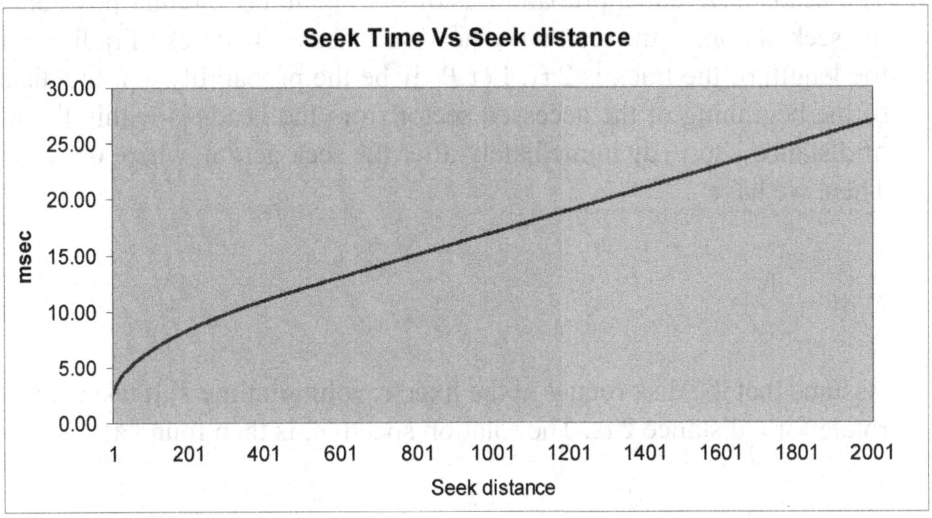

where a_1, a_2, a_3, a_4, and a_5 are parameters. These parameters vary from one disk type to another disk type depending on the actual performance.

An example of the seek time curve vs. the seek distance is shown in Figure 3.13. We can see that the seek time is almost linearly proportional to the seek distance. Anyway, the seek time increases monotonically with the seek distance (Tse, 1999; Tse & Leung, 2000).

Although we have found the seek time for random seeks, most seeks are however not random. When data are read from or written to the disk, the consecutive requests usually access consecutive sectors. Furthermore, many data placement methods increase the correlation between consecutive accesses to reduce the seek distance. For example, data that are retrieved at a similar time may be placed together on the same track or cylinder. The seek distance and seek time can thus be reduced.

Rotational Latency

After the read/write heads settle on the required track, the disk selects one of the heads to access data. It also sets up an I/O path to memory. At this time, the beginning of the accessing sector may not be at the right position for the head to access. While the disks continue to rotate, the heads will wait until the beginning of the required sector comes under the head. This period of waiting time is called the rotational latency or rotational delay.

Assume that the read/write heads are at random position after the seek action. The heads have equal probabilities of staying at any circular position after the seek action. If the read/write heads are above the track of radius x, then the length of the track is $2\pi x$. Let $P_y\,dy$ be the probability that the distance of the beginning of the accessed sector from the heads is within the range of distance y to $y+dy$ immediately after the seek action, where $0 \leq y \leq 2\pi x$. Then, we have

$$P_y\,dy = \frac{dy}{2\pi x}.$$

Assume that the disk rotates at the fixed revolution time T. It takes time T to rotate for a distance $2\pi x$. The rotation speed, a, is then found as

$$a = \frac{2\pi x}{T}.$$

When it takes time dt to rotate for a distance dy, where $0 < dt \leq T$ and $0 \leq dy \leq 2\pi x$, we have

$$dy = a\,dt.$$
$$\Leftrightarrow dy = \frac{2\pi x}{T}\,dt.$$

Thus, the rotational latency t increases linearly with the distance of the beginning of the accessed sector from the heads, y. Let P_t be the probability that the rotational latency is within the range of time t to $t+dt$, where $0 < t \leq T$, and $dt \to 0$. Obviously,

$$P_t\,dt = P_y\,dy$$
$$= \frac{2\pi x\,dt}{2\pi x T}.$$

Thus, the probability that the rotational latency is within the range t to $t+dt$ is found as

$$P_t\,dt = \frac{dt}{T}.$$

Figure 3.14. Rotational latency

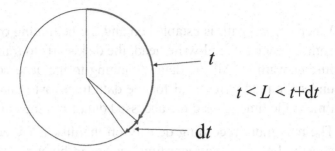

$t < L < t+\mathrm{d}t$

The mean rotational latency is found as

$$\bar{L} = \int_0^T t P_l \mathrm{d}t$$
$$= \int_0^T \frac{t\,\mathrm{d}t}{T}$$
$$= \frac{T}{2}.$$

Tse (1999) found that the variance of rotational latency is

$$\mathrm{Var}[L] = \int_0^T P_l t^2 \,\mathrm{d}t - \left(\bar{L}\right)^2$$
$$= \int_0^T \frac{t^2 \,\mathrm{d}t}{T} - \frac{T^2}{4}$$
$$= \frac{T^3}{3T} - \frac{T^2}{4}$$
$$= \frac{T^2}{12}.$$

For some disks or I/O processors that have a buffer of the size of a track, the disk may start to read as soon as the I/O path is established. The disk will read the entire track to the track buffer. Afterwards, data can be transferred to memory from the track buffer. For these disks, the disk rotational latency is then equal to the disk revolution time T. However, the data transfer time can then be ignored since only electronic transmission time from the track buffer to memory is required.

Data Transfer Time

When the I/O path is established and the beginning of the accessing sector comes under the read/write head, the disk starts to transfer data without any further waiting. All the data belonging to the accessed sector should pass under the read/write head for the data transfer to take place. Data transfer time is the time to read the accessed data from the current track.

The maximum recording density on the disk is called the maximum areal density. Let k be the recording density in bytes/unit length. On a track of radius x, the length of the track is $2\pi x$. The amount of data in this track is given by $2\pi x k$.

In one disk revolution, data on the entire track is transferred. Thus, the data transfer rate is

$$= \frac{2\pi x k}{T}.$$

To transfer R bytes of data on this track, the data transfer time (Tse, 1999) is

$$= \frac{TR}{2\pi x k}.$$

The above equation shows that the data transfer time decreases with an increase in the track radius x. Thus, the tracks on the outermost zone transfer data with the shortest time and the tracks on the innermost zone transfer data with the longest time. In addition, all tracks within the same zone store the same amount of data, and the disks rotate at the same speed. Thus, the data transfer rate is fixed for all tracks within a zone.

We have assumed that each zone has the minimum number of tracks. When the requests access data randomly, the mean data transfer time can be found (Tse, 1999) as

$$\overline{\tau} = \int_a^b P_x \frac{TR}{2\pi xk} dx$$

$$= \int_a^b \frac{2xTR}{2\pi xk(b^2 - a^2)} dx$$

$$= \frac{TR}{k\pi(a+b)}$$

The variance of data transfer time (Tse, 1999; Tse & Leung, 2000) is

$$\text{Var(t)} = \int_a^b P_x \left[\frac{TR}{2\pi xk} \right]^2 dx - \overline{\tau}^2$$

$$= \frac{T^2 R^2}{k^2 \pi^2} \left[\frac{\ln(b/a)}{2(b^2 - a^2)} - \frac{1}{(a+b)^2} \right].$$

Disk Array

In order to store more data on a storage system, multiple disks can be used. The disks may serve requests in parallel or independently. When multiple disks are used as a disk array, data are divided into data stripes. Each data stripe is a fixed number of bytes, and it is stored on multiple disks. When data are accessed, each disk is issued a request. All the requests are then served simultaneously. Each request retrieves a fraction of the data stripe. Hence, more data are transferred and large data transfers are served efficiently.

Mean time to disk failure is the average time that a disk may fail. When more disks are used, the mean time to disk failure shortens. For example, assume that the mean time to disk failure is 5 years. If we use only one disk, then we may expect to encounter a disk failure in around 5 years. If we use 10 disks, then we may expect to encounter a disk failure in around 6 months. If we use one hundred disks, then we may expect to encounter a disk failure in around 18 days. If we use 2,000 disks, then we may expect to encounter a disk failure everyday.

In order to recover data after disk failure, some redundant data are encoded and stored. Data on the failed disks can then be recovered from data storing on other disks. This arrangement of disks forms a redundant disk array

(Chen, Lee, Gibson, Katz, & Patterson, 1994; Gibson, 1992; Katz, Gibson, & Patterson, 1989; Kuratti & Sanders, 1995).

Redundant array of inexpensive disks (RAID) is an array of small and inexpensive disks that store encoded redundant data to increase data reliability and data security. When a single disk fails, data on the failed disk is recovered from data on the remaining disks. Seven RAID levels are described below.

RAID 0:   **No redundancy:** Data are simply stored on disks without any redundant information. Data can be lost when disk fails.

RAID 1:   **Mirrored disks:** The disks are arranged in pairs. Each disk in the pair contains the same data. This is the most expensive option that only half of the available disk capacity is utilized for data storage.

RAID 2:   **Bit interleaved array:** Several correction disks are added to the group of data disks similar to RAM chips. A single parity disk can detect a single error, but at least three disks are needed to correct an error. More parity disks in a group means more overheads for fault tolerance, but fewer data disks in a group means fewer I/O events/second. Since the whole group must be accessed to validate the correction codes, this is inefficient for small transfers.

RAID 3:   **Parity disk:** Data are interleaved bit-wisely or byte-wisely across the data disks. Disk controller can detect the failed bit position, and a parity disk contains the parity of the data disks. It is possible to recover data on any single lost disk by reading the contents from the surviving disks, and recomputing the parity. The disk array performance is similar to a RAID2 with a single correction disk.

RAID 4:   **Block interleaved:** Each individual block is stored on a single disk. Data are interleaved between disks at the block level instead of the bit level or byte level. The new parity is calculated as equal to (old data xor new data xor old parity). A small write request uses two disks to perform four accesses. Since all write requests access the parity disk, contentions at the parity disk would result.

RAID 5:   **Rotated parity:** Parity blocks are interleaved among the disks in a rotating manner called left-symmetric (Gibson, 1992). Two writes can take place in parallel as long as the data and parity blocks use different disks. This disk array performs better for small and large transfers, making it the most widely accepted level for transaction processing workloads. RAID5 tolerates single disk failure in each parity group of disks. Data are lost only when multiple disks in the same group of disks fail. Gibson used mean-time-to-data-loss to measure the reliability of disk arrays and showed that RAID5 can increase data reliability.

RAID 6:   **Two-dimensional parity:** The disks are arranged into a two-dimensional matrix, and a parity disk is added to each row and each column of the matrix array. This disk array can survive any losses of two disks and many losses of three disks. The only exception for three loss disks is that the data disk and both the parity disk and the column disk of this data disk fail at the same time. Since every logical write needs three disks and six accesses, the impact on I/O performance is significant. Hence, this disk array is acceptable only when the fault-tolerant requirement is very high.

In most data storage on disks, data are not differentiated into read-write or read-only types. Read-only data are static and cannot be modified by the applications. Read-write data are dynamic and are frequently modified by the application. Read-only data are easily recoverable from elsewhere, such as tertiary storage. RAID addresses the problem of losing data under the conditions of disk failures. Under the condition that read-only data are recoverable easily from other sources, the storage of redundant information of read-only data may waste storage capacity and bandwidth.

Chapter Summary

In magnetic disks, data are recorded on concentric circles on disk platters. Data are recorded on the tracks in sector units. New storage devices address the need of large capacity, short latency, high throughput, low-power consumption, and nonvolatility. We have described several new storage devices, including zoned disk layout in new magnetic hard disks, the spiral track layout in optical disks, the Millipede project, and the NRAM.

The major components of magnetic disk access time are seek time, rotational latency, and data transfer time. A continuous model provides a close approximation to the performance of the zoned disks. The mean and variance of seek distance for completely random disk accesses are found. The mean and variance of rotational latency and data transfer time are also found.

References

Chen, P. M., Lee, E. K., Gibson, G. A., Katz, R. H., & Patterson, D. A. (1994). RAID: High-performance, reliable secondary storage. *ACM Computing Surveys, 26*(2), 145-185.

Gibson, G. A. (1992). *Redundant disk arrays reliable, parallel secondary storage* (ACM 1991 Distinguished Dissertation). MIT Press.

Jeon, W. J., & Nahrstedt, K. (2002). Peer-to-peer multimedia streaming and caching service. In *Proceedings of IEEE ICME* (pp. 57-60).

Katz, R. H., Gibson, G. A., & Patterson, D. A. (1989). Disk System Architectures for High Performance Computing. In *Proceedings of the IEEE: Vol. 77*(12). 1842-1858.

Kuratti, A., & Sanders, W. H. (1995). Performance analysis of the RAID 5 disk array. In *Proceedings of the IEEE International Computer Performance and Dependability Symposium IPDS'95* (pp. 236-245).

Liao, W. J., & Li, V. O. K. (1997). The split and merge (SAM) protocol for interactive video-on-demand systems. *IEEE Multimedia, 4*(4), 51-62.

Paulson, L. D. (2002, September). Tiny punch cards boost storage capacity. *Computer*, p. 22.

Paulson, L. D. (2003, September). Nanotech RAM holds promise for universal memory. *Computer*, p. 15.

Tse, P. K. C. (1999). *Efficient storage and retrieval methods for multimedia information*. Doctoral dissertation, Victoria University, Melbourne, Australia.

Tse, P. K. C., & Leung, C. H. C. (2000). Improving multimedia systems performance using constant density recording disks. *ACM Multimedia Systems Journal, 8*(1), 47-56.

Chapter IV

Data Compression Techniques and Standards

Introduction

In the previous chapter, we see that the performance of a storage system depends on the amount of data being retrieved. The size of multimedia objects are however very large in size. Thus, the performance of the storage system can be enhanced if the object sizes are reduced. Therefore, multimedia objects are always compressed when they are stored.

In addition, the performance of most subsystems depends on the amount of data being processed. Since multimedia objects are large in size, their accessing times are long. Thus, multimedia objects are always kept in their compressed form when they are being stored, retrieved, and processed.

We shall describe the commonly used compression techniques and compression standards in this chapter. We first describe the general compression model in the next section. Then, we explain the techniques in compressing textual data. This is followed by the image compression techniques. In particular, we shall explain the JPEG2000 compression with details. Lastly, we explain the MPEG2 video compression standard. These compression techniques are helpful to understand the multimedia data being stored and retrieved.

Compression Model

A vast number of compression techniques have been designed since the 1950s. To understand different compression techniques, we here use a general model to describe data compressions as shown in Figure 4.1. Data compression is performed using two processing components. The first component is the encoder and the second component is the decoder. The encoder and the decoder components convert input data into output data according to the compression rules being specified in the compression method.

The encoder accepts some original data as input and generates a new encoded representation of these symbols. These encoded symbols are sometimes called *codewords*. The encoded symbols are created following the rules being specified by the compression method. Very often, the encoded symbols are intentionally designed to be shorter than the original input symbols.

Conversely, the decoder accepts the encoded symbols as input and outputs the restored symbols. In order to restore the original data, the decoder must use the same set of rules as the encoder, and these rules are specified by the compression method. If the decoder uses a different set of compression rules, it would not be able to restore the original data from the codewords. In addition, the codewords must be delivered unaltered from the encoder to the decoder. If any parts of the codewords are altered, the decoder also cannot restore the original data from the altered codewords.

To measure the performance of a compression technique, it is necessary to compare the size of the encoded symbols with the size of the original symbols. If the size of the encoded symbols is only one-third of the size of the original symbols, the compression ratio is said to be 3:1. Sometimes, the processing time to perform the encoding and decoding algorithms are also considered. These three metrics, including compression ratio, encoding

Figure 4.1. Compression model

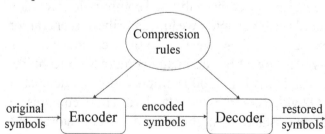

time, and decoding time, can provide good metrics of the performance of the compression techniques.

Text Compression

The Huffman coding method was created in the 1950s. The Ziv-Lempel compression and the arithmetic coding were created in the 1970s. Several popular compression algorithms, such as LZ77, LZ78, LZW, and gzip®, are variants of the Ziv-Lempel compression method. Later, the prediction by the partial matching method was designed in the 1980s. Most of the state-of-the-art compression techniques are variants of these fundamental compression methods.

In text compression, the encoder accepts some input text symbols and generates codewords. The codewords are created according to the rules being specified by the compression method in Figure 4.2. For example, if we use "a" to represent "apple," "b" to represent "boy," and "c" to represent "cat." We then represent "apple, boy, cat" with the codewords "a, b, c." This codewords are much shorter than the original input data symbols. Conversely, the decoder restores the original data from the codewords according to the rules specification of the compression method. In the above example, the decoder converts the codewords "a, b, c" back to "apple, boy, cat" according to the compression rules.

Before applying any data compressions, text symbols are represented by a fixed number of bits or bytes. In the ASCII code being used in personal computers, each text character is represented by a fixed number of eight bits.

Figure 4.2. Text compression

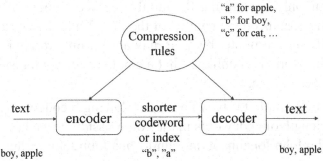

Data compression changes the number of bits in the codewords to represent each text character in the symbol.

The techniques used in the compression methods can be grouped into *symbolwise methods*, *dictionary methods*, and *hybrid methods*. The symbolwise methods, sometimes referred to as *statistical methods*, estimate the probabilities of occurrence of symbols and use shorter codewords for the more likely symbols. The dictionary methods replace words and contiguous words with an index to an entry to a "dictionary." The decoder then uses the indexes to look up the corresponding words from the same dictionary. The hybrid methods combine the two techniques of both the symbolwise methods and the dictionary methods within the same compression model. We shall explain these techniques with more details below. Afterwards, we describe the LZ77 and arithmetic coding compression techniques.

Symbolwise Methods

In a paragraph or text document, each different word or symbol usually occurs for a different number of times. Some words, such as "to," "is," and "at," occur very frequently. Other words, such as "incorrecttypo," occur rarely. If we choose a shorter codeword for the frequently occurring symbols and the longer codeword for the rarely occurring symbols, the short codewords occur more frequently, and the long codewords occur less frequently. The average length of codewords in the compressed text would then be short.

When the estimation of symbol occurrence is good, the symbolwise methods usually lead to better compression. Although the average length of codewords is usually shorter using the symbolwise method, the actual compression ratio depends on the number of occurrences of each symbol in the original text document. If the less likely symbols occur frequently in the text document, the average length of codewords in the compressed text can become long.

It is commonly known that the number of occurrences of each word in a file often depends on the context of the file. While the word "byte" appears frequently in a computer book, it may appear only rarely in a tourist guide book. Therefore, it is unlikely that a single set of compression rules works for all types of data.

We use an example to show how variable length codewords can reduce the average length of codewords in the compression. If we have a list of names "Paul John John Johanna John John Joshua John John Joshua John John John

Peter" as the input symbols, the list of uncompressed symbols are "Paul," "John," "Johanna," "Joshua," and "Peter."

Before compression, each character occupies one byte, and we ignore the space characters. The length of the list of input symbols is

$$= 10*4+1*7+2*6+1*5 \text{ bytes}$$
$$= 64 \text{ bytes.}$$

We represent the input symbols using fixed length codewords. For five different names, we need at least a 3 bits codeword to represent each name without ambiguity. For conventional purposes, we use a->b to show that codeword a represents symbol b. We choose "000" -> "Paul," "001" -> "John," "010" -> "Johanna," "011" -> "Joshua," "100" -> "Peter." As there are 14 names in the list of symbols, the total length of the symbols using fixed length codewords is

$$= 14*3 \text{ bits}$$
$$= 42 \text{ bits.}$$

We represent the symbols using variable length codewords. For five different symbols, we only need to create five different codewords with one codeword for each symbol. We choose "0" -> "Paul," "10"-> "John," "110" -> "Johanna," "1110" -> "Joshua," "1111" -> "Peter." As there is only one occurrence of "Paul," nine occurrences of "John," only one occurrence of "Johanna," two occurrences of "Joshua," and only one occurrence of "Peter," the total length of the symbols using variable length codewords is

$$= 1*1+9*2+1*3+2*4+1*4 \text{ bits}$$
$$= 34 \text{ bits}$$

The compression ratio due to using variable length codewords is thus

$$= \frac{42 \text{ bits}}{34 \text{ bits}}$$
$$= 1.235{:}1.$$

We have seen that the use of variable length codewords may change the average length of codewords. The amount of changes actually depends on the choice of codeword to represent the symbols. We can easily observe that the names appear a different number of times. The average length of codewords is minimized when the shorter codewords are chosen to represent the more frequent symbols. That is, we arrange the list of symbols according to their occurrence in the descending order. We have the ordered list of symbols as "John," "Joshua," "Paul," "Johanna," and "Peter." Let "0" -> "John," "10"-> "Joshua," "110" -> "Paul," "1110" -> "Johanna," "1111" -> "Peter," the total length of the symbols using this set of variable length codewords is

$$= 9*1+2*2+1*3+1*4+1*4 \text{ bits}$$
$$= 25 \text{ bits}$$

The compression ratio of this set of variable length codewords is thus

$$= \frac{42 \text{ bits}}{25 \text{ bits}}$$
$$= 1.68 : 1.$$

Therefore, better compression ratio can be achieved by using shorter codewords for the more frequent symbols.

Dictionary Methods

The dictionary methods replace symbols and text with an index to an entry in a "dictionary." They use simple representations to code references to entries in the dictionary. Instead of specifying one index for each symbol, an index can represent several matching symbols in the dictionary to achieve higher compressions. This is useful when several symbols often occur together.

The compression methods use a static dictionary, a semistatic dictionary, or an adaptive dictionary. A static dictionary simply uses a fixed dictionary to compress different sets of symbols. It is simple to use, but the compression ratio is not optimal in general. While a dictionary is optimal for one set of symbols, it may be suboptimal for a different set of symbols.

Some methods may use a semistatic dictionary to compress different sets of symbols. These methods construct a new dictionary or codebook for each text being compressed. This helps to optimize the compression ratio for the text or set of symbols being compressed. However, the overheads of transmitting or storing the constructed codebook are significant. As the same codebook has to be used by both the encoder and the decoder, the encoder needs to transmit the newly constructed codebook to the decoder.

Some methods use the adaptive dictionary approach. These methods use all the text prior to the current position as the codebook. While the text is reconstructed at the decoder, the codebook is reconstructed at the same time with the decompressed text. The decoder thus creates the same codebook as the encoder without the need to receive the codebook from the decoder. The dictionary is transmitted or stored implicitly at no extra cost. This codebook also makes a very good dictionary due to the same style and language used as the upcoming text after the current position.

In the dictionary methods, longer matching symbols lead to higher compression. For example, an index to two words "to be" is more efficient than two separate indexes to "to" and "be."

LZ Compressions

In the Ziv-Lempel coding, the previously occurred text is used as the "dictionary." The first occurrence of a symbol is coded as raw symbol. Repeated occurrence of a symbol is represented with the pointer to the matching location and matching length. This adaptive dictionary is used in LZ77, gzip®, LZ78, and LZW compression methods (Witten, Moffat, & Bell, 1999).

Figure 4.3. LZ77 encoder outputs codewords

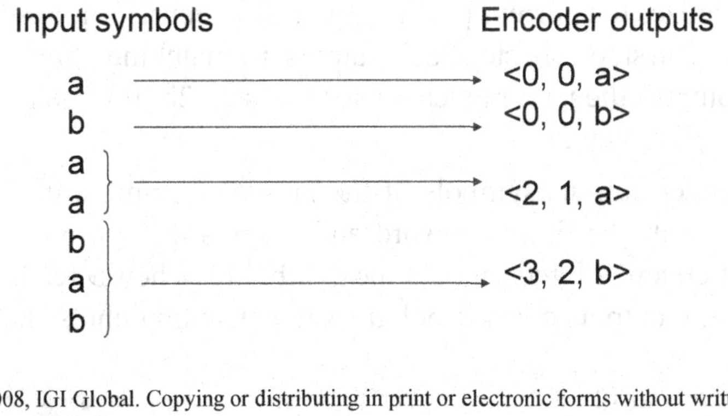

Input symbols	Encoder outputs
a	<0, 0, a>
b	<0, 0, b>
a	
a	<2, 1, a>
b	
a	<3, 2, b>
b	

In the LZ77 compressions, each compressed codeword consists of three fields, including location, length, and character. The location field describes how far back to look in the previous text to find the next phrase. The length field describes the length of the matching phrase. The character field describes the next character to follow. We describe the meaning of the codewords using an example below.

A list of text symbols is compressed using the LZ77 compression. The list of symbols are a, b, a, a, b, a, b, and so on. After the encoder reads the first symbol a, the encoder outputs the codeword <0, 0, a> as illustrated in Figure 4.3. This means that there is no matching phrase and the raw symbol is a. After the encoder reads the second symbol b, it outputs the codeword <0, 0, b>. This means that there is no matching phrase, and the second raw symbol is b. After the encoder reads the third symbol a, it matches the first symbol a, and continues to read the next symbol. After it reads the fourth symbol a and finds that it does not match with the second symbol b, it outputs the third codeword <2, 1, a>. This means that the location of the matching phrase is the one character at two symbols prior to the current position, and the next raw character to follow is an a. After that, the encoder reads the fifth symbol b which matches the second symbol b. The encoder reads the sixth symbol a which also matches the third symbol a. It then continues to read the seventh symbol b, which does not match the fourth symbol a. The encoder then outputs the codeword <3, 2, b>. This means that the matching phrase is the two characters ba, and the next raw symbol is b.

In general, the encoder reads input symbols and output codewords. The algorithm of the LZ77 encoder routine is shown in Figure 4.4. It first initializes the current position, p, to 1 in step 1. In step 2a, it loops through all the input symbols looking for the longest matching phrase from $p-W$ to $p-1$, where W is the limiting window size for matching. It then outputs the codeword in step 2b and increments the current position in step 2c.

The algorithm of the LZ77 decoder routine is illustrated in Figure 4.5. It first initializes the current position, p, to 1 in step 1. It loops through all the codewords in step 2. In step 2a, it outputs the matching phrase from $p-f$. After that, it outputs the next raw character c in step 2b. It increments the current position, p, in step 2c.

The decoder outputs symbols of the previous example in Figure 4.6. The decoder reads the first codeword and outputs the symbol a. It then reads the next codeword and outputs the symbol b. When it reads the codeword <2, 1, a>, it outputs one symbol, a, as the matching phrase and the next raw

Figure 4.4. LZ77 encoder routine

```
1. set p to 1
2. While there is text remaining to be
   coded, do
   a. Search for the longest match for
      S[p...] in S[p-W...p-1] to the matching
      at position m with length l.
   b. Output <p-m, l, S[p+l]>.
   c. Set p=p+l+1.
```

Figure 4.5. A simple LZ77 decoder routine

```
1. set p to 1
2. For each triple <f, l, c>in the input,
   do
   a. Output S[p-f...p-f+l-1] to S[p...p+l-1].
   b. Output c to S[p+l].
   c. Set p=p+l+1.
```

Figure 4.6. LZ77 decoder outputs restored symbols

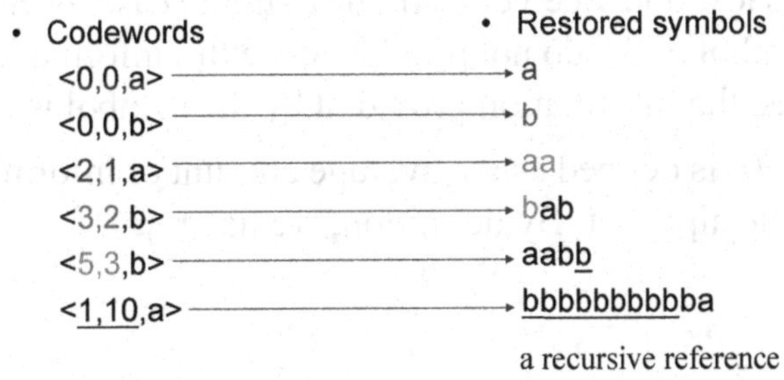

- Codewords   - Restored symbols
  <0,0,a> ——————————————→ a
  <0,0,b> ——————————————→ b
  <2,1,a> ——————————————→ aa
  <3,2,b> ——————————————→ bab
  <5,3,b> ——————————————→ aab<u>b</u>
  <u><1,10</u>,a> ——————————————→ bbbbbbbbba
                       a recursive reference

character *a*. Then it reads the codeword <3, 2, *b*> and outputs the matching phrase, *ba*, and the next raw character *b*. If it reads the next codeword <5, 3, *b*>, it outputs the matching phrase *aab* and the character *b*.

Some LZ77 decoders may support recursive references. If it reads the code-word <1, 10, *a*>, it outputs ten characters from the current position–1. Thus, the decoder recursively outputs the character *b* ten times before it outputs the next character *a*. The decoder should update the "dictionary" and output the restored symbol simultaneously.

The LZ77 compression limits the size of pointer to 13 bits and the size of the matching phrase to 8,192 characters. It avoids the need of large memory space and long searching time. Since long matching phrases is uncommon, some LZ77 encoders practically limit the length of the matching phrase to 16 characters. Some implementations use shorter codeword for recent matches and longer codeword for other matches. They use fewer bits to represent smaller numbers, but they need an extra field to indicate the number of bits for the number. Some implementations use a one-bit flag to indicate whether the next item is a pointer or a character. When there are not any matching phrases, the location and length fields are reduced to only one bit.

Arithmetic Coding

The theoretical lower bound on compression can be evaluated by considering the information content of each symbol. The whole alphabet is the set of all possible symbols. The predicted probability, $Pr[.]$, is the probability distribution for the next symbol to be coded within the whole alphabet. The information content, $I(.)$, of a symbol is defined as the number of bits a symbol, s, should be coded with $I(s) = -\log_2 Pr[s]$ bits.

When the probability of the next symbol is high, the information content of the symbol is low and vice versa. In the extreme case when the next symbol must be a symbol a, We do not provide any extra information by coding this symbol. Thus, the information provided by the symbol is 0.

The entropy, H, is defined as the average amount of information per symbol over the whole alphabet. By definition, we have

$$H = \sum_s Pr[s] \cdot I(s)$$

$$\Rightarrow H = \sum_s -Pr[s] \cdot \log Pr[s].$$

The entropy gives a theoretical lower bound on the compression ratio, measured in bits per symbol.

Consider throwing one fair dice and record the face value of the dice. The whole alphabet is {1, 2, 3, 4, 5, 6}. The predicted probability of any number,

$Pr[s] = 1/6.$
$I(s) = -\log_2(1/6) = 2.585.$

As the predicted probabilities of all symbols are the same, we have

$H = 6*[-(1/6)*(-2.585)] = 2.585.$

The arithmetic coding method optimizes the compression ratio according to the entropy of the symbols (Witten et al., 1999). Consider an alphabet consisting of numbers from 0 to 9. A fractional number with three digits can be used to specify three symbols. For instance, the number 0.245 can be used to indicate three symbols 2, 4, and 5. This is not optimal when the alphabet does not contain exactly 10 symbols or some symbols occur more frequently.

The encoding process of the arithmetic coding method finds a fractional number to represent the sequence of symbols. The decoder processing recovers the sequence of symbols from the fractional number by repeating the encoding process.

In the arithmetic coding, each symbol has an estimated probability within a range interval. Two variables, *low* and *high*, are used to specify the current range of the output fractional number. The range of the output fractional number is adjusted dynamically after each symbol is encoded. The division of the range is also adjusted dynamically according to the probabilities of the symbols.

The arithmetic coding encoder executes the following steps as illustrated in Figure 4.7:

1.   Initially, each symbol is estimated with the same probability.
2.   The range of the output fractional number is divided among the symbols according to their probabilities.
3.   After encoding a symbol, the new range of the fractional number is restricted to the range of the encoded symbol.

Figure 4.7. Arithmetic coding encoder

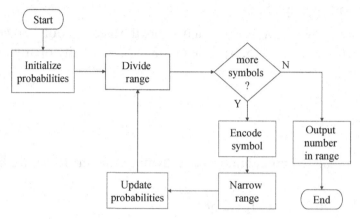

4. The probabilities of the symbols are adjusted. The range of the output fractional number is divided among the symbols according to their new probabilities.

5. The range-narrowing steps 3 and 4 are repeated until all symbols are encoded.

We use an example below to compress a string *bccb* within the set of alphabet $\{a, b, c\}$. Initially, low = 0, high = 1, probability of a = 1/3, probability of b = 1/3, and probability of c = 1/3. We divide the range according to the probabilities of the symbols. Thus, we get:

*   The symbol a is coded within the range [0, 0.333333).
*   The symbol b is coded within the range [0.333333, 0.666666).
*   The symbol c is coded within the range [0.666666, 1).

As the first input symbol is b, we narrow the range and increase the probability of the symbol b. We have low = 0.333333, high = 0.666666, probability of a = 1/4, probability of b = 2/4, and probability of c = 1/4. We subdivide the range [0.333333, 0.666666) according to the new probabilities of the next symbols to get:

- The next symbol a is coded within the range [0.333333, 0.416666).
- The next symbol b is coded within the range [0.416666, 0.583333).
- The next symbol c is coded within the range [0.583333, 0.666666).

As the second input symbol is c, we narrow the range and increase the probability of the symbol c. We have low = 0.583333, high = 0.666666, probability of a = 1/5, probability of b = 2/5, probability of c = 2/5. We subdivide the range [0.583333, 0.666666) according to the new probabilities of the next symbols to get:

- The next symbol a is coded within the range [0.583333, 0.600000).
- The next symbol b is coded within the range [0.600000, 0.633333).
- The next symbol c is coded within the range [0.633333, 0.666666).

As the third input symbol is also c, we narrow the range and increase the probability of the symbol c. We have low = 0.633333, high = 0.666666, probability of a = 1/6, probability of b = 2/6, and probability of c = 3/6. We subdivide the range [0.633333, 0.666666) according to the new probabilities of the next symbols to get:

- The next symbol a is coded within the range [0.633333, 0.638888).
- The next symbol b is coded within the range [0.638888, 0.650000).
- The next symbol c is coded within the range [0.650000, 0.666666).

As the last input symbol is b, we use the range of b, [0.638888, 0.650000), as the final range of the fractional number. The encoder just delivers any fractional number within this range to the decoder. The number 0.64 would be suitable as it falls within the range. The number 0.639 is also suitable, but it may use more digits.

A few points must be noted in performing the arithmetic coding process. First, the precision of the fractional number should be high enough to avoid ambiguity of the symbols. Second, a small final interval requires many digits to specify a number that is guaranteed to be within the final range. Third, two digits are needed to specify a number within a range of 1/100. Three digits are needed to specify a number within a range of 1/1000. The number of digits necessary is proportional to the negative logarithm of the size of the interval.

In binary digits, a symbol s of probability $\Pr[s]$ contributes $-\log_2 \Pr[s]$ bits to the output. This is equal to the information content of s, $I(s)$. Thus, the result is identical to the entropy bound. Thus, the arithmetic coding produces a near-optimal number of output bits. In practice, arithmetic coding is not exactly optimal because of the limited precision arithmetic and the whole number of bits.

Since the output number is always a fractional number, the "0." in front of the fractional number is unnecessary because the decoder knows that it always appears, and it does not provide any extra information. Thus, it can be excluded from the output bits. The output digit in the example is simply "64." In practice, binary arithmetic instead of decimal arithmetic is used. Thus, the output is a stream of bits.

Theoretically, the fractional number is determined after all the input symbols are considered. In practice, the symbols can be coded in parallel with the transmission. During the range narrowing steps, the range is $[0.633333, 0.666666)$ after the third symbol, c, is encoded. No matter what the following symbols are, the final range is within $[0.633333, 0.666666)$. The first decimal digit, 6, is already fixed and it can be transmitted to the decoder. The encoder can thus deliver digits on-the-fly before all the symbols are encoded.

Decoding is the process of recovering the string of symbols from the fractional number by repeating the encoding process. The decoding algorithm of the arithmetic coding method needs to find the range that the current fractional number belongs and cut off the tail of the string according to the number of symbols.

The decoding algorithm of the arithmetic coding method may perform the following steps as illustrated in Figure 4.8:

1. The numbers of occurrence of all symbols in the whole alphabet are first initialized to 1.

2. Calculate the predicted probabilities of all symbols in the alphabet.

3. The initial range $[0, 1)$ is divided among the symbols.

4. Find the output symbol s by mapping the fractional number from the ranges of the symbols.

5. Update the range to the range of the output symbol s.

Figure 4.8. Arithmetic coding decoder

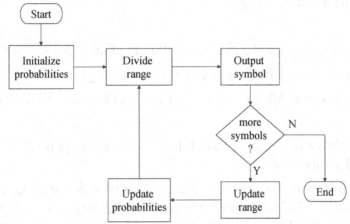

6.   Increment the occurrence of the symbol *s* and update the predicted probabilities of all symbols.

7.   Divide the range according to the predicted probabilities.

8.   Repeat step 4 to 7 until enough output symbols are obtained.

Let's consider the decoder processing in the above example. The decoder restores a string of four symbols from the set of alphabet {*a*, *b*, *c*} on receiving the two digits 64 to indicate a fractional number 64.

Initially, low = 0, high = 1, probability of *a* = 1/3, probability of *b* = 1/3, and probability of *c* = 1/3. We divide the range according to the probabilities of the symbols. Thus, we get:

- The symbol *a* is coded within the range [0, 0.333333).
- The symbol *b* is coded within the range [0.333333, 0.666666).
- The symbol *c* is coded within the range [0.666666, 1).

The fractional number 0.64 falls within the range for the symbol *b*. Thus, the first symbol is *b*.

After encoding the first input symbol *b*, we narrow the range and increase the probability of the symbol *b*. We have low = 0.333333, high = 0.666666, probability of *a* = 1/4, probability of *b* = 2/4, and probability of *c* = 1/4. We subdivide the range [0.333333, 0.666666) according to the new probabilities of the next symbols to get:

- The next symbol *a* is coded within the range [0.333333, 0.416666).
- The next symbol *b* is coded within the range [0.416666, 0.583333).
- The next symbol *c* is coded within the range [0.583333, 0.666666).

As the fractional number 0.64 falls within the range for the symbol *c*, the second symbol is *c*.

We then narrow the range and increase the probability of the symbol *c*. We have, low = 0.583333, high = 0.666666, probability of *a* = 1/5, probability of *b* = 2/5, probability of *c* = 2/5. We subdivide the range [0.583333, 0.666666) according to the new probabilities of the next symbols to get:

- The next symbol *a* is coded within the range [0.583333, 0.600000).
- The next symbol *b* is coded within the range [0.600000, 0.633333).
- The next symbol *c* is coded within the range [0.633333, 0.666666).

As the fractional number 0.64 falls within the range for the symbol *c*, the third symbol is also *c*.

We continue to narrow the range and increase the probability of the symbol *c*. We have low = 0.633333, high = 0.666666, probability of *a* = 1/6, probability of *b* = 2/6, and probability of *c* = 3/6. We subdivide the range [0.633333, 0.666666) according to the new probabilities of the next symbols to get:

- The next symbol *a* is coded within the range [0.633333, 0.638888).
- The next symbol *b* is coded within the range [0.638888, 0.650000).
- The next symbol *c* is coded within the range [0.650000, 0.666666).

As the fractional number 0.64 falls within the range for the symbol *b*, the fourth symbol is *b*. Now, we have decoded all four symbols, *bccb*, within the alphabet {*a*, *b*, *c*} on receiving the two digits 64 from the encoder.

Image Compression

The main objective of image compression is to reduce the amount of data in representing an image. As uncompressed images are large in size, images are often kept in a compressed format. This helps to save storage space in keeping the images and time to retrieve the images from the storage media. The main approach in image compression methods is to reduce redundancy in encoding images. The images may be decompressed and retrieved in parallel to hide the processing time in decompression.

Image compression methods can be roughly divided into lossless compression methods, lossy compression methods, and hybrid compression methods. The most well-known image compression standards include the Joint Photographic Expert Group (JPEG) and JPEG2000 methods.

Lossless compression, or noiseless compression, encodes data in a form that represents the original images with fewer bits. The original representation can be perfectly recovered. If the original images must not be lost, the images should be compressed using lossless compression methods only. The Huffman coding, arithmetic coding, Ziv-Lempel, and run length encoding belong to this category.

Lossy compression methods encode images into a form that can be decoded into a representation that humans find similar to the original image. The difference between the original images and restored images should be unnoticeable or not important to the human viewer. Lossy compression methods can be applied on image, audio, and video objects.

The main advantage of lossy compression methods is that they can usually compress images at a much higher compression ratio. Using the lossless compression techniques, JPEG can compress images to the just noticeable quality at the compression ratio of 15:1. The Motion Picture Expert Group (MPEG) standard can compress video at compression ratio of 200:1. The H.261 or px64 compression methods can compress video at the compression ratio up to 2000:1.

The hybrid compression methods use both lossless and lossy compression techniques. These include most compression standards, including JPEG, JPEG 2000, MPEG-1, and MPEG-2. Compression standards help to avoid complexity in handling heterogeneous methods.

Lossy compression methods compress images and video objects by predictive, frequency oriented, and importance oriented techniques. The motion

Figure 4.9. Lossy compression techniques

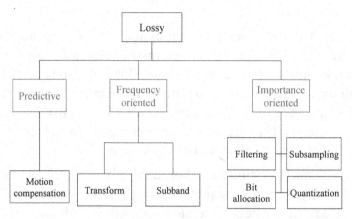

compensation method is a predictive technique. The transform coding and subband coding are frequency oriented techniques. The filtering, bit allocation, subsampling, and quantization methods are importance oriented techniques. These techniques are used in JPEG, JPEG2000, and MPEG compressions.

JPEG2000 Compression

The JPEG compression methods encode images using one of the four modes of operations. The four modes of operations include sequential encoding, progressive encoding, lossless encoding, and layered encoding.

In the lossless encoding, the images are encoded to guarantee exact recovery of every source image sample value. In the sequential encoding, each image component is encoded in a single left-to-right, top-to-bottom scan. In the progressive encoding, the images are encoded in multiple scans for applications in which transmission time is long. In the layered encoding, also called hierarchical encoding, the images are encoded at multiple resolutions. The lower resolution versions of the images may be accessed without first having to decompress the image at its full resolution.

The JPEG2000 compression method is a hybrid compression method which uses both lossless and lossy compression techniques (Adams, 2002). It implements compression of low bit rate. It is designed for images over low bandwidth transmission. Each image is divided into several image components. Each image component is subdivided into tiles that cover less than or equal to 4096 pixels. It performs colour transform, wavelet/subband coding,

Figure 4.10. Processing components of the JPEG encoder

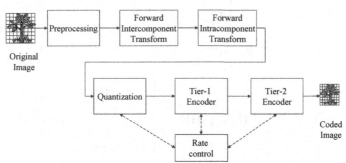

Source: Michael Adams, "The JPEG-2000 Still Image Compression Standard"

quantization, progression, and rate control on the images as illustrated in Figure 4.10.

A source image can be composed of several overlapping components. JPEG supports 1 to 255 image components. Each image component consists of one colour channel or spectral band. The colour of a full colour image can be decomposed into three colour components, such as red, green, and blue. The image formed by the red component is the red component image. Similarly, the images formed by the green or blue component are the green or blue component image. Thus, a colour image is decomposed into three overlapping images.

In the preprocessing step, the encoder adjusts the pixel values so that the nominal dynamic range is approximately centred at about zero. This is done by subtracting a bias of 2^P-1 to move the samples to the range [-2^{P-1}, 2^{P-1} −1].

JPEG defines two intercomponent transforms, including irreversible colour transform (ICT) and reversible colour transform (RCT) to change the colour representation of the images. The irreversible colour transform (ICT) is a Lossless compression using real-to-real transform. The reversible colour transform (RCT) is a lossy compression using integer-to-integer transform. The ICT converts image colours from the RGB representation to the YCbCr transform. The RCT approximates the ICT to perform a reversible integer-to-integer transform.

Afterwards, the encoder performs an intracomponent transform using the 2D wavelet/subband coding as illustrated in Figure 4.11. A low (L) subband image of half resolution of the original image is formed by using the mean of the sample values in the higher resolution. Then, another subband, the high

Figure 4.11. Wavelet intracomponent transform

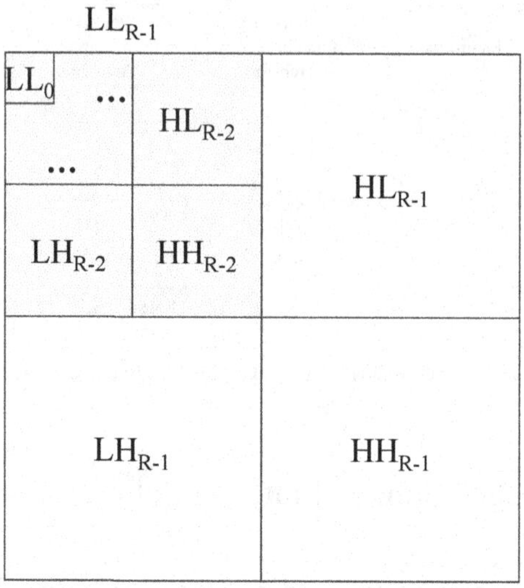

(H) subband, image of half resolution is formed by using the difference of the subband image with the original image. Thus, an image is transformed into two subband images. This subband coding is applied in both horizontal and vertical directions to form four subband images, including the LL, LH, HL, and HH subbands. The subband images are formed recursively on the LL subband of the previous level to generate the wavelet image.

The transformed wavelet image is then quantized. Mathematically, the quantization process is

$$V(x,y) = \lfloor |U(x,y)| / \Delta \rfloor \, \text{sgn}\left(U(x,y)\right)$$

where Δ is the quantization step size, $U(x, y)$ is the value of the pixel at position (x, y) before quantization, and sgn() is the sign function returning either +1 or -1.

Conversely, the dequantization process is:

$$U(x,y) = \left(V(x,y) + r \, \text{sgn}\left(V(x,y)\right)\right)\Delta$$

where $r = 0.5$ is the bias parameter.

In the Tier-1 Coding, the image is divided into blocks of rectangular tiles with size ≤ 4096 pixels per tile. Thus, the largest square tile covers 64x64 pixels. The pixel values are retrieved at a scan height of four samples per vertical column. Three passes per bit plane to get the sample values in the scan order. In the first pass, only the most significant bits of the sample values are obtained. In the second pass, the refinement bits are used. In the third cleanup pass, all other least significant bits are used.

The sample values are obtained in this scanning order to support multiple passes encoding. This is particularly suitable for images being transmitted at a low transmission rate. The resolution of images increases progressively as more passes of data are received.

The Tier-2 Coding builds packets with passes. Each packet is comprised of two parts, header and body. The encoded data for each tile is organized into a number of layers. Five sorting orders of packets called progressions are specified in JPEG2000. The five sorting orders are layer-resolution-component-position, resolution-layer-component-position, resolution-position-component-layer, position-component-resolution-layer, and component-position-resolution-layer. The encoder may choose the most suitable sorting order for the image or application.

JPEG2000 supports bit rate controlling. The bit rates can be controlled by choosing suitable quantization step sizes or including only a suitable subset of coding passes. JPEG2000 allows the region of interest (ROI) coding. Different regions of an image may be coded with differing fidelity. While synthesized from its transformed coefficients in the decompression process, each coefficient contributes only to a specific region. The encoder may identify the coefficient contributing to the ROI. It can then encode some or all of these coefficients with greater precision than the others.

JPEG2000 defines a structure for the encoded data. A code stream is a sequence of marker segments. Each marker segment has three fields, including type, length, and parameter. The code stream has one main header, a number of tile-part header body pairs, and one main trailer. The JPEG2000 files use the .JP2 file extension. A JP2 file contains a number of boxes. Each box has box length, box type, the true length of box when the box length is 1, and box data.

The JPEG2000 decoder reverses the process of JPEG 2000 encoder. It goes through the following processing components as illustrated in Figure 4.12.

Figure 4.12. Processing components of the JPEG2000 decoder

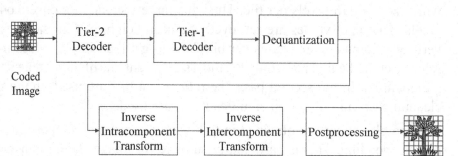

1. The compressed code stream is fed through Tier-2 and Tier-1 decoders.
2. The decoded values go through the dequantizer.
3. The dequantized values go through the inverse intracomponet transform and the inverse intercomponent transform.
4. The postprocessing restores the pixel values.
5. The image component is reconstructed from the pixel tiles.
6. The image is reconstructed from the colour components.

Video Compression

Several video compression standards were developed by the International Telecommunications Union and the Motion Picture Expert Group. ITU alone developed the video compression standards H.261, H.263, H.263+, and H.263++. MPEG alone developed the MPEG1, MEPG4, MPEG7, and MPEG21. The ITU and MPEG worked together to develop the MPEG2 and H.264.

MPEG1 is the first video compression standard from MPEG, and it was released in 1993. Its main purpose is to compress a video into a sequence of image frames. MPEG2 is an enhanced video compression standard, and it was released in 1994. MPEG4 is an object based video compression standard in 1999, and it compresses video into composing objects. MPEG7 is a multimedia content description standard based on the eXtensible Markup Language (XML). MPEG21 is an open multimedia framework standard.

MPEG-1 compresses the source intermediate formats (SIF) video. The characteristics of a SIF format video are 4:2:0 subsampling, progressive scan, and 30 mbps. A SIF format video may display either 352×240 pixels/frame at 30 frames/seconds or 352×288 pixels/frame at 25 frames/second. MPEG-1 compresses SIF video with raw data rate of 30 mbps to about 1.1 mbps at the VHS VCR quality

MPEG compression is suitable for digital storage media and channels. Different types of applications may compress and decompress video different number of times. Some applications may compress an object only once and decompress them several times. Other applications may compress and decompress objects in similar number of times.

Depending on the frequency of compressions and decompressions being performed, a compression technique can be classified as symmetric and asymmetric. The symmetric compression methods compress objects and decompress objects with similar processing times. They are more suitable for use in applications such as video e-mail and video conferencing. In these applications, video objects are compressed and decompressed a similar number of times. The asymmetric compression methods compress video objects with varying processing times. They are more suitable for use in applications including movies, video-on-demand, education-on-demand, and e-commerce. In these applications, the video objects are compressed only once at production of the objects. The compressed objects are decompressed more frequently, usually once when the objects are being viewed or displayed.

MPEG2 Compression

MPEG2 is an asymmetric compression. It strikes a balance between intraframe and interframe coding. For interframe coding, it performs block based motion compensations to reduce temporal redundancy. For intraframe coding, it performs DCT based transformations to reduce spatial redundancy.

An MPEG stream consists of many group-of-pictures (GOPs). Each GOP consists of three types of frames, including I-frame, P-frame, and B-frame. I-frames are intrapictures, and they are compressed using JPEG. They are independently compressed, and they can be used as the starting points for random access. P-frames are predicted pictures, and they are coded by referring to past pictures. They may also be used as reference pictures for future predicted pictures. B-frames are bidirectional predicted pictures, and they are coded by interpolating from the past and future pictures.

The MPEG I-frame encoders compress pictures using the JPEG compression as illustrated in Figure 4.13. The encoder first converts the colour space of the picture from RGB to YUV. The encoder then performs a forward discrete cosine transform (FDCT). The transformed sample values are quantized. After that, the quantized values are encoded using Huffman coding. MPEG achieves moderate compression on the I-frames.

The MPEG P-frames and B-frames are compressed by referring to other frames (Figure 4.14). P-frames only refer to the previous I-frame or P-frame, whereas B-frames refer to the previous I-frame or P-frame as well as the future I-frame or P-frame. P-frames are encoded using motion estimations, and B-frames are encoded using interpolations.

Motion estimation uses the block matching techniques to compensate the interframe differences due to motion as shown in Figure 4.15. For each block inside the current frame, the encoder finds the best matching block from the reference frame. If this block is found, it encodes the location of the matching block and the difference between this block and the matching block. P-frames are thus compressed at higher compression ratio than the I-frames.

MPEG uses interpolations to perform motion compensations on B-frames (Figure 4.16). For each block in the current frame, the encoder finds the best matching block in the previous reference frame and the best matching block in the future reference frame. These two blocks are interpolated to generate the interpolated block. The difference between the current block and this interpolated block is then encoded. MPEG thus achieves the highest compression on the B-frames.

As the B-frames depend on the previous and future frames, the sequence of storing and retrieving frames is different from the sequence of displaying frames. Each B-frame is stored after the previous and future pictures that it depends on.

Chapter Summary

Data compressions are vital to the storage and retrieval of multimedia information. While compression on textual documents is optional, it is mandatory to compress multimedia objects. In general, image compression techniques can be categorized into lossless and lossy compressions. Lossless compressions do not lose information in the encoding and decoding processes. They

Figure 4.13. MPEG I-frame encoder

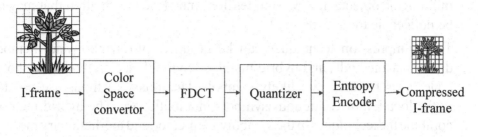

Figure 4.14. MPEG P-frame and B-frame encoder

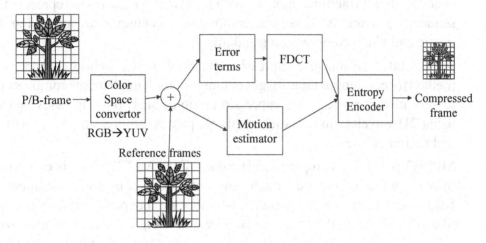

Figure 4.15. MPEG motion estimation

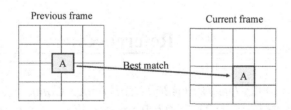

Figure 4.16. MPEG interpolation

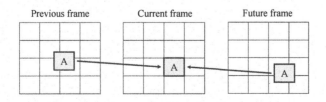

are used in handling textual documents, medical images, and originals of multimedia objects. Lossy compressions may lose information that may not be noticeable to humans.

Text compression techniques can be grouped into symbolwise methods, dictionary methods, and hybrid methods. Symbolwise methods use shorter codewords for the more likely symbols. Dictionary methods use pointers to the location of contiguous symbols in a dictionary. The hybrid methods combine the techniques in the symbolwise method and the dictionary methods within the same compression model. The arithmetic coding method optimizes the compression close to the entropy of the symbols. The arithmetic coding encoder finds a fractional number with sufficient precisions to represent the sequence of symbols. These text compression techniques are applied to the image and video compression standards.

JPEG2000 is an image compression standard. It is a hybrid compression method for continuous tone images compressions. It implements compression to very low bit rate at the compression ratio of 50:1. It compresses images using 2D wavelet, quantization, multiple passes, progression, rate control, and region of interest.

MPEG2 is a video compression standard. Each MPEG video is composed of many group-of-pictures. Each group of picture consists of a number of I-frames, P-frames, and B-frames. I-frames are independently compressed like JPEG images. P-frames are compressed using motion estimation with reference to the previous frames. B-frames are compressed using interpolation between previous and future I-frames or P-frames.

References

Adams, M. (2002) *The JPEG-2000 Still Image Compression Standard*. Retrieved November 21, 2007, from http://www.jpeg.org/wgln2412.pdf

Witten, I., Moffat, A., & Bell, T. (1999). *Managing gigabytes: Compressing and indexing documents and images* (2nd ed.). Morgan Kaufmann.

Summary to Section I

Background

This book is divided into the following six sections:

1. Background information in Section I.
2. Data placement on disks in Section IIa.
3. Data placement on hierarchical storage systems in Section IIb.
4. Disk scheduling methods in Section III.
5. Data migration methods in Section IV.
6. Cache replacement policies in Section V.

Multimedia data can be used in many types of applications. These applications include broadcasting, video-on-demand, communications, monitoring and control, and even information systems. The design of multimedia systems should consider the storage system, delivery network, and the scheduling algorithms. Most of these systems store large multimedia objects in their storage system for future retrievals. Inside the storage system, multimedia objects are stored as large binary data files, and they are accessed and delivered using streams. Multimedia streams can be classified by their periodicity, regularity, and continuity.

In magnetic disks, data are recorded on concentric circles on disk platters. Data are recorded on the tracks in sector units. New storage devices address the need of large capacity, short latency, high throughput, low power consumption, and nonvolatility. We have described several new storage devices, including zoned disk layout in new magnetic hard disks, the spiral track layout in optical disks, the Millipede project, and the NRAM.

The major components of magnetic disk access time are seek time, rotational latency, and data transfer time. A continuous model provides a close approximation to the performance of the zoned disks. The mean and variance of seek distance for completely random disk accesses are found. The mean and variance of rotational latency and data transfer time are also found.

Data compressions are vital to the storage and retrieval of multimedia information. While compression on textual documents is optional, it is mandatory to compress multimedia objects. Lossless compressions do not lose information in the encoding and decoding processes. They are used in handling textual documents, medical images, and originals of multimedia objects. The arithmetic coding method optimizes the compression close to the entropy of the symbols. It finds a fractional number with sufficient precisions to represent the sequence of symbols. JPEG2000 is an image compression standard for continuous tone images. Its encoder performs compression using 2D wavelet, quantization, multiple passes, progression, rate control, and region of interest. MPEG2 is a video compression standard. The MPEG encoders perform compression using FDCT, quantization, entropy coding, motion estimation, and interpolation.

Section IIa

Data Placement on Disks

Introduction

In the previous chapter, we have described how to apply compression techniques to reduce the size of multimedia objects. The performance of storage systems is efficient when data are carefully organized on the storage system. Thus, we describe the data placement on disks in this part.

Storage organization is also known as data placement. The storage organization methods are methods that place data on to the storage devices. These methods make use of the characteristics of access patterns on the type of storage device.

A method that is suitable for one type of storage device may not be suitable for another type of storage device. However, different storage devices may share some overheads in access data from various locations. Thus, the same placement strategy may be applied to different storage devices.

Many intelligent storage organizations, or data placement methods, have been designed for traditional data files and database systems. Traditional file placement methods are grouped into the following strategies (Kuvayev, Giles, Philbin, & Cejtin, 1997):

1. **Random placement.** Each data file is split into file blocks, and the file blocks are randomly placed on any storage locations. This is the simplest strategy to handle random accesses to file blocks.

2. **Contiguous placement.** Each data file is stored to contiguous physical locations. This strategy performs best when the entire file is accessed by consecutive requests. However, fragmentation prohibits the placement of large files.

3. **Type based placement.** Files containing the same type of data are grouped to a category. Files belonging to the same category are placed close to each other. This strategy trades off the seek distance of consecutive requests on data of the same type with that on data of different types.

4. **Frequency based placement.** Files are sorted according to the stationary probabilities of their accesses. Frequently accessed files are placed in the locations with low average access overheads. This strategy needs to record the access frequency of files in order to reorganize the data files.

5. **Markovian placement.** The pattern of consecutive accesses to data files is investigated. Two data files that are accessed by consecutive accesses are correlated. The data files with the highest correlation probabilities are stored to consecutive locations. This strategy optimizes the seek distance of requests according to the access history.

Many data placement methods are specifically designed for multimedia data. These data placement methods can be grouped according to their strategies into the following categories (Tse, 1999):

1. **Random placement.** Data stripes are stored randomly. This simple method is used for comparison only. Practical systems usually use this strategy due to its simplicity and flexibility.

2. **Statistical placement.** Objects are stored according to the stationary or transition probabilities.

3.   **Striping.** Objects are divided into stripes to allow round robin or parallel retrievals.

4.   **Replication.** Objects are fully or partially replicated to increase availability of data, or redundant codes are encoded and stored to increase data reliability and security.

5.   **Constraint allocations.** The physical storage locations to store consecutive data stripes are restricted so that the maximum overheads between consecutive requests are reduced.

These data placement strategies, except the random placement strategy, are described in the following chapters. The random placement strategy is skipped because it is simple and it does not provide any promises to the performance of the storage systems.

References

Kuvayev, L., Giles, C. L., Philbin, J., & Cejtin, H. (1997). Intelligent methods for file system optimization. In *Proceedings of the 14th National Conference on Artificial Intelligence and 9th Innovative Applications of Artificial Intelligence Conference* (pp. 528-533). Cambridge, MA: MIT Press.

Tse, P. K. C. (1999). *Efficient storage and retrieval methods for multimedia information.* Doctoral dissertation, Victoria University, Melbourne, Australia.

Chapter V

Statistical Placement on Disks

Introduction

The access pattern on each multimedia object can have very different characteristics. Some multimedia objects are more popular and they are more frequently accessed by more users. The user may concern the average access time on the objects. Thus, the storage systems can make use of the popularity of multimedia objects to optimize the average access time. Some objects need to be accessed at a higher data rate than the other objects. The users may concern the continuity of these objects. The storage systems may store the high data rate objects at the locations where data transfer rates are higher.

The statistical placement methods place the multimedia objects according to the characteristics of their access patterns. We shall describe the frequency based placement or popularity based placement method which optimizes the mean access time as the performance metric in the next section. After that, we shall describe the bandwidth based placement which uses the object continuity as the performance metrics.

When two placement methods are compared on the same storage system, each one of the methods may show better performance according to different metrics. System builder may choose the appropriate method according to the method that shows better performance in the preferred metrics. Thus, both placement methods have their significance.

Frequency Based Placement

Multimedia streams access objects and display them directly to users. Different users may access the same object stream. The same user may access an object more than once. This produces an observable characteristic of access pattern at the multimedia server called popularity of the objects. We will explain below that the access frequency of objects depends on the popularity of objects, thus the frequency based placement method is also called the popularity based placement or the temperature based placement.

When an object is popular, more users access the object for display. The time interval between consecutive requests on this object becomes short. The object is said to have high temperature or hot. The object is frequently accessed by the users. Thus, the access frequency of an object depends on the popularity of the object. The storage system can place the hot objects in the most convenient locations so that it may serve the request streams on the hot objects efficiently.

If an object is unpopular, only a few users or not any users access the object for display. The time interval between consecutive requests on this object is long. The object is rarely accessed by anyone. The object is said to have low temperature or cold. The storage system may remove the cold objects from the convenient locations to free space for the hotter objects. The higher overheads in accessing the cold object have little impact on the mean access time.

Many objects are neither popular nor unpopular. These objects are sometimes accessed by users. The time intervals between consecutive requests on these objects are of medium length. These objects are said to be warm. The storage system should place these objects at the medium convenient locations so that the requests on these objects can be served efficiently.

According to the Zipf-like distribution of object popularity, there are only a small number of hot objects, but there are many warm or cold objects. If the

80/20 rule is applicable, 80% of the requests access only 20% of the objects. The storage system can place only 20% of the objects at the most convenient locations to serve 80% of requests efficiently. However, the storage system also needs to efficiently store 80% of the objects in order to improve the access time of the last 20% of requests. This also shows that the 20% of objects should be placed with minimum access time. The objective of the frequency based placement is to reduce the mean access time of objects to its minimum. The mean access time logically becomes the performance measure for the placement method.

In Chapter III, we have shown that the access time is mainly composed of seek time, rotational latency, and data transfer time. The rotational latency is half of the disk revolution time. Data transfer time is shorter for objects residing on the outer zones. Seek time of an object depends on the seek distance traveled by the disk heads. This means that the seek time to serve a request depends on the track location accessed by the immediate previous request.

The frequency based placement methods assume that the objects are accessed randomly from the disks according to their access frequencies. When objects are randomly accessed, the immediate previous request may access data from any random track location. Thus, it is logical to minimize the mean seek distance from a random track.

In order to reduce the average seek time of disk requests, access probabilities have been considered in designing optimal file locations (Ford & Christodoulakis, 1991; Triantafillou, Christodoulakis, & Georgiadis, 1996). Since the access frequencies or data temperatures of multimedia data can be obtained from prediction or access history, movie data can be distributed among disks according to their access frequencies (Little & Venkatesh, 1995). Multimedia objects on zoned disks can be distributed according to their access frequencies (Chen & Thapar, 1996; Tewari, King, Kandlur, & Dias, 1996; Wang, Tsao, Chang, Chen, Ho, & Ko, 1997).

We define the middle zone as the zone to which the middle track of all tracks belongs. The zones containing tracks with shorter radius than the middle track are called inner zones. The zones that consist of tracks with longer radius than the middle track are called outer zones.

The middle track has the shortest distance from other tracks. Thus, it has the shortest mean seek distance. Since the seek time increases with the seek distance as we have shown in Chapter III, the middle track has the shortest mean seek time.

We have also shown in Chapter III that the data transfer time of tracks in outer zone is shorter than the data transfer time of tracks in inner zones. Thus, the tracks on the outermost zone transfer data with the shortest time, and the tracks on the innermost zone transfer data with the longest time.

In the frequency based placement methods, the hottest object, V_1, is placed at the optimal position that has the minimum random access time from all positions on the disks. The next hottest object, V_2, is then placed at the next available optimal position and so on (Figure 5.1). The objects are then placed similarly in a organ-pipe pattern, and the organ-pipe is skewed in the outward direction (Chen & Thapar, 1996). When the objects are independently and randomly accessed, the mean data access time would be minimal.

Where is the optimal location? The position of the optimal location varies from disk to disk depending on the disk parameters. Tracks of middle zone or the outer zone may be the optimal location, but tracks of the inner zones cannot be the optimal location. This is because the requests to the middle track are served with smaller mean seek time and mean data transfer time than the requests to any one track of the inner zones.

Consider two requests to the innermost track of two neighbouring zones that are in the middle or outer zones. The request that accesses a track from the inner one of the two zones will be served with shorter mean seek time but longer data transfer time. The other request will be served with longer mean seek time but shorter data transfer time. Depending on the difference between their mean seek times and data transfer times, the request that access a track from the outer one of the two zones may be served with shorter access time. Thus, the optimal location may be present in the outer one instead of in the inner one of the two zones.

If the reduction of data transfer time is larger than the increase in mean seek time for every pair of neighbouring zones, the optimal location will be in the outermost zone, and the hottest object will be placed in the outermost zone. Alternatively, if the reduction of data transfer time is smaller than the increase in mean seek time for every pair of neighbouring zones, the optimal location will be in the middle zone, and the hottest object will be placed in the middle zone.

Which track has the smallest mean access time among all tracks within a zone? The data transfer rate is fixed for all tracks within each zone. The mean seek time of a track increases when the track is further away from the middle track. The innermost track of an outer zone has the shortest mean access time than all other tracks within the same zone. The middle track has

Figure 5.1. Frequency based placement

$$V_1 \; V_2 \; V_3 \; V_4 \; V_5 \; V_6 \; V_7 \; V_8 \; V_9 \; V_{10} \; V_{11} \; V_{12}$$

decrease in popularity

inner zone   outer zone

V_{12}	V_{11}	$V_{10}V_9$	V_5V_4	$V_1V_2V_3$	$V_6V_7V_8$
1	2	3	4	5	6 zone

increase in radius

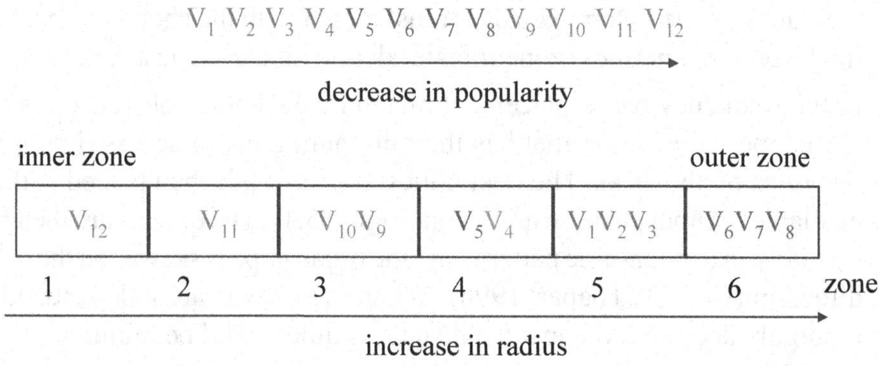

shorter mean access time than all other tracks within the middle zone. The outermost track of an inner zone has the shortest mean access time than all other tracks within the same zone. Thus, if the optimal location is in the middle zone, the optimal track should be at the middle track. If the optimal location is within an outer zone, the innermost track of this zone should be the optimal location.

If the object access frequencies are obtained from access history, some extra disk storage space is required to store the access history. Fortunately, the data temperatures of objects in some multimedia applications can be predicted. However, their data temperature dynamically changes over time but the placement methods are static (Griwodz, Bär, & Wolf, 1997). To maintain the optimal performance, data on the disks need to be frequently reorganized.

The frequency based placement strategy assumes that objects are independently and randomly accessed. However, a stream of requests sequentially accesses data stripes of the same multimedia object. When there are multiple concurrent streams, the disk heads traverse to-and-fro between storage locations of objects. Therefore, this strategy should be refined to a finer granularity in order to handle concurrent multimedia streams.

However, the multimedia objects are not accessed independently in most cases. In these situations, the correlation between object accesses must be considered. The Markov chain is used to model the access patterns for browsing graphs with low connectivity. A heuristic algorithm has been proposed to place the objects (Chen, Kashyap, & Ghafoor, 1992). The running time of the proposed heuristic algorithm is however in $O(n^3)$.

When objects are stored or temporarily placed on staging buffers, objects are only written and read back once. After these two data accesses, the objects may be deleted to release disk space. Thus, the number of data accesses of each object on the disk is different from the object temperature in the placement. In addition, the individual access frequency of these objects may be very low, but the staged buffers are accessed more frequently than other resident objects. If these buffers are allocated at the two ends of the disk, the mean seek distance would be very long. Therefore, these placement methods need to be refined for the optimal placement on staging buffers.

In frequency based placement, extra storage space is required to store the access history. The presence of concurrent streams and the continuous display requirement render that the statistical placement methods should be enhanced to handle streams of requests for multimedia data.

Bandwidth Based Placement

Different multimedia objects may have different access bandwidth requirements. High bandwidth multimedia objects, such as video, may consume more bytes per second than low bandwidth multimedia objects, such as voice. In order to meet the continuous display requirement of data streams, high bandwidth streams should be served with higher data rates than low bandwidth streams (Tse, 1999; Tse & Leung, 2000). Apart from the multimedia objects, computer programs and text files may also reside on the same group of disks. Discrete requests will access these files and these requests can be served with any data transfer rates.

As shown in Chapter III, the same amount of data are transferred in less time from outer zones than from inner zones of zoned disks; the throughput of accessing data from different zones varies. This variation in data transfer rates can be used to create new placement methods for the multimedia objects. The bandwidth based placement helps to maintain continuity of streams by placing the objects according to their necessary data rates.

The bandwidth based placement method stores objects in two steps. First, the multimedia objects to be stored on disks are grouped together based on their bandwidth requirement. Other binary and textual data files are grouped as an arbitrary bandwidth group. The bandwidth groups are then sorted from the highest to the lowest bandwidth. Second, each zoned disk is divided into

Figure 5.2. Bandwidth based placement

$$V_1 \ V_2 \ V_3 \ V_4 \ V_5 \ V_6 \ V_7 \ V_8 \ V_9 \ V_{10} \ V_{11} \ V_{12}$$

decrease in access bandwidth

inner zone   outer zone

V_{12}	V_{11}	$V_9 V_{10}$	$V_7 V_8$	$V_4 V_5 V_6$	$V_1 V_2 V_3$
1	2	3	4	5	6 zone

increase in radius

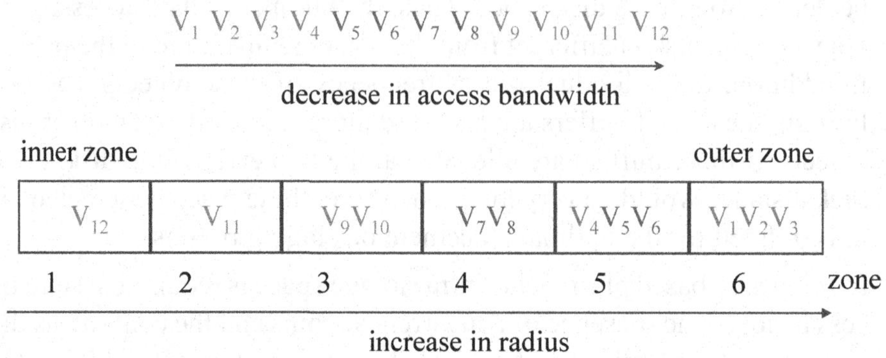

a number of groups of zones. The number of zone groups is ideally more than or equal to the number of bandwidth groups. Objects belonging to the highest bandwidth group are stored at the outermost zone group on all disk platters. Objects belonging to the next highest bandwidth group are stored at the next outermost zone group on all disk platters and so on. After the objects in all bandwidth groups are stored, the binary and textual data are stored at the innermost zone group. An example of bandwidth based placement using four zone groups is illustrated in Figure 5.2.

In the bandwidth based placement method, multimedia objects can be stored together with traditional data files on the same group of disks. Since high bandwidth data are stored at outer zones more than low bandwidth data, the transfer rate of higher bandwidth data are always higher. It reduces the data transfer time in accessing high bandwidth objects at the expense of longer data transfer time in accessing low bandwidth objects. Therefore, the access time to high bandwidth objects is reduced at the expense of longer access time to low bandwidth objects.

This trade-off may seem to be unfavourable for binary and textual data objects. In fact, not much is lost for the requests on binary and textual data. Since the binary and textual data are normally accessed in small blocks, only a few kilobytes of data are often sufficient to satisfy each request. These requests still enjoy a similar number of I/Os per second, and they are not much worse off. It is a reasonable trade-off so that the continuous media objects can be accessed with their necessary data rates.

As the data rate of each object is static, this object characteristic does not change over time. Once the storage organization is optimized for the highest performance according to the data rates, there is no need to perform reorganizations of the storage systems. The objects are properly placed on the preferred location until they are no longer needed.

Chapter Summary

The statistical placement methods consider the characteristics of the multimedia objects and place them accordingly. This allows the system administrator to optimize the storage system performance according to the administrator's preferred metrics. A combination of the statistical characteristics may also be combined into a priority function that determines the optimal locations of placing objects onto the disks.

We have described two statistical placement methods that base on different access characteristics. The frequency based placement method optimizes the average request response time. It uses an algorithm to place the objects according to their access frequencies. The hottest object is placed at the storage location with the least average access time. The next hottest object is placed at the next available storage location with the least average access time and so on. The objects are then placed in a skewed organ-pipe manner on the disks.

The bandwidth based placement method places objects according to their data rates. The storage system maintains its optimal performance according to the object data transfer time without reorganizations. The bandwidth based placement method adapts the data transfer time of objects according to their necessary data rates.

References

Chen, Y. T., Kashyap, R. L., & Ghafoor, A. (1992). Physical storage management for interactive multimedia information systems. In *Proceedings of IEEE International Conference on Systems, Man, and Cybernetics* (Vol. 1, pp. 1-6).

Chen, S., & Thapar, M. (1996). Zone-bit-recording-enhanced video data layout strategies. In *Proceedings of the IEEE MASCOTS Conference* (pp. 29-35).

Ford, D. A., & Christodoulakis, S. (1991). Optimal placement of high-probability randomly retrieved blocks on CLV optical discs. *ACM Transactions on Information Systems, 9*(1), 1-30.

Griwodz, C., Bär, M., & Wolf, L. C. (1997). Long-term movie popularity models in video-on-demand systems. In *Proceedings of the ACM Multimedia Conference* (pp. 349-357).

Little, T. D. C., & Venkatesh, D. (1995). Popularity-based assignment of movies to storage devices in a video-on-demand system. In *Proceedings of ACM Multimedia Systems* (Vol. 2, pp. 280-287).

Tewari, R., King, R., Kandlur, D., & Dias, D. M. (1996). Placement of multimedia blocks on zoned disks. In *Proceedings of SPIE Multimedia Computing and Networking 1996* (Vol. 2667, pp. 360-367).

Triantafillou, P., Christodoulakis, S., & Georgiadis, C. (1996). *Optimal data placement on disks: A comprehensive solution for different technologies* (Tech. Rep.). Technical University of Crete.

Tse, P. K. C. (1999). *Efficient storage and retrieval methods for multimedia information*. Doctoral dissertation, Victoria University, Melbourne, Australia.

Tse, P. K. C., & Leung, C. H. C. (2000). Improving multimedia systems performance using constant density recording disks. *ACM Multimedia Systems Journal, 8*(1), 47-56.

Wang, Y. C., Tsao, S. L., Chang, R. Y., Chen, M. C., Ho, J. M., & Ko, M. T. (1997). A fast data placement scheme for video server with zoned-disks. In *Proceedings of SPIE Conference on Multimedia Storage and Archiving Systems* (Vol. 3229, pp. 92-102).

Chapter VI

Striping on Disks

Introduction

Multimedia streams need continuous data supply. The aggregate data access requirement of many multimedia streams imposes very high demand on the access bandwidth of the storage servers. The *disk striping* or *data striping* methods spreads data over multiple disks to provide high aggregate disk throughput (Chua, Li, Ooi, & Tan, 1996; Hsieh, Lin, Liu, Du, & Ruwart, 1995).

In addition to the popularity of multimedia objects that we have described in the last chapter, multimedia streams consume an object in a sequential manner. The striping methods make use of this access pattern to evenly spread the workload across disks. This can increase aggregate disk throughput so that high bandwidth streams can be delivered continuously.

We first describe the simple striping method that places data stripes on a set of disks in the next section. After that, the staggered striping method that places data on a set of disks in a rotating manner is described. The pseudorandom placement method that stores data stripes on random disks is explained before we summarize this chapter.

Simple Striping

The main objective of simple striping method is to increase the storage system throughput so that the objects with high data rates can be accessed from the disks. In order to use the simple striping method, multiple disks should be available to store the multimedia objects.

The simple striping method divides an object into multiple data stripes of fixed size (Chua et al., 1996). The stripes are placed on multiple disks on a disk array. Each data strip is placed on one disk in the round robin manner. When an object is striped across N disks, the first data stripe is placed on disk 1, the second data stripe is placed on disk 2, and so on. In general, the ith data stripe is placed on disk $1 + (i\text{-}1)$ mod N (Figure 6.1).

When the data stripes are accessed from the disk array, one request is sent to every disk in the array at the same time. While the first disk is repositioning its read/write heads to the desired location, the second to the last disks are also repositioning their read/write heads to the desired locations. One data stripe is then transferred back from each disk to the memory buffers.

Hence, the time required to retrieve N data stripes from N identical disks takes about the same amount of time as retrieving one data stripe from only one disk. In this way, the throughputs of all N disks are summed up to provide high data bandwidth. Letting β be the throughput of each single disk and N be the number of disks, the total throughput of the disk array can be up to $N\beta$. When the data rates of objects are high, the storage system should increase the number of disks proportionally.

In order to retrieve a data stream from the disks, a minimum buffer to store $N+1$ data stripes is required. The size of the display buffers increases with the number of disks. Initially, N data stripes are fetched from the disks to the N buffers before the first data stripe can be displayed. This initial time to fill N buffers is called the start-up latency of the simple striping method.

Figure 6.1. Simple striping

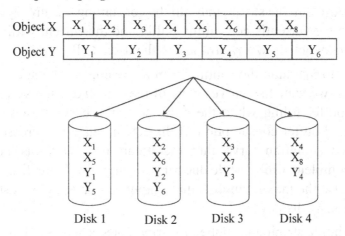

After the initial N buffers are filled, the stream may begin to display. The data consumption begins at the first data stripe. The $(N+1)$th buffer is also starting to fill data from disk while the first data strip is being consumed. After the first data stripe is displayed, the buffer space that is containing the first data stripe is freed. Then, the $(N+2)$th data stripe starts to fill into the first buffer while the second data stripe is then started to be consumed. Similarly, after the jth data stripe is consumed, the buffer space that is containing the jth data stripe is freed. Then, the $(N+j+1)$th data stripe is being retrieved while the $(j+1)$th data stripe is being consumed. In this way, the whole stream is retrieved using $N+1$ buffers.

When the data stripes are placed across more disks, more disks can be accessed in parallel to achieve a higher throughput. The actual disk throughput for the stream is however controlled by the current data consumption rate of the stream. When the buffer containing the jth data stripe is still in use, the $(N+j+1)$th data stripe cannot be retrieved. Thus, data are accessed from the disks at the rate that the data are consumed from the buffers.

If the data consumption rate is higher than the aggregate disk bandwidth, all buffers might be consumed and freed. All N disks are still busy accessing data to the buffers. The stream will then become starved and will not continue to display the media stream properly. The user will then observe an artifact that a video may freeze at a frame or an audio may become silent at an inappropriate point of time. Thus, the system should use enough disks to maintain the aggregate disk bandwidth higher than the data rate of the streams.

If the data consumption rate is only temporarily higher than the aggregate disk bandwidth; the stream may still be consuming the already-filled buffers between the currently consuming buffer and the currently filling buffers. A stream may not show any artifacts to the user at all.

In order to maintain the continuity of a stream, the actual data curve stays between two stair-like curves. One of the stair-like curves shows the completed buffer filling while the other stair-like curve shows the currently completed buffer consumption. If the actual data curve crosses the current buffer consumption curve, then the stream may starve as the buffers are still incomplete, filling while due for consumption. More disks may be used to increase the maximum disk throughput so that the object stream can be continuously displayed.

When simple striping is applied to stripe objects across a disk farm, the object may be striped across a number of disks. The number of striping disks should be enough to provide a disk bandwidth that can support the object's data rate requirements. The maximum number of striping disks is the number of disks in the disk array.

When an object is striped across all disks, all streams are concurrently served by all the disks. Each disk will access one data strip for each stream. Since each service of request consumes one seek and latency overhead, the amount of seek and latency overhead is equal to the number of concurrent streams. If each object is striped across a subset of disks, the concurrent streams are shared among different subsets. Thus, the number of seek and latency overheads on each disk is reduced. Therefore, it is more efficient to create data stripes across the smallest number of disks which can support the object's data rate requirements.

If the actual data curve hits the current buffer consumption curve, then the stream consumes data so slowly that all disks are waiting. The actual data access rate is very slow. The object stream can still continue to display properly.

Staggered Striping

Simple striping divides each object into data stripes and spreads them across a subset of disks. These subsets of disks overlap with each other within the set of disks. When concurrent streams are served, some disks may need to serve more streams while other disks serve fewer streams. This skews the total throughput of the disks. In addition, the busy disks may become unavailable for a long period of time when many objects are being accessed concurrently.

Berson, Ghandeharizadeh, Muntz, and Ju (1994) proposed a staggered striping method that aims at avoiding the continuous unavailability of disks in a disk array. The staggered striping method removes the constraint that two consecutive sub-objects must be assigned on non-overlapping disks. The staggered striping method can also accommodate objects of heterogeneous display bandwidth with little loss of disk throughput.

In the staggered striping method, each multimedia object is partitioned into a number of sub-objects. Each sub-object is placed on a cluster of disks (Figure 6.2). The number of disks in a cluster is chosen in a way that it can support the required bandwidth of the object. The next sub-object is then placed in the next disk cluster. The next cluster of disks is selected as the next k disks being shifted by r disks, where $0 \leq r \leq k$. The number of shifted disks, r, is called the *stride*.

In Figure 6.2, the multimedia object, X, is partitioned into three sub-objects, X_1, X_2, and X_3. In order to support the data rate requirements, the object X needs to be stored on three disks. The sub-object X_1 is further divided into X_{11} to X_{13}. These data stripes X_{11}, X_{12}, and X_{13} are placed on disk 1, disk 2, and disk 3, respectively. The sub-object X_2 is further divided into X_{21} to X_{23}. The stride of 1 is used so that the next cluster of disks is shifted by one disk. Thus, the data stripes X_{21}, X_{22}, and X_{23} are placed on disk 2, disk 3, and disk 4, respectively. Similarly, the sub-object X_3 is further divided into X_{31} to X_{33}. The next cluster of disks is also shifted by one disk. Thus, the data stripes X_{31}, X_{32}, and X_{33} are placed on disk 3, disk 4, and disk 1, respectively.

Similarly, the multimedia object Y is partitioned into three sub-objects, Y_1, Y_2, and Y_3. In order to support the data rate requirements, the object Y needs to be stored on two disks. The sub-object Y_1 is further divided into Y_{11} and Y_{12}. These data stripes, Y_{11} and Y_{12} are placed on disk 4 and disk 1, respectively. The sub-object Y_2 is further divided into Y_{21} and Y_{22}. The stride of 1 is also used so that the next cluster of disks is shifted by one disk. Thus, the data stripes Y_{21} and Y_{22} are placed on disk 1 and disk 2, respectively. Similarly, the sub-object Y_3 is further divided into Y_{31} and Y_{32}. The next cluster of disks is also shifted by one disk. Thus, the data stripes Y_{31} and Y_{32} are placed on disk 2 and disk 3, respectively.

Figure 6.2. Staggered striping

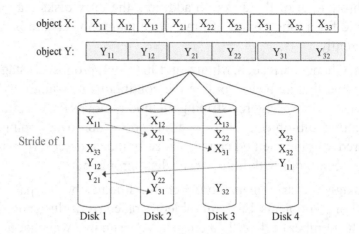

While an object is being retrieved in parallel, the cluster of disks in use changes from time to time. The subset of disks being used for a stream shifts by the stride value. Hence, each disk becomes free periodically. As long as a new stream can be served within the time gap, another object can be retrieved within the time gaps.

The staggered striping method provides effective support for multiple streams accessing different objects from a group of striped disks, and it automatically balances the workload among disks. The staggered striping method is actually a generalization of the simple striping method. When the stride is equal to zero or k, the stagger striping method becomes the same as the simple striping method.

Application Note: *Unfortunately, the staggered striping method still suffers from the disk bandwidth fragmentation problems. Since continuous disk bandwidth must be obtained from the participating disks, the disk bandwidth can become fragmented, and new streams are rejected. This bandwidth fragmentation problem could be alleviated by efficient scheduling methods that alter the service order of requests.*

Although data on tertiary storage devices may also mismatch the staggered striping arrangement on disks, data on tertiary storage can be pre-arranged to alleviate this problem. Unfortunately, the objects are not always presented in the normal display rate. When an object is presented in fast forward mode or rewind mode, data are retrieved in a different rate from the cluster of disks. Berson et al. (1994) proposed creating a replica in order to support objects retrieved at abnormal rates. However, each rate would require an extra replica and the system is obviously limited to a small number of display rates predicted in advance.

Pseudorandom Placement

In the data striping methods, the data stripes are stored onto a number of disks. The choice of which disk to store a data stripe depends on the number of disks. The striping methods assign disk numbers sequentially to data stripes in cycles. For a storage system with d disks, the disks are numbered from D_0 to D_{d-1}. An object Y with n data stripes is placed on the d disks. The $i+1$th data stripe Y_i is placed on D_j if

$D_j = i \bmod d$,
where $j = 0, 1, \ldots, d-1$ and $i = 0, 1, \ldots, n-1$.

When new disks are added to the disk farm, the data stripes become incorrectly placed according to the new number of disks. Thus, all the disks need to be reorganized, and the data stripes of all the objects are moved to new locations in order to maintain the integrity of the storage system. This reorganization of all the objects on the disks incurs heavy workload on the storage system.

In Figure 6.3, object Y is originally stored on two disks, D_0 and D_1. The object Y is split into six data stripes, Y_0 to Y_5, and these data stripes are already placed on the appropriate disks. A new disk, D_2, is now added to the disk farm. The data stripes Y_2 to Y_5 need to be moved to their new disk location. This cycle repeats for every six (=2*3) data stripes when the third disk is added. Thus, four out of every group of six data stripes should be moved.

The addition of the second disk to a single disk involves moving half of all data stripes. The addition of the third disk involves moving two thirds of all data stripes. The addition of the fourth disk involves moving three fourths of all data stripes. Since d and $d-1$ are relatively prime for all $d > 1$, the addition of the dth disk involves moving $d*(d-1)/d^2 = (d-1)/d$ of all data stripes.

Figure 6.3. Pseudorandom placement. In adding a new disk D_2, Y_3 to Y_6 are moved.

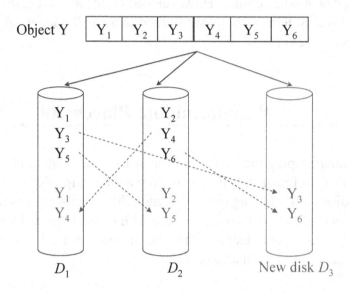

Apart from disk additions, disk reorganization is required when disks are removed. When one of the disks is removed, the number of disks decreases. The data stripes on all disks should be moved to other disks in order to maintain the integrity of the striping method. Furthermore, removing a disk in the middle of a group of disks may result in a gap within the range of disk numbers. The disks should be renumbered so that the data stripes can be retrieved from the correct disk. Although disks are seldom removed, failed disks are often directly replaced with a new one. The workload on disk reorganization for disk removals is however heavy.

The objective of the pseudorandom placement method is to reduce the workload in reorganization when disks are added or removed from the disk array. It reduces the number of data stripes being moved after adding a disk. It also reduces the number of data stripes being moved to remove a disk.

Instead of assigning sequentially a fixed disk number to the data stripe when a new disk is added, the pseudorandom placement method uses the pseudorandom function to generate the new disk numbers so that the data stripes can be evenly distributed (Goel, Shahabi, Yao, & Zimmermann, 2002; Santos, Muntz, & Ribeiro-Neto, 2000).

The pseudorandom function is not truly random. It returns a random number within the range 0 to 1 uniformly. When a seed number is provided as the parameter to the pseudorandom function, the pseudorandom function always returns the same random number. If a random number within a range of 0 to N-1 is required, the return random number is simple multiplied by N, and the fractional part is truncated away.

By controlling the new disk numbers for the data stripes, the pseudorandom striping method reduces the number of movements of data stripes (Goel et al., 2002). After a new disk is added, it regenerates a new disk number for every data stripe. If the generated disk number for a data stripe is within the original disks before adding, it keeps the old disk number as the new disk number and avoids moving the data stripe. If the generated disk number is on the newly added disk, then the new disk number is the generated disk number and the data stripe is moved to the new disk.

Consider that a seed X_s is chosen. The pseudorandom function, RF(.), can be used to generate the new disk numbers D_1 and D_2 as follows.

$D_1 = RF(X_s)$, and
$D_2 = RF(D_1) = RF(RF(X_s)) = RF^2(X_s)$,
where X_s is the initial seed for the pseudorandom function. Similarly, the new disk number D_j is generated within the range 0 to d-1 as

$D_j = RF(D_{j-1})$.
D_{j-1} is then further expanded repeatedly to get

$D_j = RF(RF(D_{j-2})) = \ldots = RF^j(X_s)$.

When the same initial seed number X_s is used, it always generates the same sequence of numbers D_j such that each D_j is within the range of 0 to d-1. This also implies that if we know the value of the initial seed, X_s, we can calculate an entire sequence of seed numbers D_j.

If we define $q_j = (X_j \text{ div } N_j)$ and $r_j = X_j \text{ mod } N_j$, then q_j and r_j are the quotient and remainder of X_j divided by N_j. Thus, we have

$$X_j = q_j * N_j + r_j.$$

Let X_j be the seed for the jth application of the random number function on a data stripe, Y_i. For simplicity, the index of a data stripe, i, may be used as the initial seed for the data stripe. After adding a new disk, the previous X_{j-1} is used as the seed of random number function to generate the new X_j. Thus, we can always get the same sequence of seed numbers, X_j, for all $j > 1$. The following disk addition algorithm is used to generate the sequence of seed numbers after adding a new disk (Goel et al., 2002).

Disk addition algorithm to generate, X_j, the jth seed number of a data stripe after adding a new disk:

If $(RF(X_{j-1}) \bmod N_j) < N_{j-1}$, then
$$X_j = RF(X_{j-1}) * N_j + r_{j-1}$$
Otherwise,
$$X_j = RF(X_{j-1}) * Nj + RF(X_{j-1}) \bmod N_j.$$

The above disk addition algorithm uses $RF(X_{j-1})$ to generate a new random number so that the data stripes can be evenly distributed to N_j disks. If the remainder of this random number divided by N_j is less than N_{j-1}, then the remainder is within the original number of disks before adding the new disk. The new seed number X_j is then calculated as a multiple of N_j plus the previous remainder r_{j-1}. The new disk number, r_j, is equal to the old disk number, r_{j-1}, since

$$
\begin{aligned}
r_j \quad &= X_j \bmod N_j \\
&= (RF(X_{j-1}) * N_j + r_{j-1}) \bmod N_j \\
&= r_{j-1}.
\end{aligned}
$$

If the remainder of the random number divided by N_j is equal to N_{j-1}, then the data stripe should be placed in the new disk. The new X_j is calculated as a multiple of N_j plus the remainder of the random number modulo N_j. Thus, the new disk number, r_j, can be found as

$$
\begin{aligned}
r_j \quad &= X_j \bmod N_j \\
&= (RF(X_{j-1}) * Nj + RF(X_{j-1}) \bmod N_j) \bmod N_j \\
&= RF(X_{j-1}) \bmod N_j.
\end{aligned}
$$

Therefore, the data stripe will be placed in the newly added disk if $RF(X_{j-1})$ mod N_j is equal to N_{j-1}. Since the random number function always generates random numbers that spread uniformly over the range of values from 0 to

N_{j-1}, only one of N_j return random number values will be equal to N_{j-1}. Thus, only one of N_j data stripes will be moved to the new disk.

Similar to adding disks, the pseudorandom placement method also provides the means to reduce data stripes movements for disk removals. Before a disk is removed, the previous X_{j-1} is used as the seed of random number function to generate the new disk number. The following disk removal algorithm is executed to generate new sequence of seed numbers (Goel et al., 2002).

Disk removal algorithm to generate, X_j, the jth seed number of a data stripe before removing a new disk:

If r_{j-1} is not removed, then
$X_j = \text{RF } (X_{j-1}) * N_j + \text{new}(r_{j-1})$
Otherwise,

$X_j = \text{RF}(X_{j-1})$,
where new(.) is a mapping function that maps from previous disk numbers to new disk numbers.

The disk removal algorithm uses the previous X_{j-1} as seed to generate a new seed number for the data stripe. It uses a new(.) to map the previous disk numbers to new disk numbers so that no gaps exist in the disk numbers after mapping. The input parameter to this new( ) function is a disk number in the range before disk removal. It thus returns a disk number in the range after disk removal.

The above disk removal algorithm checks if the data stripe originally resides on the removing disk. If it is not on the removing disk, the new X_j is calculated as a multiple of N_j plus the mapping of the previous remainder r_{j-1}. Thus, the data stripe thus stays on the original disk.

If the data stripe is on the removing disk, a new X_j is calculated as $\text{RF}(X_{j-1})$. The data stripe will then be moved to a random one of the remaining disks. Since the pseudorandom function is used to generate the new random number, the data stripe has the same probability to reside on anyone of the remaining disks. Thus, the data stripes originally residing on the removing disk are thus evenly distributed to the N_{j-1} disks.

The pseudorandom placement method changes the traditional striping methods that assign disk numbers sequentially in cycles. When disks are added or removed, only a small fraction of all data stripes need to be moved. The data stripes continued to be evenly distributed across the disks.

In order to find the sequence of seeds and random numbers, the pseudorandom placement method needs to use the random number function many times. Fortunately, the random number function mainly looks up entries from the random number table. The function can perform efficiently.

Chapter Summary

The simple striping methods increase the efficiency of serving concurrent multimedia streams. These methods consider the characteristics of multimedia streams in the design of the techniques. Multimedia streams can access the data stripes according to their actual data consumption rates. Thus, the disk bandwidth and the memory buffer are used efficiently. However, the actual participating streams may not access objects exactly as expected. Thus, the increase in efficiency is not as much as expected.

The staggered striping method provides effective support for multiple streams accessing different objects from a group of striped disks, and it automatically balances the workload among disks. Unfortunately, the staggered striping method still suffers from the disk bandwidth fragmentation problems, and new streams may be rejected.

The pseudorandom placement method maintains that the data stripes are evenly distributed on disks. In addition, it reduces the number of data stripes being moved when the number of disks increases or decreases. It uses the pseudo-random number function to generate new disk numbers that are independent of the disk number of other data stripes. The pseudorandom placement reduces the workload on data reorganization when disks are added or removed.

References

Berson, S., Ghandeharizadeh, S., Muntz, R., & Ju, X. (1994). Staggered striping in multimedia information systems. In *Proceedings of the ACM SIGMOD Conference* (pp. 79-90).

Chua, T. S., Li, J., Ooi, B. C., & Tan, K. L. (1996). Disk striping strategies for large video-on-demand servers. In *Proceedings of the ACM Multimedia Conference* (pp. 297-306).

Goel, A., Shahabi, C., Yao, S.-Y. D., & Zimmermann, R. (2002). SCADDAR: An efficient randomized technique to reorganize continuous media blocks. In *Proceedings of the 18th International Conference on Data Engineering (ICDE'02)*.

Hsieh, J., Lin, M., Liu, J. C. L., Du, D. H. C., & Ruwart, T. M. (1995). Performance of a mass storage system for video-on-demand. In *Proceedings of the 14th Annual Joint Conference of the IEEE Computer and Communications Societies INFOCOM'95* (Vol. 2, pp. 771-778).

Santos, J. R., Muntz, R., & Ribeiro-Neto, B. (2000). Comparing random data allocation and data striping in multimedia servers. In *ACM Sigmetrics 2000* (pp. 44-55).

Chapter VII

Replication Placement on Disks

Introduction

When extra storage space is available on the striping disks being described in the last chapter, the storage system may keep extra copies of the stored objects to enhance the performance of the storage system. If any one of the copy or the original copy is corrupted, the corrupted copy can possibly be recovered by comparison with its replicas. The replication strategy thus increases reliability of the storage system by applying redundancy on the stored objects.

Extra copies of objects may be created and stored on the storage system to increase the storage system performance. The presence of replicas on light loading disks may be able to reduce the period of time that an object is inaccessible. Thus, the replication strategy increases the availability of the stored objects.

The replication strategy can have several advantages. First, the replica on idle disks can increase the availability of data on corrupted and busy disks. Second, the replica on local server can reduce the network load to access objects from remote servers. Third, the replica on local server can also reduce the need to wait for the filling of initial buffer prior to consumption. Fourth, replica can avoid disk multitasking by avoiding the need to serve multiple streams from the same disk head.

We will describe the streaming redundant array of inexpensive disks (RAID) method that increases availability and fault tolerance in the next section. After that, we present the Lancaster storage server to reduce network load. Then, we show two data replication methods to reduce start-up latency. Afterwards, we explain how the data replication method can avoid disk multitasking. Before we conclude this chapter, we describe the replication method that balances the space and workload of storage devices.

Replication to Increase Availability

Redundant array of inexpensive disks has become widely accepted in recent years. Similar to RAID disks, the streaming RAID was proposed to serve multimedia streams. The objective of streaming RAID is to increase reliability and availability of multimedia data. The approach to achieve these objectives is by storing redundant information (Cohen & Burkhard, 1996; Tobagi, Pang, Baird, & Gang, 1993). Performance of multimedia streams is maintained by using multiple disks like the striping methods. A disadvantage of streaming RAID is that even more data are stored on the storage system.

Multimedia data are large, and each stream accesses data of an object for a long time. Thus, the disk containing the accessed object will become busy for a long period of time. When other streams try to access other objects residing on the same disk, the disk becomes too busy to serve them. As a result, new request streams will not be served until the disk becomes free. This disk outage problem limits the storage system's ability to serve multimedia streams without degrading their quality.

Streaming RAID is an interdisk, strip-based method. In the streaming RAID method, every data object is divided into a number of blocks. Each block is a fixed number of bytes, and the data blocks are stored on multiple disks. One block from each disk forms a group. A parity bit is formed by XOR of one bit from every block in the group. The parity information is created as the redundant information. This parity information is then stored onto a separate parity disk (Tobagi et al., 1993).

For example, an object X is stored on three disks. Block X is divided into many blocks. X_{3i} is the $3i$th block of X and it is stored on disk 1. X_{3i+1} is the $3i+1$th block of X, and it is stored on disk 2. X_{3i+2} is the $3i+2$th block of X, and it is stored on disk 3. P_i is the ith parity block. Then, the jth bit of the parity block, $P_{i,j}$ is found as:

$$P_{i,j} = X_{3i,j} \oplus X_{3i+1,j} \oplus X_{3i+2,j},$$

where $X_{3i,j}$, $X_{3i+1,j}$, $X_{3i+2,j}$ are respectively the jth bit of the $3i$th block, $3i+1$th block, and $3i+2$th block of object X.

Multiple data disks are used as a disk array, and the disks serve requests in parallel. When data are accessed, each disk is issued a request. All the requests are then served simultaneously. Each request retrieves a data block from the disk. If one of the disks is not available, or some data on the disk are corrupted, the redundant information on the parity disk is accessed. The unavailable or corrupted block is then reconstructed from the data from other data disks and the parity disk.

For example, a data block, X_{3i+2}, is unavailable when the object X is being accessed. This block can be recovered from the data blocks X_{3i+2}, X_{3i+2}, and the parity block P_i. The jth bit of the missing block, $X_{3i+2,j}$, can be recalculated using the equation:

$$X_{3i+2,j} = X_{3i,j} \oplus X_{3i,j} \oplus P_{i,j}.$$

The streaming RAID method is designed to increase the reliability of multimedia streams by storing redundant information. It also enhances the storage disk performance through controlling the storage location of objects. The streaming RAID method is similar to the RAID-3 level disk in keeping the parity information on separate parity disks. This is suitable for large data transfers but not efficient for small data transfer. Since multimedia objects are large and a large amount of data are transferred each time, the streaming RAID is an efficient method for multimedia object streaming.

A limitation of streaming RAID is its lack of control on the placement of multimedia data in storage. Hence, the data bandwidth cannot be effectively controlled, and large variations in data bandwidth require more read-ahead buffer.

A disadvantage of streaming RAID is that it increases the data storage usage. Since multimedia objects are large in size, storage of the objects' data already exhausts many storage systems. The creation of redundant information increases the burden on the storage system.

Storing redundant information obviously increases the security of data during disk failure. Although the security of multimedia data should not be neglected, proper backing up and archiving data can also achieve the data security. Since most multimedia data are not frequently modified and storing the redundant information would reduce the available user data bandwidth, it would be nice to consider redundant codes when surplus bandwidth is available or other means to provide data security are not available.

Replication to Reduce Network Load

Multimedia objects are large in size. The workload to deliver multimedia objects across the networks is heavy. Objects may be stored on storage servers that are distributed over a wide geographic area network. It would be nice if some objects can be fetched from neighbouring storage servers that have stored the object. Thus, data replication is one of the approaches to distribute objects across the network in order to reduce the network load.

In the Lancaster continuous media storage server, object files are replicated according to their distance from the originating site (Lougher, Shepherd, & Pegler, 1994). If an object's originating site is far from the local media storage server, the object has a higher priority of being replicated in the local server. If an object's originating site is close, the object has a low priority of being replicated. The Lancaster storage server provides a method to differentiate the priority of objects being replicated in the local server. This method provides a mechanism to evenly spread the objects across a number of servers over a geographical area. The most important advantage of the Lancaster server design is that network load can be reduced. This is similar to reduce network load using proxy servers.

Replication to Reduce Start-Up Latency

When multimedia streams are initiated, the storage server delivers the first part of the object to the clients. The client program uses these initial data to fill up the memory buffer. Before enough data are received to fill the buffers, the client program cannot start to display the stream. Thus, the client program needs to wait for the delivery of the initial part of the objects. This waiting time is the start-up latency. The start-up latency is a delay time that is directly observed by the user. When multimedia objects are being accessed over a high delay network, the start-up latency may be significant.

Data replication is one of the approaches to reduce the start-up latency. Ghandeharizadeh, Kim, Shi, and Zimmermann (1997) proposed to migrate requests with data replication across disk clusters in order to reduce start-up latency. Chang and Molina (1997) replicated the leaders of multimedia objects on a separate disk to reduce start up latency in constraint allocation methods.

A limitation of the leader replication is that this method only reduces the start-up latency. After a stream is started, the leader in storage does not make additional contributions in the delivery of the object. More methods to reduce start-up latency will be discussed in the cache replacement policies.

Replication to Avoid Disk Multitasking

In magnetic hard disks, the disk heads are connected together like a hair comb. All the disk heads move at the same time to the accessed tracks and cylinders. Each object may be stored contiguously onto a few cylinders. When one of these objects is accessed, the disk heads only need to move one long seek action. Subsequent seek actions are very short if there is not any other concurrent streams. Thus, the aggregate seek overhead is very low. However, if the disk heads need to serve multiple concurrent streams, the disk heads move up and down across the disk surface to serve one request for each stream. The disk head is then multitasked among multiple streams. This disk multitasking involves significant seek overheads that erode the disk performance.

Separate replica on multiple disks may avoid disk multitasking by avoiding the need to serve multiple streams from the same disk head. Ghandeharizadeh and Ramos (1993) proposed data replication to avoid disk multitasking that could reduce disk throughput.

When multimedia objects are declustered across a group of disks, all the disks in the group must be accessed simultaneously in order to retrieve the objects in real-time. In order to maintain the disk retrieval throughput at the desired level, the number of disks to decluster each multimedia object is limited. Due to the limitation of disk throughput, each disk can only support a limited number of streams. The contention of streams for disk bandwidth could reduce the throughput. In Ghandeharizadeh and Ramos (1993), data are replicated in other disks to reduce this contention.

Apart from avoiding disk multitasking, objects may be duplicated on randomly selected disks to avoid disk multitasking. The number of replica being created is directly proportional to the access frequency of the object (Korst, 1997). More replicas may be created on frequently accessed objects and few replicas are created on rarely accessed objects. Since more streams access the hot objects, more copies of the hot object can help the object to be accessed from more disks. Thus, the hot objects can be accessed with low overheads to increase the efficiency of the storage system.

For example, Figure 7.1 shows two objects X and Y being stored on six disks, disk 1 to disk 6. Object X is divided into $X1$ to $X4$ and they are stored on disk 1 and disk 2. Object Y is split into $Y1$ to $Y6$ and they are stored on disk 1 to disk 4. Some data stripes of object Y that are stored on disk 1 and disk 2, including $Y1$, $Y2$, $Y5$, and $Y6$, are replicated onto disk 5 and disk 6. While user A is accessing object X from disk 1 and disk 2, another user B may send requests to access object Y. The disk 1 and disk 2 may not have the disk bandwidth to be able to access data stripes for stream X and stream Y concurrently. During this period of time, disk 5 and disk 6 may be idle. Instead of using disk multitasking to serve both stream X and stream Y from disk 1 and disk 2, the replica of object Y on disk 5 and disk 6 may be accessed. Thus, the storage system can serve both stream X and stream Y concurrently. This shows a successful situation that replication can be used to increase disk throughput and serve more concurrent streams.

The replication of objects may need a large number of disks. If each disk serves only one stream, then the number of disks should not be less than the number of concurrent streams. Thus, one disk is needed to serve one additional concurrent stream. Unless each disk can store only one object, the disk storage space is thus not efficiently used. When several replicas residing on several disks are available, it is necessary to choose an appropriate

Figure 7.1. Data replication to avoid disk multitasking

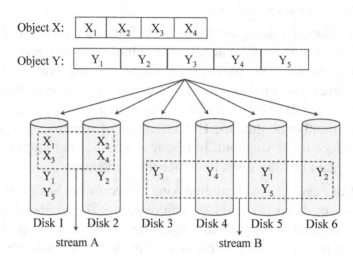

disk to serve an incoming stream. This choice increases the complexity in retrieving the objects.

Since the access frequency of objects changes dynamically, the number of objects cannot be increased without additional workload to create copies. Thus, it is not an easy task to maintain the optimal number of objects on the appropriate disks.

Replication to Maintain Balance of Space and Load

The access bandwidth of an object is affected by access frequency of the object and the required bandwidth to deliver the object. If all the objects are accessed with the same number of megabytes per second, the access bandwidth of the objects is linearly proportional to their access frequency. If all the objects have the same access frequency, the access bandwidth of the objects should be linearly proportional to their data rate. Thus, the access bandwidth of an object is equal to the data rate weighted by the access frequency of the object. In the following paragraphs, a hot object is an object with high access bandwidth, and a cold object is an object with low access bandwidth.

Replication of objects consumes both storage space and access bandwidth. When a replica of an object is stored on a storage device, the replica may be accessed by request streams. The replica cannot be accessed if the storage device does not have enough bandwidth to deliver it. Thus, it is more appropriate to place the replica on other storage devices with sufficient bandwidth. We shall explain using the four undesirable conditions on a storage system below.

First, when hot objects are stored on a low bandwidth disk, the disk does not have sufficient bandwidth to serve the streams on the hot object. Otherwise, the disk becomes overloaded. The hot objects should be replicated to high bandwidth disks, and the hot objects can then be accessed without delay.

Second, when cold objects are stored on a high bandwidth disk, the disk has spare bandwidth to serve more streams. However, the disk does not have more requests to the cold objects. Thus, the disk utilization is low. The cold objects may be moved to another disk with low bandwidth to release storage space so that the high bandwidth disk can have storage space to store and serve hot objects.

Third, a high bandwidth disk needs to have sufficient storage capacity to store the hot objects. If the high bandwidth disks have stored many cold objects and do not have sufficient storage space, the hot objects still cannot be stored.

Fourth, a low bandwidth needs to have sufficient storage capacity to store the cold objects. If the low bandwidth disks have already stored many hot objects and do not have sufficient storage space, the cold objects need to be stored on disks with higher bandwidth. As a result, the disk bandwidth utilization is low.

The above four situations show that hot objects should be stored on high bandwidth disks, and cold objects should be stored on low bandwidth disks. The optimal condition is maintained if all the disks consume their storage space and spare bandwidth in similar proportions. The objective of the bandwidth-to-space ratio (BSR) replication is to maintain the same percentage of space and load consumptions on all storage devices.

The bandwidth-to-space ratio replication is an interdisk, object-based replication method for heterogeneous storage devices. In the BSR replication method, the storage capacity and access bandwidth of each storage device may be different. It maintains the balance of access bandwidth to storage space ratio for every storage device (Dan & Sitaram, 1995).

The storage system keeps the allocated bandwidth to space ratios for every storage device. When a replica of an object needs to be stored on the storage system, it needs to find a storage device to store the new replica. If the replica

Figure 7.2. BSR replication. Both the consumed storage space and allocated bandwidth increase after adding a new object.

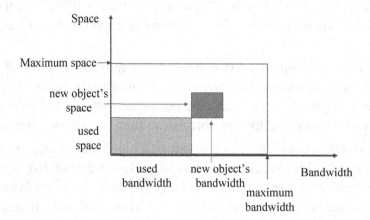

is stored onto the storage system, the storage system allocates both access bandwidth and storage space for the object. This allocated bandwidth and allocated storage space come from the same storage device. Thus, the allocated bandwidth and the allocated storage space would increase (Figure 7.2).

Depending on the allocated bandwidth-to-space ratio and the bandwidth-to-space ratio of the new object, the allocated bandwidth-to-space ratio of the selected storage device may increase or decrease. The bandwidth-to-space ratio of other storage devices however remains the same since they are not affected.

The BSR of a storage device is defined as the bandwidth-to-space ratio of the storage device. The actual BSR of a storage device is defined as the bandwidth-to-space ratio of the storage device when it is empty. Thus,

$$ActualBSR = \frac{AccessBandwidth}{StorageCapacity},$$

where *AccessBandwidth* and *StorageCapacity* are the access bandwidth and the storage capacity of the storage device respectively.

The allocated BSR of a storage device is defined as the allocated bandwidth divided by the allocated storage capacity of the storage device. Thus,

$$AllocatedBSR = \frac{AllocatedAccessBandwidth}{AllocatedStorageCapacity},$$

where *AllocatedAccessBandwidth* and *AllocatedStorageCapacity* are the allocated bandwidth and the allocated storage capacity of the storage device respectively.

The BSR deviation of a storage device is defined as the difference between the actual BSR and the allocated BSR of the storage device. Thus:

BSRDeviation = AllocatedBSR − Actual BSR.

The storage device with a high BSR deviation value is hot. The storage device with a low BSR deviation value is cold. Sometime, the BSR deviation value can be negative.

The BSR replication method first checks if any storage devices have the storage capacity and bandwidth to store the new object. Any storage devices with insufficient space or bandwidth are excluded. It then calculates the allocated BSR of the remaining storage devices on the speculative condition that the replica is stored on the storage device. Afterwards, it chooses the storage device such that the storage of the new replica results in the smallest BSR deviation. When there is a tie, any one among the storage devices with the smallest BSR deviations can be chosen.

For example, a storage system has five disks, D_1 to D_5. Each disk has a storage capacity of 600MB and bandwidth 60 MB/s. After some objects are stored on the disks, the disks now have 100MB, 300MB, 300MB, 500MB, 500MB of free space and 10MB/s, 35MB/s, 30MB/s, 45MB/s, 50MB/s of free bandwidth, respectively.

The actual BSR of the disks is

= 60MB/s ÷ 600MB.
= 0.1 /s.

The allocated bandwidths of the first disk, D_1, is

= 60MB/s − 10MB/s

= *50MB/s.*

The allocated storage space of the first disk, D_1, is

= *600MB − 100MB*
= *500MB.*

The allocated BSR of the first disk, D_1, is

= *50MB/s ÷ 500MB.*
= *0.1 /s.*

The BSR deviations of the first disk, D_1, is

= *0.1/s − 0.1/s = +0/s.*

Similarly, the allocated bandwidths of the other disks, D_2 to D_5, are

= *25MB/s, 30MB/s, 15MB/s, and 10MB/s.*

The allocated storage spaces of the other disks, D_2 to D_5, are

= *300MB, 300MB, 100MB, and 100MB.*

The allocated BSR of the other disks, D_2 to D_5, are

= *25/300, 30/300, 15/100, and 10/100.*
= *0.8333/s, 0.1/s, 0.15/s, and 0.1/s.*

The BSR deviations of the other disks, D_2 to D_5, are
= *-0.0167/s, 0/s, +0.05/s, and 0/s.*

By comparing the BSR deviations of the disks, we can see that D_2 is a cold disk and D_4 is a hot disk.

An object X_1 of size 100MB and bandwidth 15 MB/s is now stored on the disk. The storage system will find the new BSR deviations of the disks after the new object is stored.

The available storage space and bandwidth of the disks are first checked. D_1 is excluded because it does not have enough bandwidth to store the new object.

If we place X_1 on D_2, the allocated bandwidths of D_2 would become

$= 25MB/s + 15MB/s$
$= 40MB/s.$

The allocated storage spaces of the disk, D_2, would become

$= 300MB + 100MB$
$= 400MB.$

The allocated BSR of the disk, D_2, would become

$= 40MB/s \div 400MB$
$= 0.1 /s.$

The new BSR deviations of the first disk, D_2, would become

$= 0.1/s - 0.1/s$
$= +0 /s.$

Similarly, if the object X_1 is stored on other disks, the allocated bandwidths of the other disks, D_3 to D_5, would become

$= 45MB/s, 30MB/s, and 25MB/s.$

The allocated storage spaces of the other disks, D_3 to D_5, would become

$= 400MB, 200MB, and 200MB.$

The allocated BSR of the other disks, D_3 to D_5, would become

= 45/400, 30/200, and 25/200.
= 0.1125/s, 0.15/s, and 0.125/s.

The new BSR deviations of the other disks, D_3 to D_5, would become

= +0.0125/s, +0.05/s, and +0.025/s.

As D_2 has the lowest new BSR deviation, the object X_1 is stored on the disk D_2. After the object is stored, the allocated BSR of the disks, D_1 to D_5, becomes

= 0.1/s, 0.1/s, 0.1/s, 0.15/s, and 0.1/s.

The new BSR deviations of the disks, D_1 to D_5, become

= +0/s, +0/s, +0/s, +0.05/s, and +0/s.

We can see that by storing the hot object X_1 to the disk D_2, the bandwidth-to-space ratio of the cold disk D_2, increases. If we add another cold object with BSR lower than 0.1, it would decrease the BSR deviations of the disks.

The BSR replication method maintains a balance of the bandwidth to space ratio of all the storage devices. This helps to store the hot objects on high bandwidth storage devices and cold objects on low bandwidth storage devices. When a storage device becomes cold, the storage device would then be chosen to store the hot objects. When a storage device becomes hot, the storage device would reduce the chance of choosing it to store new objects.

Chapter Summary

A general requirement of all data replication methods is that extra storage space is used. When the disk array is bandwidth bound, the usage of vacant space to raise throughput is possible. This strategy is thus limited by the amount of free space available. Fortunately, the recent trend of technology shows that storage capacity is increased at a faster pace than the access bandwidth. Storage capacity may not be a problem when compared to the access bandwidth.

Unfortunately, multiple data copies should be maintained the same while they are modified. This coherence of multiple data copies on disks increases program complexity and workloads. The index entries to link the multiple data copies need to be stored, processed, and maintained. The selection of data to replicate and the selection of disks to place the replica should be optimized to achieve the sufficient gain against the extra workloads.

Fortunately, the replication of multimedia objects can increase the availability of objects. Objects lost on corrupted disks can be recovered from the redundant information or the replica of the original object. The replica on neighbouring servers can reduce the network load similar to proxy servers. The replica of leaders on local servers can hide the start up latency that is visible to the users. When many disks are available like a disk array, proper replication of data stripes can improve the efficiency of the storage systems.

References

Chang, E., & Molina, H. G. (1997). Reducing initial latency in media servers. *IEEE Multimedia, 4*(3), 50-61.

Cohen, A., & Burkhard, W. A. (1996). Segmented information dispersal (SID) for efficient reconstruction in fault-tolerant video servers. In *Proceedings of the ACM Multimedia Conference* (pp. 277-286).

Dan, A., & Sitaram, D. (1995). An online video placement policy based on bandwidth to space ratio (BSR). In *Proceedings of the ACM SIGMOD International Conference on Management of Data* (pp. 376-385).

Ghandeharizadeh, S., Kim, S. H., Shi, W., & Zimmermann, R. (1997). On minimizing startup latency in scalable continuous media servers. In *Proceedings of SPIE Multimedia Computing and Networking Conference* (Vol. 3020, pp. 144-155).

Ghandeharizadeh, S., & Ramos, L. (1993). Continuous retrieval of multimedia data using parallelism. *IEEE Transactions on Knowledge and Data Engineering, 5*(4), 658-669.

Korst, J. (1997). Random duplicated assignment: An alternative to striping in video servers. In *Proceedings of ACM Mulitmedia 97* (pp. 219-226).

Lougher, P., Shepherd, D., & Pegler, D. (1994). The impact of digital audio and video on high-speed storage. In *Proceedings of the 13th IEEE Symposium on Mass Storage Systems* (pp. 84-89).

Tobagi, F. A., Pang, J., Baird, R., & Gang, M. (1993). Streaming RAID: A disk array management system for video files. In *Proceedings of the 1st ACM Conference on Multimedia* (pp. 393-400).

Chapter VIII

Constraint Allocation on Disks

Introduction

Most existing storage servers store data stripes on magnetic hard disks. These magnetic hard disks are accessed by moving the disk heads to random disk tracks. A significant amount of overhead is spent in moving the disk heads across the disk tracks. The access time of a request would be significantly reduced if the seek time is reduced.

In the normal placement of data stripes on disks being described in the two previous chapters, data stripes can be placed on any tracks with free space. There is not much consideration on the distance among data stripes of concurrent streams. Separation distances between data stripes of an object are not sufficiently constrained. Thus, the only guarantee on the upper bounds of access times is very high.

Constraint allocation methods limit the available locations to store the data stripes. This helps to control the access time within media playback requirements. The data stripes are also evenly spread across the surface of the storage media. This reduces the overheads of serving concurrent streams from the same storage device. Therefore, the maximum overheads in accessing data from the storage devices, such as seek time, become lowered.

In this chapter, we shall describe two constraint allocation methods that are designed for magnetic hard disks. These methods may also be applicable to other storage media that use the disk format. When many streams access the same hot object, the phase based constraint allocation supports more streams with less seek actions. We shall describe the phase based constraint allocation method in the next section. The region based allocation limits the longest seek distance among requests. After that, we describe the region based allocation method.

Phase Based Constraint Allocation

Multimedia objects are stored on and accessed from storage systems. The concurrent streams send requests to access data stripes. If the disk heads serve all the requests of one stream before another, the latter stream waits for a long time before it can start. If the disk heads serve requests of streams in an interleaving manner, the disk heads move across the disk heads many times. The storage locations of these objects could be very far away. Thus, the disk heads take a long time to seek the required tracks of each request. The overheads in serving concurrent streams are heavy, and the storage system cannot retrieve the objects efficiently.

When the overheads are heavy, the upper bounds on the access time are high. The maximum access time to serve a stream becomes very long. Thus, the storage system can only accept a small number of streams to be served. Other streams have to be rejected from being served.

Özden, Biliris, Rastogi, and Silberschatz (1994) proposed the *phase based constraint allocation method* to serve multiple concurrent streams efficiently (Özden et al., 1994; Özden, Rastogi, & Silberschatz, 1996). It shares the seek time overheads among the requests of concurrent streams. Instead of storing the data stripes belonging to an object on nearby locations, the phase based constraint allocation stores together the data stripes that are accessed by requests belonging to concurrent streams. Therefore, the phase constraint allocation method can place a tighter upper bound on the mean seek time of the requests.

In order to share the overheads among requests of concurrent streams, the access patterns of the streams are restricted. First, these streams may be homogeneous in nature. That is, all the streams may access data at the same period of time. Second, the streams are scheduled in advance before the objects are stored. In broadcasting and near video-on-demand systems (NVOD), all the streams start at the predefined time according to the time schedule. A stream thus accesses data according to the predefined time schedule only.

In near video-on-demand systems, a number of channels are delivered to the viewers. Each channel shows a video object being delivered from the system. The starting time of these streams are separated at a fixed time interval. An object may be delivered on several channels, and it is accessed by multiple streams. Thus, a user may join one of the streams to view a video. If the user misses the starting time of a video, he may wait to join the next starting time. He may also jump to the preceding or following streams to view a different part of the object.

In the phase based constraint allocation method, all the objects are interleaved together to form a super object. The super object is viewed by users starting at fixed and regular intervals called *phases*. A user may join one of the phases to view the super object being displayed continuously within the phase. Since the multimedia streams are homogeneous, each multimedia object can be split into short data stripes that will be consumed for a fixed period of time. Thus, only one data stripe per stream is required for this fixed period of time.

The super object is then placed on the storage system. Let m be the number of disks in the storage system and let p be the number of phases. The super object is organized as an $(n \times (m \times p))$ matrix of data stripes. The data stripes are evenly distributed among the m disks using the simple striping method. Thus, consecutive data stripes of the super object are stored sequentially from disk 1 to disk m and so on. Each column of p data stripes is stored contiguously on a disk (Figure 8.1).

The super object serves multiple streams with a phase shift at the same time. After the disk arm moves the disk heads to the required track with only one disk read, one data stripe per phase is then accessed from the contiguous locations on the disk (Figure 8.2). These data stripes are then delivered to the streams of the specific user phases. Since the super object is composed of all the objects, the objects are then accessed periodically.

Figure 8.1. Phase constraint allocation

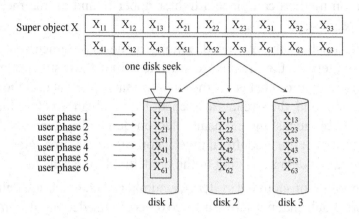

For example, the storage system delivers six streams, and each stream is separated from the previous stream with a phase time T. The data stripes of the super object are placed on three disks as shown in Figure 8.1. The data stripes X_{11} to X_{61} are stored on the same track of the disk 1. The data stripes X_{12} to X_{62} are stored on the same track of the disk 2. The data stripes X_{13} to X_{63} are stored on the same track of the disk 3.

The data stripes X_{11} to X_{61} are accessed after only one disk seeking action. The near video-on-demand streams can then deliver one data stripe per stream for six different streams. The six streams can display for a time not shorter than $T/3$.

Afterwards, the data stripes X_{12} to X_{62} are accessed after one seeking action on the second disk. The near video-on-demand streams can then deliver the second data stripe per stream to the six streams. The six streams can display for another time interval not shorter than $T/3$.

Similarly, the data stripes X_{13} to X_{63} are accessed after one seeking action on the third disk. The near video-on-demand streams can then deliver the third data stripe per stream for the six streams. The six streams can display for another time interval not shorter than $T/3$.

Afterward, the data stripes X_{14} to X_{64} are accessed from the first disk and so on. Repeatedly, the data stripes are accessed from the storage system and delivered to the streams. The phase based constraint allocation method is good at delivering multiple object streams efficiently. It delivers multimedia objects with minimum overheads to the near video-on-demand systems. Therefore, it is particularly suitable for the storage subsystem of near video-on-demand systems.

Figure 8.2. Phase based constraint allocation method for the near VOD streams

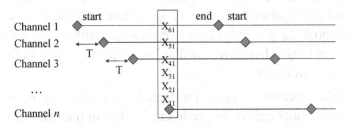

$X_{11} ... X_{61}$: corresponding data stripes in the super video X

The seek time is shared among the number of phases. The maximum storage system throughput is then limited by the number of phases instead of being limited by the number of streams. When the number of phases is high, it alleviates the disk bandwidth contention on delivering many hot multimedia objects.

Unfortunately, the start-up latency is being traded off. Since there is a gap between the start of any two phases, new streams must wait for the beginning of the next phase before they can be served. On average, a new stream waits for half of the phase period.

Application Note: *The phase based constraint allocation method is tailored for near video-on-demand systems. The delivery schedule of data streams needs to be fixed and predetermined in advance. Thus, this is not flexible, and the schedule cannot be changed easily. If changes in the time schedule are required, the NVOD system may need two disk arrays. While one disk array serves the streams according to the current schedule, the objects should be prepared and stored at the other disk array for the next schedule.*

Region Based Constraint Allocation

Multimedia objects are stored on the magnetic disks. When the data stripes are randomly stored on any tracks or cylinders of a disk, the disk heads may need to move across all the other tracks in between the storage location of two data stripes to serve a request. The maximum of seek distance is thus very long. As the seek time increases with the seek distance traveled by the disk heads, the upper limits on the seek time and the access time are very long. To provide guarantees for continuous display, the maximum access time is very long. Therefore, the disk bandwidth is low, and the disks cannot be utilized efficiently.

Multimedia streams of video-on-demand systems may be initiated at any time. The streams cannot be predetermined as in the near video-on-demand systems. During the quiet period, the system may not receive any requests for data accessing services. During the busy period, the system may receive many requests for data accessing services. Thus, it is not sure which objects will be accessed concurrently and should be stored together.

Moreover, multiple streams access data stripes concurrently. In order to provide a guarantee of continuous display, the supply of data should be provided continuously and smoothly. In addition, only a few requests should be served prior to the display of the streams. Otherwise, the start-up latency is undesirably long. Therefore, the requests of concurrent streams should be served in an interleaving manner. This incurs heavy seek overheads due to disk multitasking.

For each request, the seek time overheads are already heavy. This results in long access time. When many requests are served concurrently, the total access time is calculated as the access time multiplied by the number of concurrent requests. Thus, the storage system cannot give a tight upper bound on the total access time. Even if the seek time overheads may be shared among requests using efficient disk scheduling algorithms, the guaranteed upper limit on the total access time is still very long. Therefore, the storage system cannot provide guaranteed delivery to many streams.

The objective of the region based constraint allocation method is to increase the number of streams that can be served by the storage system. It limits the maximum separation distance among data stripes that will be accessed by consecutive requests to tighten the upper limits on the seek time and access time (Oyang, Lee, Wen, & Cheng, 1995). After the upper limits on the access time are reduced, the storage system can accept more multimedia streams to be served.

The region based constraint allocation method partitions each disk into a linear array of logical regions. Each region consists of a number of neighbouring tracks. The number of regions and the size of each region may vary from disk

Figure 8.3. Region based constraint allocation places data stripes in re-gions.

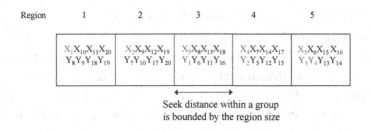

to disk depending on the preferred maximum seek distance and the maximum start-up latency. When many small regions are created, the maximum seek distance is short, but the maximum start up latency is high. Alternatively, the maximum seek distance is long, but the maximum start-up latency is low when only a few large regions are created. The normal placement method without any constraints is the same as the case when only one region is created. At the extreme case that each track is considered as a region, the maximum seek distance is very short, but the maximum start-up latency is very long. The disk heads would traverse track by track to access data.

The data stripes of objects are stored into the regions one by one (Figure 8.3). After the first data stripe of an object is stored within a region, the second data stripe of this object is stored into its neighbouring region. The third data stripe of the object is then stored onto the following region in the same direction. The data stripes are stored in the regions in the same direction until it reaches the last region in a direction. Instead of storing one data stripe in the last region, two data stripes are stored in the last regions. After two data stripes are placed in the last region, the algorithm changes direction and store one data stripe in each region again.

An example is shown in Figure 8.3. The data stripes of two objects, X and Y, are stored. Object X and object Y are split into data stripes X_1 to X_{20} and Y_1 to Y_{20}. The data stripes of object X are stored on the disk, beginning with X_1 in region 1, X_2 in region 2, and so on until region 5. In region 5, both X_5 and X_6 are stored in the same region to change direction. Then, X_7 is stored in region 4, X_8 is stored in region 3, and so on until region 1. Both X_{10} and X_{11} are stored in region 1, and it changes direction again. The data stripes of object X are stored in regions until all the data stripes are stored.

Similarly, object Y is stored in regions of the same disk. The only difference is that the placement of object Y begins in region 3. The data stripes of object Y are stored on the disk, beginning with Y_1 in region 3, Y_2 in region 4, both Y_3 and Y_4 in region 5, Y_6 in region 4, and so on.

We may wonder why two data stripes are stored in the regions at the two ends. This is to balance the size of the regions. When the data stripes are placed, the regions are visited in cycles. The regions at the two ends are visited only once per cycle. Other regions are however visited once in every direction, so they are visited twice per cycle. If we place only one data stripe in the regions at the two ends every time, half of the storage space in these regions would be wasted. If we place two data stripes in these regions, these regions would be consumed at the similar rate as other regions.

The data stripes can be stored on any tracks within the constraint region. The storage system thus has the freedom to store the data stripes on tracks close to or far from the centre of disks. A region may cover more than one zone in the zoned disks or the entire region may reside within a zone. Thus, the storage system may store data stripes according to the bandwidth based placement policy within a zone. For the regions at the two ends, the data stripes of hot objects may be stored on tracks that are close to the middle region according to the frequency based placement method. This would slightly reduce the average seek distance when the storage system only serves streams that access hot objects.

A stream access data stripes in the same sequence as the order of data stripes. The stream sends a request to access the first data stripe. After a data stripe is accessed, the disk heads stay on the storing track of this data stripe. The stream then sends the next request to access the second data stripe from the disk. If the disk heads serve the next request of this stream, they access the next data stripe for this stream. Since the next data stripe is either in the same region or in the neighbouring region, the disk heads only stay in the same region or move to its neighbouring region. It is clear that the starting track and the destination track are both within these two regions; the seek distance, D, is then bounded above as

$$\leq 2k\text{-}1,$$

where k is the number of tracks in each region. Since the seek time increases with the seek distance, using the seek time equation in Chapter III we get an upper bound on the seek time as

$$s \leq \begin{cases} a_1 + a_2 \ (2k-1), & 2k > a_5 + 1, \\ a_3 + a_4 \sqrt{2k-1}, & 2k \leq a_5 + 1, \end{cases}$$

From the above equation, we can see that the maximum seek time is also bounded above. Since the value of k is smaller than the number of tracks on the disk surface, the upper bound on the seek time is also smaller than the worst case seek time when the disk heads traverse across all tracks on the disk surface.

When multiple streams are concurrent, the request within the same region would be served consecutively. Each request that access data from the same region belongs to one of the concurrent streams. Thus, the concurrent streams are served in an interleaving manner. One request of each concurrent stream accesses one data strip from a region in each round. Each region is visited once in each direction in each cycle. For each concurrent stream, $2g$ requests are served in each cycle, where g is the number of regions. We shall explain more details about how concurrent streams are served in the group sweeping scheduling policy in Chapter VIII.

Multimedia streams that provide some VCR-like interactive functions may be supported. Apart from normal displaying streams that access data stripes from the beginning to the end, a stream may jump to start displaying from positions other than the current displaying position. The stream only needs to skip $2g$ requests and sends the next request to access the data stripes within the next region of the same cycle. The streams may also repeat this request skipping to provide fast forward and rewind like interactive VCR functions. It may even be possible to preview the objects by skipping a large number of data stripes at different times.

If the region based constraint allocation method is used to place data stripes, the disk scheduling method should be chosen to serve requests in the waiting queue. The disk scheduling method should serve requests according to their distance from the disk heads. Requests that are close to the disk heads are served before the request that far away from the disk heads. The SCAN and group sweeping scheduling policies serve requests according to their track locations. Thus, the storage system should use either the SCAN policy or the group sweeping scheduling policy to serve requests. If the unidirectional SCAN is used, the data stripes should be placed in regions in the same unidirectional order as the direction of the SCAN policy. Details of the disk scheduling policies would be described in Chapter VIII.

The region based constraint allocation method is efficient. It increases the efficiency in accessing multimedia objects. It provides an upper bound on the maximum seek distance of disk requests to limit the retrieval time of each requests below the displaying time. The seek time overheads are bounded; more concurrent streams are acceptable; and the system throughput is raised.

The region based constraint allocation method is flexible. It can be used for general multimedia systems. The multimedia streams can display objects sequentially from the beginning to the end. They can jump to display at any data stripes in the other cycles. They can skip cycles of data stripes to provide VCR-like interactive functions. They can send multiple requests to access data and the service order of these requests is controlled by the disk scheduling method. The region based constraint allocation method is particularly suitable for storing multimedia objects on disks. It may also be applied to other storage systems such as hierarchical storage system.

Application Note: *Although new streams may only start when the region containing the first data stripe is being scanned, the maximum start-up latency of new streams is limited to the period of traversing all regions once. Since the start-up latency is proportional to the number of regions, it can be very long if too many regions are created. Chang and Molina (1997) proposed to reduce this start-up latency by replicating the data stripes of the leaders.*

Chapter Summary

Multimedia systems store objects on and accessed from storage systems. The concurrent streams send requests to access data stripes. The storage systems should serve requests belonging to different concurrent streams in an interleaving manner, leading to long seeks and heavy overheads. Therefore, only a few streams can be served concurrently from each disk.

The constraint allocation methods place limits on the storage locations of objects and usage patterns of streams to reduce the access times of multimedia storage systems. They increase the efficiency of the storage systems so that the storage systems can serve more streams.

In near video-on-demand systems, the delivery schedule of data streams are fixed and predetermined in advance. The phase based constraint allocation method can be used to deliver multiple object streams efficiently. It shares the disk seek time among the number of requests belonging to different phases. It alleviates the disk bandwidth contention on delivering many hot multimedia objects.

For general video-on-demand systems, the region based constraint allocation method may be used in their storage systems. The region based constraint allocation method partitions the disks tracks into regions and store data stripes into specific regions. The data stripes of objects are stored into the regions one by one. This limits the maximum separation distance among data stripes belonging to the same object so that the upper bounds on the seek time and access time are tightened. It increases the maximum number of streams that can be served concurrently. It serves multimedia streams efficiently to raise the storage system throughput. It can support some interactive streams on top of the normal displaying streams. The region based constraint allocation method is flexible that it can be applied in other storage systems such as hierarchical storage systems.

In both constraint allocation methods, the start-up latency is being traded off. The average start-up latency of new streams is half of the phase period when the phase based constraint allocation method is used. The average start-up latency of new streams is the period of time to serve one request for all the concurrent streams when the region based constraint allocation method is used.

References

Chang, E., & Molina, H. G. (1997). Reducing initial latency in media servers. *IEEE Multimedia, 4*(3), 50-61.

Oyang, Y. J., Lee, M. H., Wen, C. H., & Cheng, C. Y. (1995). Design of multimedia storage systems for on-demand playback. In *Proceedings of the 11th International Conference on Data Engineering* (pp. 457-465).

Özden, B., Biliris, A., Rastogi, R., & Silberschatz, A. (1994). A low-cost storage server for movie on demand databases. In *Proceedings of the 20th International Conference on Very Large Data Bases* (pp. 594-605).

Özden, B., Rastogi, R., & Silberschatz, A. (1996). On the design of a low-cost video-on-demand storage system. *ACM Multimedia Systems, 4,*

Summary to Section IIa

Data Placement on Disks

The statistical placement methods consider the characteristics of the multimedia objects and place them accordingly. This allows the system administrator to optimize the storage system performance according to the adminiatrator's preferred metrics. A combination of the statistical characteristics may also be combined into a priority function that determines the optimal locations of placing objects onto the disks. We have described two statistical placement methods based on different access characteristics.

The frequency based placement method optimizes the average request response time. It uses an algorithm to place the objects according to their access frequencies. The hottest object is placed at the storage location with the least average access time. The next hottest object is placed at the next available storage location with the least average access time and so on. The objects are then placed in a skewed organ-pipe manner on the disks.

The bandwidth based placement method places objects according to their data rates. The storage system maintains its optimal performance according to the object data transfer time without reorganizations. The bandwidth based placement method adapts the data transfer time of objects according to their necessary data rates.

The simple striping methods increase the efficiency of serving concurrent multimedia streams. These methods consider the characteristics of multimedia streams in the design of the techniques. Multimedia streams can access the data stripes according to their actual data consumption rates. Thus, the disk bandwidth and the memory buffer are used efficiently. However, the actual participating streams may not access objects exactly as expected. Thus, the increase in efficiency is not as much as expected.

The staggered striping method provides effective support for multiple streams accessing different objects from a group of striped disks, and it automatically balances the workload among disks. Unfortunately, the staggered striping method still suffers from the disk bandwidth fragmentation problems, and new streams may be rejected.

The pseudorandom placement method maintains that the data stripes are evenly distributed on disks. In addition, it reduces the number of data stripes being moved when the number of disks increases or decreases. It uses the pseudo-random number function to generate new disk numbers that are independent of the disk number of other data stripes. The pseudorandom placement reduces the workload on data reorganization when disks are added or removed.

A general requirement of all data replication methods is that extra storage space is used. When the disk array is bandwidth bound, the usage of vacant space to raise throughput is possible. This strategy is thus limited by the amount of free space available. Fortunately, the recent trend of technology shows that storage capacity is increased at a faster pace than the access bandwidth. Storage capacity may not be a problem when compared to the access bandwidth. Unfortunately, multiple data copies should be maintained the same while they are modified. This coherence of multiple data copies on disks increases program complexity and workloads. The index entries to link the multiple data copies need to be stored, processed, and maintained. The selection of data to replicate and the selection of disks to place the replica should be optimized to achieve the sufficient gain against the extra workloads.

Fortunately, the replication of multimedia objects can increase the availability of objects. Objects lost on corrupted disks can be recovered from the redundant information or the replica of the original object. The replica on neighbouring servers can reduce the network load similar to proxy servers. The replica of leaders on local servers can hide the start up latency that is visible to the users. When many disks are available like a disk array, proper replication of data stripes can improve the efficiency of the storage systems.

Multimedia systems store objects on and accessed from storage systems. The concurrent streams send requests to access data stripes. The storage systems should serve requests belonging to different concurrent streams in an interleaving manner, leading to long seeks and heavy overheads. Therefore, only a few streams can be served concurrently from each disk. The constraint allocation methods place limits on the storage locations of objects and usage patterns of streams to reduce the access times of multimedia storage systems. They increase the efficiency of the storage systems so that the storage systems can serve more streams.

In near video-on-demand systems, the delivery schedule of data streams is fixed and predetermined in advance. The phase based constraint allocation method can be used to deliver multiple object streams efficiently. It shares the disk seek time among the number of requests belonging to different phases. It alleviates the disk bandwidth contention on delivering many hot multimedia objects.

For general video-on-demand systems, the region based constraint allocation method may be used in their storage systems. The region based constraint allocation method partitions the disk tracks into regions and store data stripes into specific regions. The data stripes of objects are stored into the regions one by one. This limits the maximum separation distance among data stripes belonging to the same object so that the upper bounds on the seek time and access time are tightened. It increases the maximum number of streams that can be served concurrently. It serves multimedia streams efficiently to raise the storage system throughput. It can support some interactive streams on top of the normal displaying streams. The region based constraint allocation method is flexible that it can be applied in other storage systems such as hierarchical storage systems.

In both constraint allocation methods, the start-up latency is being traded off. The average start-up latency of new streams is half of the phase period when the phase based constraint allocation method is used. The average start-up latency of new streams is the period of time to serve one request for all the concurrent streams when the region based constraint allocation method is used.

Section IIb

Data Placement on Hierarchical Storage Systems

Introduction

Storage system stores data objects on different storage devices. When these storage devices are of the same type, the objects may be stored and retrieved with similar access latency. When these storage devices are of different types, the objects may be stored and retrieved with different access latencies. Thus, the type of storage devices that contain the stored object affects the access latency in accessed a stored object.

A common method to arrange the storage devices of different types is the hierarchical storage systems (HSS). All or most objects are stored on the storage devices with longer access latency. When these data objects are accessed, the objects are moved from these storage devices with longer access latency to the storage devices with shorter access latency. This is called data migration.

Similar to storage organizations on disks, there are many data placement methods being designed to improve the performance of hierarchical storage systems. These techniques use different strategies to optimize the HSS performance. We group these data placement methods according to the following four strategies:

1. Contiguous placement strategy
2. Statistical placement strategy
3. Striping strategy
4. Constraint allocation strategy

Readers may find that these strategies have been described in the last part. Similar techniques on disks have been discussed in previous chapters. Readers should notice that the same technique on disks may not be directly applicable to the tertiary storage devices. Even if the same efficient technique can be applied on HSS, it may deteriorate the HSS performance instead of enhancing it.

We will first describe the tertiary storage devices that store data objects in the tertiary storage level in Chapter IX. The contiguous placement strategy minimizes the overheads in accessing the objects in their entirety. We shall describe the contiguous placement and the log structure placement on HSS in Chapter X. The statistical placement method optimizes the average performance by placing data according to their access characteristics. We will show the frequency based placement method on hierarchical storage systems in Chapter XI. Afterwards, we will describe the striping strategy which divides a multimedia object into shorter segments and retrieves them in parallel using separate requests. Two striping methods on HSS, including the parallel tape striping and the triangular placement method, are described in Chapter XII. Lastly, we will explain in Chapter XIII the constraint allocation strategy which limits the physical locations to place objects and segments. We will explain the interleaved contiguous placement and the concurrent striping methods.

Chapter IX

Tertiary Storage Devices

Introduction

The main objective of the tertiary storage level is to provide huge storage capacity at low cost. Several types of storage devices are available to be used at the tertiary storage level in Hierarchical Storage Systems (HSS). They include:

- Magnetic tapes
- Optical disks
- Optical tapes

These storage devices are composed of fixed storage drives and removable media units. The storage drives are fixed to the computer system. The removable media unit can be removed from the drives so that the storage capacity can be expanded with more media units. When data on a media are accessed, the media unit is accessed from their normal location. One of the storage drives on the computer system is chosen. If there is a media unit in the storage drive, the old media unit is unloaded and ejected. The new media unit is then loaded to the drive.

Each type of storage drive may handle the storage drives and media units differently. The magnetic tapes are described below in the next section. Then, the optical tapes are presented. Afterwards, the optical disks are briefly described before this chapter is summarized.

Magnetic Tapes

Magnetic tapes have been in use before the magnetic hard disks became popular. Although magnetic disks are low latency, inexpensive disks, magnetic tapes are cheap and of large capacity. Thus, the magnetic tapes are still used in practical storage systems for backup and archival applications. They are used to store objects that are large and rarely accessed.

Multimedia objects are large in size, and some objects are mainly stored for the back up purpose. These objects are rarely accessed. Thus, the large capacity of magnetic tapes helps to store multimedia objects cheaply. In addition, a multimedia stream accessed a data object sequentially. When a multimedia object is sequentially accessed from the tapes, the tape storage format allows the storage system to deliver data at high throughput. Thus, magnetic tapes have been investigated to store multimedia objects.

Magnetic tape drives access data tapes in two forms. These include the tape reels and the tape cartridges. When tapes are wound on reels, the drive uses two reels. They include the supply reel and the take-up reel. The magnetic tape is unwound from the supply reel. It passes through several tape guides to the read-write heads. It then passes through more tape guides to the take-up reel to be wound as illustrated in Figure 9.1. It usually needs human intervention to lead the tape through all the guides and wind it at the take-up reel. It is difficult to perform the tape loading operation automatically.

When tapes are kept on cartridges, the supply reel, the tape guides, and the take-up reel are all included in one cartridge. To load a tape, the drive extracts some tape between the supply reel and the take-up reel and winds it around the read-write heads. It is easier to perform the tape loading operation automatically.

Magnetic tapes record data in three formats. They include:

- Linear
- Longitudinal
- Helican scan

This tape format stores data on data tracks. As shown in Figure 9.2, the read/write heads assembly may be able to move. The different directions in moving the read/write heads lead to different tape formats. These tape formats are used in different types of storage devices.

Figure 9.1. Magnetic tape drive

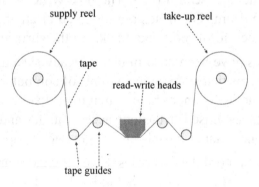

Figure 9.2. Magnetic tape formats

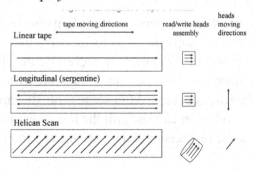

Traditional computers record data on magnetic tapes in the linear tape format. The tapes move horizontally. The read/write heads assembly is fixed inside the tape drive. Computer data are recorded horizontally along with the tape moving direction. Several read/write heads are mounted along perpendicularly to the tape moving direction. Thus, several bits are recorded by the read/write heads on the tape at the same time.

Digital linear tapes record data using the serpentine tape format. Data are recorded in the longitudinal direction like the linear tapes. Similar to the linear tape format, the tape read/write heads are fixed when data are recorded on the tape to form a track. After the tape comes to one end, the heads move at perpendicular direction to the tape moving direction. The tape then moves backwards to record another data track in the opposite direction. The movement of the read/write heads are repeated to record several data tracks on the tape. Thus, the width of the tape is used to increase the storage capacity of the magnetic tape.

Video cassette recorders (VCR) record video data onto VHS tapes. The VHS tapes use the helican scan format. The read/write heads are mounted on a cylinder like a drum. The heads are mounted at an angle and rotate like a wheel. Thus, they form short data tracks on the surface of the tape.

Magnetic tapes have been used in many legacy systems. They offer cheap storage to systems that store large amounts of computer data. The storage of data that are practically impossible on magnetic disks can be implemented using magnetic tapes. Based on the long access latency and low storage cost per gigabyte, magnetic tapes have been used in backup applications for years.

Magnetic tapes record data on tapes. Since the tapes are wound around the reels, the tape recording surface is hidden from the read/write heads. This leads to long access latency when the tape is unwound to reveal the hidden surface. It also results in a high storage capacity to physical dimension ratio when compared to the disk format.

In recent years, the improvements in recording density in magnetic disks are also implemented on magnetic tapes to increase their storage capacity and throughput. Thus, the improvement in recording density does not make the magnetic tapes obsolete. Unfortunately, the read/write heads touch the tape surface when data are accessed. After some time, the tape can become wound out or torn. This and other causes limit the life span of magnetic tapes. Thus, the tapes need to be replaced and data are moved to new tapes.

Optical Disks

Optical disks record data that can be read by optical beams. Optical disks can record data at very high recording density. Compact disks (CD) and digital versatile disks (DVD) are commonly used optical disks. The DVD disks are sometimes called digital video disks.

Optical disks can be classified as read-only disk, write-once disk, rewriteable disk, and read-write disk according to the modification ability of the recording material. Read-only disks can only be read by the optical drive. The data on the disks cannot be changed. Write-once disks can be modified only once and read many times. After a bit of data is modified, the bit of data cannot be changed again. Similar to write-once disks, the rewriteable disks can be modified only once and read many times. In addition, the entire disk can be erased. After the disk is erased, the disk can be modified again. Read-write disks can be read and modified many times.

The optical disks are covered with clear polycarbonate. Data are recorded on the recording material under the disk surface. A thin layer of aluminium is coated on the substrate below the recording material. The optical disks are circular in shape. Data are recorded on a spiral track. The disk drive uses the servo to control the position of the optical drive automatically.

Optical disks read and write data using laser beams. Some optical disks are recorded using red laser beams, and some other optical disks are recorded using blue laser beams. The laser beam is diffracted into the recording layer of the optical disk. It is then focused at the recording track. The status of the recording material at the recording layer is modified by high intensity laser beams. The status of the recording material is read by low intensity laser beams.

At one status of the recording bit position, the laser beam directly passes through the recording layer to the aluminium coating underneath. The aluminium coating then reflects the laser beam to the reading head. At another status of the recording bit position, the laser beam is deflected at the recording layer. The reading head thus does not receive any reflected beams from the aluminium coating.

Like magnetic disks, optical disks store data on rigid disk platters. The optical disk head can be moved along the radius of the circular disk to locate the accessed data quickly. Thus, the optical disk drives can access data on the track with low latency. This makes the disk format superior to the tape format.

Since optical drives record data on the disk recording layer using laser beams, the drives do not need to touch the optical disks at all. This avoids scratching the disk surface. When moisture or fingerprints gather on the disk surface, the disk can easily be wiped away. These features allow the optical disks to have a long life span.

Optical Tapes

Optical tapes are designed to maximize the storage capacity of a media unit. Optical tapes record data on tapes using laser beams to maximize the recording density. Most of the recording surface is wound and hidden using a tape form.

Unlike magnetic tapes, optical tapes record data in the transverse format. The tape moves horizontally and the optical read/write head moves at the perpendicular direction to the tape moving direction as shown in Figure 9.3. The tape stops while the optical head records a track of data. The head records data from one edge to another edge along the width of the tape. After a track of data is recorded, the tape moves a step and the head springs back. The tape stops again, and the optical head writes another data track. These data tracks are perpendicular to the tape moving direction. The length of the data track is shorter than the width of the tape.

Figure 9.3. Optical tape format

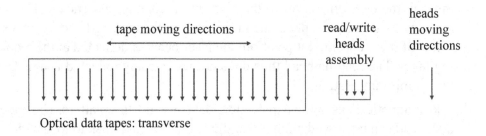

tape moving directions   read/write heads assembly   heads moving directions

Optical data tapes: transverse

Robotic Tape Library

Large hierarchical storage systems need to store many objects. These HSS need to exchange tapes quickly so that they can serve many requests. Robotic tape libraries perform the exchange operation automatically so that manual operations are avoided.

As shown in Figure 9.4, the robotic tape library consists of the:

1. tapes,
2. tape drive,
3. robotic arm, and
4. tape cells.

As in manual tape drives, the objects are stored on the tapes, and the tapes are loaded to the tape drives for accessing. The number of tape drives in the robotic tape library determines the access bandwidth of the library. The tapes are usually kept in the tape cells. The number of tape cells in the robotic tape library determines the total storage capacity of the library. The robotic arm performs the exchange of tapes automatically.

Figure 9.4. Robotic tape library

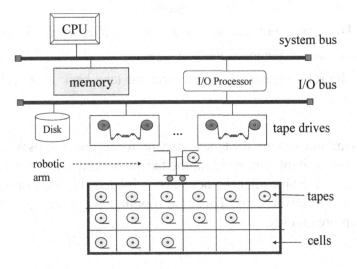

When a tape is required, the robotic tape library performs the following steps:

1.   The robotic arm moves to the tape drive.
2.   The tape drive ejects the original tape.
3.   The robotic arm fetches the original tape.
4.   The robotic arm moves the original tape back to its own cell or a vacant cell.
5.   The robotic arm moves to the cell containing the new tape.
6.   The robotic arm fetches the new tape.
7.   The robotic arm moves the tape to the tape drive.
8.   The robotic arm puts the tape inside the tape drive.
9.   The tape drive loads the tape.

The above exchange operation uses only one robotic arm. If the tape library has two robotic arms that are mounted together, it can exchange tapes using fewer steps as follows.

1.   The robotic arm moves to the tape cell.
2.   The robotic arm fetches the tape from the cell.
3.   The robotic arm moves the tape to the tape drive.
4.   The tape drive ejects the original tape.
5.   The robotic arm exchanges the tape with the original tape.
6.   The tape drive loads the new tape.
7.   The robotic arm moves the original tape back to its cell or a vacant cell.

From the above steps, the tape library performs fewer steps when two robotic arms are available. In addition, the tape drive can start its next operation to reposition the tape after the new tape is loaded. The tape drive receives the new tape in fewer steps. Thus, the robotic tape library can thus exchange tapes more quickly.

Performance of the Tertiary Storage Devices

Similar to the disk performance, the tertiary storage devices mainly spend their time on the mechanical steps. Other steps also consume some time, but they are comparatively less significant. The major mechanical steps in serving a request are shown in Figure 9.5 and they include:

1. Time to exchange or switch the tape in the tape drive.
2. Time to reposition the tape to the first data block of the required file or object.
3. Time the transfer data blocks from tape to memory.

Let ω be the exchange time, α be the reposition time, γ be the tape transfer rate, and X be the size of the object. Then, the access time can be found as the sum of exchange time, reposition time, and data transfer time (Tse & Leung, 1998).

$$= \omega + \alpha + \frac{X}{\gamma}. \tag{9.1}$$

Some assumptions are made to analyze the performance of magnetic tape drives and optical tape drives. First, the exchange time can be assumed to be uniformly distributed over a mean value. Since the times to unload and load tapes are almost constant, it is valid to make this assumption. Second, the tape drive runs at a fixed speed in skipping a certain length of tape since the tape skipping time increases with the length of the tape being skipped from reading. The reposition time thus increases linearly with the amount of data being skipped. Third, the tape drive transfers data at a fixed data transfer rate since the tape passes the read/write heads at a fixed speed. The data transfer time thus increases linearly with the amount of data accessed.

These time components show that:

1. the time to access an object has a minimum overhead,
2. the overheads increase linearly with the amount of data being skipped, and
3. the access time increases linearly with the object data size.

Figure 9.5. The major time spent in serving a request at the tertiary storage devices

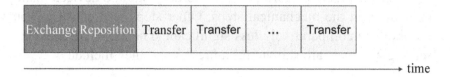

First, the time to access an object has a minimum overhead. Since the exchange time is uniformly distributed, a minimum overhead is required unless the object already resides on the loaded tape in the drive. Second, the overheads increase linearly with the amount of data being skipped in the reposition step. When some other objects need to be skipped, the skipping time increases linearly with the size of the skipped data. It is more efficient to place the objects near the unloading position on the tape. Thus, an efficient data placement method can avoid the overheads from escalating. Third, the access time increases linearly with the object data size. Thus, it takes longer time to access large objects.

Chapter Summary

The main objective of the tertiary storage level is to provide huge storage capacity at low cost. The tertiary storage devices in use include magnetic tapes, optical disks, and optical tapes. The media units are removable from the drive so that the storage capacity can be expanded by using more media units. The media units take the tape form so that the physical dimension of the media unit is small. Optical disks and tapes record data the laser beam to provide the highest recording density.

Large hierarchical storage systems may use robotic tape libraries to store many large objects. Robotic tape libraries use the robotic arms to exchange tapes automatically and quickly. When data are accessed from the tape drives, the drives spend much time in performing the mechanical steps. The drives have a minimum overhead to access data. The overheads are affected by the data placement method in use. It also takes longer time to access large objects.

References

Tse, P. K. C., & Leung, C. H. C. (1998). A low latency hierarchical storage organization for multimedia data retrieval. In *Proceedings of the IAPR International Workshop on Multimedia Information Analysis and Retrieval* (LNCS, 1464(8), pp. 181-194). Springer-Verlag.

Chapter X

Contiguous Placement on Hierarchical Storage Systems

Introduction

The contiguous placement is the most common method to place traditional data files on tertiary storage devices. The storage space in the media units is checked. The data file is stored on a media unit with enough space to store the data file.

When tertiary storage devices are used to store multimedia objects, the objects are stored and retrieved similar to traditional data files. Since the main application of the tertiary storage devices is to back up multimedia objects from computers, the objectives of the contiguous method are:

1.   supporting back up of multimedia objects efficiently, and
2.   reducing the number of separate media units that are used to store an object.

We will describe in the next sections the simple contiguous placement method. Afterwards, the log structured placement method is explained before we summarize this chapter.

Contiguous Placement

Similar to traditional data files, multimedia objects can be stored in a contiguous manner to the media units. Each media unit stores the whole object as a file. When a media unit is partially occupied and the available storage space is not enough, a separate media unit is used. If the object is larger than the storage capacity of a media unit, the object spans across multiple media units. The object is partly stored on each media unit.

The contiguous placement is simple to implement. The storage system only checks for the available storage space in each media unit beforehand. If the object is consumed on another computer, only a few media units need to be taken away.

The exchange overheads on accessing an object are light. When the objects are accessed in their entirety, it takes only one exchange per object. The amount of reposition overheads depend on the number of media units available. If each object is stored on a separate media unit, each object can be stored from the loading position of the media unit. Thus, the overhead in skipping over other objects on the same media unit are light. If multiple objects are stored on a media unit, the reposition time to skip over unwanted objects is significant.

The throughput of the storage system depends on the size of the stored objects. If the objects are large in size, the tertiary drive exchanges and repositions once for every accessed object. Although the exchange and reposition overheads are heavy, the large object size would make the transfer time more significant. Thus, the storage system can deliver the object at high throughput. However, if the objects are small in size, the tertiary drive would also exchange and reposition once for every accessed object. The heavy exchange and reposition overheads become more significant than the data transfer time. Thus, the throughput of the storage system is low.

Since it is efficient to access each object as a whole, the storage system may access the entire object to the staging buffer during data migration. The storage space requirement on the secondary storage level would become large.

This leads to inefficient usage of staging buffer space since a large portion of the object is accessed well ahead of its displaying time. These prefetched data are kept in the staging buffer for later consumption.

If the streams are served in a sequential manner, the streams are served one after another. A stream would only be served after the previous stream has completely been served. Since the multimedia objects are large in size, the tertiary drive takes a long time to access the whole object. Thus, a stream would occupy the tertiary drive for a long time. Other streams can only wait while the tertiary drive is busy serving the stream. Therefore, the response times of the waiting streams are long.

If the concurrent streams are served in a time sharing manner, the storage system would switch to serve the request for another stream after it has served requests of a stream for some time units. If each object is stored on a separate media unit, the tertiary drive would access these objects in an interleaving manner. It exchanges the media units once for every change in the serving stream. Thus, the overheads in accessing the objects from the tertiary storage level would be heavy. It is therefore inefficient to serve concurrent streams in a time sharing manner when the objects are stored using the contiguous placement method. We shall explain different methods to migrate multimedia objects from the tertiary storage level in the data migration part later.

As the multimedia objects are stored contiguously, the entire object is over-written when a small part of it is modified. Partial updating of the objects is not supported. Thus, the workload on updating the objects is heavy.

When the small objects are deleted after they are stored for some time, the free space on the media units cannot be filled by larger objects. As a result, the media units become fragmented. This fragmentation problem erodes the storage space of the tertiary storage system. The fragmented storage space can be recovered after reorganization.

Log Structured Placement

In the back up and data archival applications, object files are backed up to the media units so that they can be accessed when the original data are corrupted or lost. As modified objects are also backed up to the media units, an object may be overwritten many times before it is retrieved again. Thus, the data objects are written more often than they are read in these applications.

A simple log structured placement treats the entire storage space as a log. All the object files are written by appending to the storage space only. A log structured placement method was designed to write object files to a hierarchical storage system (HSS) in Kohl, Stonebraker, and Staelin (1993). The access ranges within an object are tracked to determine whether the object is often accessed sequentially or randomly. Random accessed objects may be stored to many locations on the media units. Sequential object files are stored contiguously. When new objects are created, they are appended to the end of the media units. When an object is modified, the modified data blocks are appended to the end of the media unit and the data blocks being modified are deleted. When the entire object is overwritten, the entire object is appended to the end of the media unit.

If the tertiary drive only writes data objects without reading them back, the tertiary drive only receives write data requests. After the tertiary drive has served the previous requests, it stays at the end of the written object files. As the next request is also a write data request, the tertiary drive can immediately write data without repositioning the media unit. Thus, the append-only method optimizes the tertiary drive performance by minimizing the reposition overheads.

The append-only operation improves the efficiency in serving consecutive writing requests. Unfortunately, the presence of reading operations and delete operations breaks the list of writing operations. When the tertiary drive serves the reading request, it exchanges the media units and moves the current position to the accessed object. After serving a reading request, the tertiary drive stays at the end of the accessed object. The tertiary drive needs to reposition the media unit again to serve the next writing request. Thus, the tertiary storage performance is not optimized when the tertiary drive needs to read objects as well.

The log structured placement is efficient only for the back up and archival applications where data are more often being modified than retrieved. If data are not retrieved after writing, then the reasons to write these data become doubtful. In most applications, the data files are more often read than modified. In particular, multimedia objects are seldom modified. Therefore, the log structure placement is not an efficient method for general purpose multimedia storage systems.

Chapter Summary

The contiguous placement method stores the whole object in the same media unit. It is simple and efficient when the objects are written and retrieved in their entirety. Unfortunately, it suffers from large staging buffer consumption and long response time.

The log structured placement is an efficient placement method for the back up and archival applications. It optimizes the writing performance by providing the append-only operations. However, the performance is not optimized due to the presence of reading requests that are present in multimedia storage systems.

References

Kohl, J., Stonebraker, M., & Staelin, C. (1993). HighLight: A File System for Tertiary Storage. In *Proceedings of the Twelfth IEEE Symposium on Mass Storage Systems* (pp. 157-161).

Chapter XI

Statistical Placement on Hierarchical Storage Systems

Introduction

We have described the contiguous placement in the previous chapter and the statistical strategy to place objects on disks in Chapter IV. In this chapter, we describe the statistical strategy to place them on hierarchical storage systems. The objective of the data placement methods is to minimize the time to access object from the hierarchical storage system. The statistical strategy changes the statistical time to access objects so that the mean access time is optimal.

The objective of the frequency based placement method is to differentiate objects according to their access frequencies. The objects that are more frequently accessed are placed in the more convenient locations. The objects that are less frequently accessed are placed in the less convenient locations.

We will describe the frequency based placement method in the next section. Afterwards, we will analyze its performance. Last, we summarize this chapter.

Frequency Based Placement

Inside the tertiary storage library, the media units are physically placed in the cells. Some of these cells are near the drive while other cells are far from the drive. When objects are being accessed, the media unit that contains the object is exchanged to the drive. The time to exchange the media unit depends on the distance of the media unit from the drive. If the media unit is far from the drive, the exchange time would be long. If the cell containing the media unit is close to the drive, the exchange time is short.

The exchange time is a significant overhead in accessing an object. If the object is large, the transfer time is long and the exchange time is relatively a small fraction of the object access time. If the object is small, the transfer time is short and the exchange time becomes a significant percentage of the object access time. The frequency based placement method has been applied to reduce the average exchange time in accessing objects from hierarchical storage systems.

The frequency based placement has been applied to place objects across media units on the tertiary storage library. To reduce the average exchange time, the hot objects should be placed on the media units in the cells that are near the drive. For convenience, we would say in below paragraphs that the distance of a media unit from the drive is the distance of the cell that contains the media unit from the drive. The nearest media unit actually means the media unit in the cell that is the nearest to the drive. The farthest media unit actually means the media unit in the cell that is the farthest away from the drive.

The frequency based placement method places the objects according to their access frequencies or popularity and fills the media units according to their distance from the drive (Tse & Leung, 2000). First, the objects are sorted in the decreasing order of their access frequencies or popularities. The objects are placed in the order from the hottest object to the coldest object. Second, the media units are sorted in the increasing order of their distances from the drive. The media units are filled in the order from the nearest media unit to the farthest media unit.

The frequency based placement method places the first, hottest, objects onto the first, nearest, media unit. After the first object is stored, it then stores the next hottest objects on the first media unit until the first media unit becomes full. The next hottest object is then placed on the second media unit and so on. Thus, it places as many hot objects as possible together onto the same media unit until the media unit becomes full.

Inside a media unit, the objects are stored according to the distance from the loading position. Among the objects that are stored on a media unit, the hotter objects are stored before the colder objects. Thus, the hotter objects are stored closer to the loading position than the colder objects.

For example, a tertiary storage library has one drive and six media units. Each media unit can store two objects. The multimedia objects V_1 to V_{12} are sorted in the order of popularity as shown in Figure 11.1. The object V_1 is the most popular object, and the object V_{12} is the least popular object.

The six media units are sorted in the order of their distances from the drive as illustrated in Figure 11.2. The media unit T_1 is the nearest to the drive, and the media unit T_6 is the farthest away from the drive. According to the frequency based placement method, the hottest object, V_1, is first placed on the first media unit, T_1. After V_1 is placed, there is still storage space on the media unit, T_1. Since T_1 still has enough storage space, the second hottest object, V_2, is also placed on it. After V_2 is placed, the media unit, T_1, becomes full and it does not have enough storage space to store the next object V_3. Thus, the next media unit, T_2, is chosen to store the next object, V_3. After storing V_3, the media unit T_2 can also store V_4. Similarly, V_5 and V_6 are stored on the media units T_3 and so on.

Figure 11.1. Frequency based placement

$$V_1 \ V_2 \ V_3 \ V_4 \ V_5 \ V_6 \ V_7 \ V_8 \ V_9 \ V_{10} \ V_{11} \ V_{12}$$

decrease in popularity

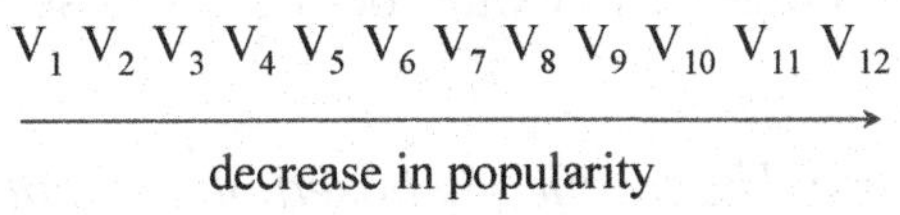

Figure 11.2. Frequency based placement

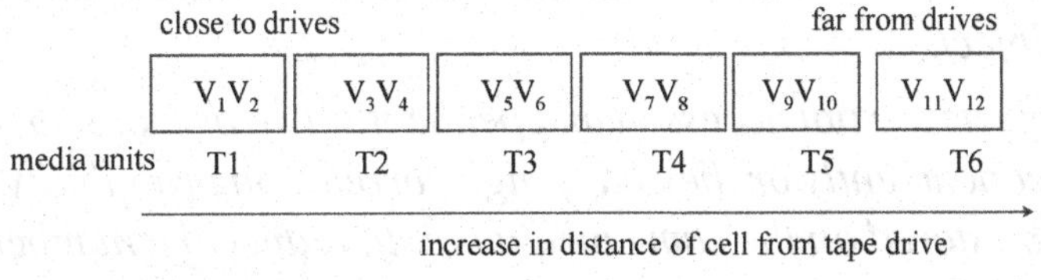

close to drives					far from drives
V_1V_2	V_3V_4	V_5V_6	V_7V_8	V_9V_{10}	$V_{11}V_{12}$
T1	T2	T3	T4	T5	T6

media units

increase in distance of cell from tape drive

Discussion

The frequency based placement method assumes that the objects are accessed independently. This means that the access probability of an object is the same no matter which object has just been accessed. If the objects are independently accessed, the probability to exchange a media unit to the drive can easily be found as the sum of the probabilities of the objects that are stored on this media unit.

The frequency based placement method stores the hot objects on the media unit that are exchanged with shorter time. Since the hot objects are accessed with the high access probability, the average exchange time is short when the hot objects are stored on the media unit near the drive.

If we consider the media unit already loaded in the drive, then this media unit is at zero distance from the drive since this media unit can be accessed without exchanges. Thus, the media unit in the drive becomes the most convenient location to store new objects after it is loaded to the drive.

The frequency based placement method places the hottest object on the media unit nearest to the drive. This media unit has the highest probability of being exchanged to the drive than other media units. As the nearest media unit is exchanged with the shortest time, the hottest object would incur the lightest overheads when it is placed on the nearest media unit. Thus, the hottest object should be placed on the nearest media unit to achieve the shortest exchange time.

For the same reason, the next hottest object is placed to the nearest media unit until it becomes full. After the nearest media unit is filled up, the next nearest media unit with available space would become the nearest media unit to store the next object. All the objects are thus stored on the media units so that the mean exchange time would be the shortest.

Application Notes: *The frequency based placement is applicable when the objects are independently accessed and the objects are of the similar size. If objects are different in size, a media unit that stores two colder objects may have a higher exchange probability than another media unit that stores one hotter object.*

If the objects are not accessed independently, two or more objects may be accessed concurrently or they have high correlation probability. These objects should be stored on the same media unit to reduce the number of exchanges and the mean exchange time. Unfortunately, multimedia objects, such as video and audio, may have high correlation probability if they are stored as separate objects.

The frequency based placement stores the hottest objects on the nearest media unit. Thus, many requests are directed towards this media unit. If the tertiary storage system has more than one drive, there may be more than one stream which would like to access an object from this media unit. Thus, a contention for the media unit is incurred. All other streams need to wait for the media unit in the drive, and the waiting time is long. Thus, the hot objects may be distributed onto a few media units so that all the drives can serve concurrent streams efficiently.

Besides moving the media units to the drive and their cells, the robotic arms may be able to swap the positions of media units among the cells. This is called the background migration. After the access probability of objects has changed, the probability to exchange a media unit may be changed. The original optimal placement of objects may become sub-optimal. The robotic arm can be used to swap the media units among cells to improve the average exchange time. This background migration restores the order of the media units according to the probability that the media unit is exchanged. This background migration should be performed when the workload on the tertiary storage library is light. Background migration moves the media units to the most desirable location depending on the frequency of exchanging the media unit when the workload is light.

If the optimal performance needs to be restored, a complete reorganization is needed. Objects are first copied to new media units according to their access frequencies. The media units are then migrated according to the exchange probability with the media unit with the highest exchange probability placed at the cell nearest to the drive (Tse, 1999).

Chapter Summary

We have explained the statistical placement method using the frequency based placement of objects on media units. The frequency based placement method places the objects to the media units according to the access frequency of the objects and the distance of the cell containing the media unit from the drive. The performance of the frequency based placement method is optimized when the objects are accessed independently and the objects are of the same size.

References

Tse, P. K. C. (1999). *Efficient storage and retrieval methods for multimedia information.* Doctoral dissertation, Victoria University, Melbourne, Australia.

Tse, P. K. C., & Leung, C. H. C. (2000). Improving multimedia systems performance using constant density recording disks. *ACM Multimedia Systems Journal, 8*(1), 47-56.

Chapter XII

Striping on Hierarchical Storage Systems

Introduction

The data striping technique has been successfully applied on disks to reduce the time to access objects from the disks as shown in Chapter VI. Similarly, the striping technique has been investigated to reduce the time to access objects from the tape libraries.

Similar to the striping on disks, the objective of the parallel striping method is to reduce the time to access objects from the tape libraries. The parallel tape striping directly applies the striping technique to place data stripes on tapes. The triangular placement method changes the order in which data stripes are stored on tapes to further enhance the performance.

In the next section, the parallel tape striping method will be described. The performance of the parallel tape striping follows. After that, the triangular placement method is explained, and it is followed by the performance of the triangular placement method.

Parallel Tape Striping

The objective of the parallel tape striping method is to reduce the time to access objects from the tape library. Parallel tape striping places objects using the following steps:

1. Divide the object into data stripes.
2. Distribute the data stripes across several tapes.
3. Access the data stripes from the tapes in parallel.

The parallel tape striping method divides the object into data stripes of constant data length approach. The size of each data stripe is fixed. Large objects are divided into more data stripes. Small objects are divided into fewer data stripes (Drapeau & Katz, 1993).

The data stripes are then distributed across multiple tapes. The number of tapes being used to store an object should be fewer than or equal to the number of drives. If an object is distributed across more tapes, some data stripes of the object cannot be accessed in parallel.

The tape drives perform the I/O operation in parallel. When an object is written to the tapes, the robotic arm first exchanges the tapes to the drives. The tertiary drives then reposition to the beginning of an empty space on the tapes. Afterwards, the drives transfer data to the tapes with the same number of data block on each tape. Thus, the object is written to the tapes in parallel.

Similarly, the objects are retrieved in parallel from the tapes. When an object is being accessed, the robotic arm first exchanges the required tapes to the drives. The tertiary drives then reposition to the beginning of the object being accessed. After that, the drives transfer data from the tape to the memory. Therefore, the object is accessed in parallel from the tapes.

For example, the robotic tape library has three drives and five tapes. The objects X, Y, and Z are to be stored on the robotic tape library. Object X is divided into nine data stripes X_1 to X_9. Object Y is divided into six data stripes Y_1 to Y_6. Object Z is also divided into six data stripes Z_1 to Z_6 as shown in Figure 12.1.

When object X is being stored, the robotic arm exchanges three tapes, T_1, T_2, and T_3, to the three drives. The drives then reposition the tapes to the beginning of empty storage space. Three data stripes, X_1, X_2, and X_3, are then stored on the three tapes, T_1, T_2, and T_3, respectively, with one data stripe on each tape. After that, the next set of three data stripes, X_4, X_5, and X_6, are then stored on the three tapes, T_1, T_2, and T_3, respectively. Last, X_7, X_8, and X_9, are stored on the three tapes, T_1, T_2, and T_3, as well. As a result, data stripes X_1, X_4, and X_7, are stored on the tape T_1. Data stripes X_2, X_5, and X_8 are stored on the tape T_2. Data stripes X_3, X_6, and X_9 are stored on the tape T_3.

Similarly, object Y is also distributed across the tapes T_1, T_2, and T_3. When object Z is stored, the three tapes T_1 to T_3 are full and they cannot store any more data stripes. The robotic arm thus exchanges the tapes T_4 and T_5 to two drives. The drives then reposition the tapes T_4 and T_5 to the beginning of empty space. Two data stripes Z_1 and Z_2 are stored on the tapes T_4 and T_5, respectively. Similarly, the data stripes Z_3 and Z_4 are stored on the tapes T_4 and T_5 again. Last, the data stripes Z_5 and Z_6 are stored on the tapes T_4 and T_5, as well. Therefore, the data stripes Z_1, Z_3, and Z_5 are stored on the tape T_4. The data stripes Z_2, Z_4, and Z_6 are stored on the tape T_5.

When object X is being retrieved, the robotic arm exchanges three tapes, T_1, T_2, and T_3, to the three drives. The drives then reposition the tapes to the beginning of the object on the tapes. The first drive repositions T_1 to the beginning of X_1. The second drive repositions T_2 to the beginning of X_2. The third drive repositions T_3 to the beginning of X_3. Three data stripes, X_1, X_2, and X_3, are then read from the three tapes, T_1, T_2, and T_3, respectively. After

Figure 12.1. Parallel tape striping

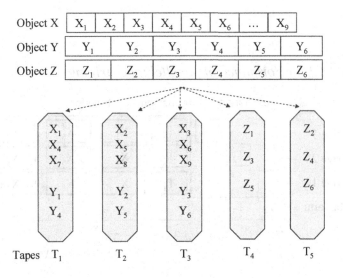

that, the next set of three data stripes, X_4, X_5, and X_6, are read from the three tapes, T_1, T_2, and T_3, respectively. Last, X_7, X_8, and X_9, are read from the three tapes, T_1, T_2, and T_3. After all the data stripes are retrieved from the tapes, all three drives are released. The objects Y and Z are retrieved similarly. Details of how the objects are kept when they are retrieved will be described in the data migration part.

Performance of Parallel Tape Striping

When the drives access an object in parallel, the time to perform each input/output (I/O) operation overlaps with each other. Since each drive accesses only a fraction of the object, the time to access an object is split among several drives. In particular, the data transfer time is reduced by split among the drives. Thus, the object request is served with a shorter service time. Therefore, the time spent by each drive to access an object is overlapped to reduce the response time of each request.

In the example above, the objects are accessed in parallel. When the object X is being accessed, the time when the drive exchanges, repositions, and transfers data stripes is illustrated in Figure 12.2.

Let ω be the tape exchange time, α be the tape reposition time, and γ be the data transfer rate. Let X be the size of the object X being accessed without losing clarity.

Figure 12.2. Performance of parallel tape striping

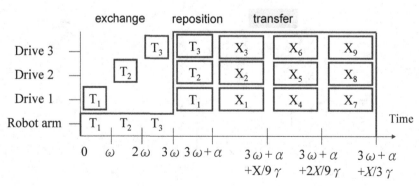

In the above example, the object X is striped across three tapes. As shown in Figure 12.2, the time to access the object X from the tape library using parallel tape striping

$$= 3\omega + \alpha + \frac{X}{3\gamma}$$

Alternatively, if the object X is placed contiguously onto a single tape, then the access time of the object X is found as

$$= \omega + \alpha + \frac{X}{\gamma}$$

Thus, the access time of the object X is reduced if

$$\omega + \alpha + \frac{X}{\gamma} > 3\omega + \alpha + \frac{X}{3\gamma}$$

$$\Leftrightarrow \frac{2X}{3\gamma} > 2\omega$$

That is, the access time is reduced by using the parallel tape striping if the decrease in data transfer time is more than the increase in exchange time.

In general, the time to access objects from the robotic tape library can be compared in a similar way. If none of the tapes needed are already loaded to the tape drives, the time to access an object of size X using parallel tape striping is

$$= N * \omega + \alpha + \frac{X}{N * \gamma} \tag{12.1}$$

where the object X is striped across N tapes.

Thus, the access time of the object X is reduced if

$$\omega + \alpha + \frac{X}{\gamma} > N * \omega + \alpha + \frac{X}{N * \gamma}$$

$$\Leftrightarrow \frac{(N-1)X}{N\gamma} > (N-1)\omega$$

$$\Leftrightarrow \frac{X}{N\gamma} > \omega$$

$$\Leftrightarrow N < \frac{X}{\omega\gamma} \qquad\qquad (12.2)$$

Therefore, we have found an upper bound on the number of tapes that an object can be striped across. If an object of size X is striped across fewer than $\frac{X}{\omega\gamma}$ tapes, the access time of the parallel tape striping method is shorter than the contiguous placement method. If the object is striped across more than $\frac{X}{\omega\gamma}$ tapes, the access time of the parallel tape striping method becomes longer than the contiguous placement method. If the object is striped across $\frac{X}{\omega\gamma}$ tapes, the access time of the parallel tape striping method is equal to the access time of the contiguous placement method. However, more drives are used to provide the parallel tape striping. Thus, the objects should be striped across fewer than $\frac{X}{\omega\gamma}$ tapes.

For example, if the robotic tape library has as many drives as we need, an object of 1000MB is stored on the tape library. The time to exchange a tape is 20 seconds and the drives transfer data at the rate of 10MB/sec. From equation (12.2), the object should not be striped across more than N tapes where N is

$$= \frac{X}{\omega\gamma}$$

$$= \frac{1000}{(20)*(10)},$$

$$= 5.$$

That is, the object should not be striped across more than five tapes. Otherwise, the data access time would increase instead of decrease. We could find the optimal number of drives in another approach below. Let θ be the access time of the object. From equation (12.1), we have

$$\theta = N * \omega + \alpha + \frac{X}{N * \gamma} \qquad (12.3)$$

Looking at this equation, we can see that the value of θ increases with N due to the term $N*\omega$, and decreases due to the term $\dfrac{X}{N * \gamma}$. The first order derivative of θ with respect to the number of striping tapes N is

$$\frac{d\theta}{dN} = \omega - \frac{X}{\gamma * N^2} \qquad (12.4)$$

Setting the first order derivative of θ to zero, we have

$$\omega - \frac{X}{\gamma * N^2} = 0$$

$$\Leftrightarrow \omega = \frac{X}{\gamma * N^2}$$

$$\Leftrightarrow N^2 = \frac{X}{\omega * \gamma}$$

$$\Leftrightarrow N = \pm \sqrt{\frac{X}{\omega * \gamma}} \qquad (12.5)$$

As N is greater than 1, we reject the negative value of N to get the optimal number of striping tapes as

$$N_{optimal} = + \sqrt{\frac{X}{\omega * \gamma}} \qquad (12.6)$$

The second order derivative of θ with respect to N is

$$\frac{d^2\theta}{dN^2} = \frac{2X}{\gamma * N^3}$$

(12.7)

As all the parameters X, γ, and N are all greater than 0, the second order derivative of θ is greater than zero. Therefore, the optimal access time is the minimum access time. The minimum access time is achieved when the object is striped across $+\sqrt{\dfrac{X}{\omega * \gamma}}$ tapes.

If the value of $+\sqrt{\dfrac{X}{\omega * \gamma}}$ is not an integer, then the floor function or the ceiling function may be applied to find the minimum access time. Thus, the optimal number of striping tapes is either equal to $\left\lfloor +\sqrt{\dfrac{X}{\omega * \gamma}} \right\rfloor$ or $\left\lceil +\sqrt{\dfrac{X}{\omega * \gamma}} \right\rceil$ depending on the actual access time when the floor function or ceiling function is applied.

The minimum access time and the optimal number of striping tapes of parallel tape striping are plotted in Figure 12.3. The nonstriping access time of the contiguous placement method is also shown in the figure for comparison. We can see that larger objects can be striped across more tapes to reduce the object access time. However, smaller objects should be striped across fewer tapes to avoid too much exchange overheads. When the objects are very small, the number of optimal striping tapes can be equal to one. Thus, the object should be stored on only one tape without striping. When the object

Figure 12.3. Performance of parallel tape striping

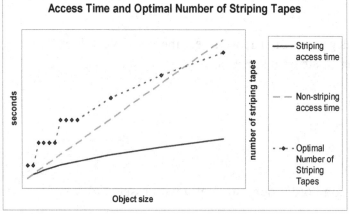

is large, the optimal number of striping tapes may be more than the number of tape drives in the library. Since the tapes are access in parallel, the object should not be striped across more tapes than the number of tape drives.

In addition, the optimal access time of parallel tape striping is always lower than or equal to the access time of nonstriping. Therefore, the parallel tape striping method reduces the time to access an object from the tape library. Although the access time of the parallel tape striping method is always lower than the access time of the nonstriping methods, the parallel tape striping method uses several drives simultaneously to serve one stream. The tape drives cannot serve requests from other streams. Therefore, the nonstriping method should be used when its access time is the same as the striping access time.

The parallel tape striping uses multiple drives to transfer an object from several tapes at the same time. The transfer time of an object is reduced by splitting among the striping tape drives. Thus, the access time is greatly reduced. Unfortunately, the parallel tape striping method synchronizes the reading and writing operations. When data are read or written from the tapes, the synchronization is impaired by the presence of a bad segment. The read and write operations are retried leading to variable access times. The synchronization of the read or write operation on each drive is delayed. Thus, the practical throughput of the storage system is lower than the theoretical achievable value.

In addition, the parallel tape striping method exchanges the tapes in parallel. When the number of robotic arms is fewer than the number of tape drives, the fewer robotic arms receive all the exchange requests at the same time. It should be noted that robotic tape libraries usually has only one robotic arm to serve one exchange request at a time. Thus, some exchange requests need to wait in the waiting queue. Therefore, parallel tape striping incurs contention at the robotic arms leading to reduced system throughput. We shall explain how the contention of exchange requests in the triangular placement method in the next section.

Triangular Placement

The parallel tape striping method reduces the transfer time in delivering objects from tapes. It however induces contentions on switching tapes. The performance of parallel tape striping is limited by the ability of the robotic arms in switching tapes. The triangular placement method relaxes the strict synchronization in accessing objects to reduce the switching overheads.

Consider that a tape library has four drives and only one robotic arm. For objects that are striped across four tapes, the drives start to reposition and transfer after the robotic arm has exchanged four tapes. The time to exchange the four tapes is four times of the time to exchange one tape. Since the robotic arm serves the exchange requests sequentially, it exchanges the tapes to the drives one by one. After the first tape is loaded to the first drive, the drive waits for the robotic arm to exchange other tapes. This tape is already ready for repositioning and transfer. As shown in Figure 12.4, these drives have some usable bandwidth that can be utilized.

The triangular placement method assumes that the tape drives share a robotic arm. The robotic tape library can only serve exchange requests one by one (Chiueh, 1995). In addition, the exchange time should be predictable.

The triangular placement method relaxes the synchronization constraint that the exchange step should be completed on all drives before the next step to reposition the tapes on all drives. Instead, each drive starts to reposition the tape immediately after the tape on this drive is exchanged (Chiueh, 1995). Thus, the tape drive does not wait for the other drives to complete their exchanging operation.

Similar to parallel tape striping, an object is divided into fixed length data stripes. The number of data stripes depends on the size of the object. Large objects are divided into many data stripes. Small objects are divided into few data stripes.

Figure 12.4. Usable bandwidth in parallel tape striping

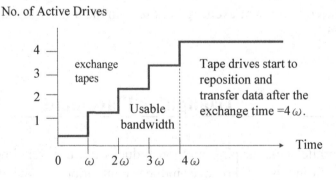

The tape drives perform the I/O operation in parallel with relaxed synchronization. They do not synchronize individual exchange, reposition, and data transfer operations. They only synchronize when all the data stripes of the object is transferred.

When an object is written to the tapes, the robotic arm first exchanges a tape to the first drive. After the tape is exchanged, the first drive is initiated to reposition to an empty space. The first drive immediately starts to transfer data stripes to the tape after repositioning. While the first drive is repositioning and transferring data, the robotic arm starts to exchange the second tape to the second drive. After the tape is exchanged, the second drive is initiated to reposition to an empty space. The second drive immediately starts to transfer data stripes to the tape after repositioning. The third drive and other drives perform similarly and so on. Therefore, the object is written in parallel with relaxed synchronization to the tapes.

Similarly, the objects are retrieved in parallel with relaxed synchronization. When an object is written to the tapes, the robotic arm first exchanges a tape to the first drive. After the tape is exchanged, the first drive is initiated to reposition to the beginning of the object being accessed. The first drive immediately starts to transfer data stripes from the tape after repositioning. While the first drive is repositioning and transferring data, the robotic arm starts to exchange the second tape to the second drive. After the tape is exchanged, the second drive is initiated to reposition to the beginning of the object being accessed. The second drive immediately starts to transfer data stripes from the tape after repositioning. The third drive and other drives perform similarly and so on. Therefore, the object is accessed in parallel with relaxed synchronization from the tapes.

Since the drive with an early exchanged tape starts to transfer data at an earlier time, more data stripes can be stored on this tape. The storage space on these tapes is consumed more quickly.

Consider the same example as in the parallel tape striping method. The objects X, Y, and Z are stored to the robotic tape library with three drives and five tapes. Object X is divided into nine data stripes X_1 to X_9. Object Y is divided into six data stripes Y_1 to Y_6. Object Z is also divided into six data stripes Z_1 to Z_6 as shown in Figure 12.5.

The four devices, including the robotic arm and the three drives, write object X to the tapes by performing the following operations. Each operation below lasts for a considerable period of time at the devices.

1. The robotic arm exchanges the tape T1 to the first drive. The second and third drives are idle.

2. The first drive repositions T1 to an empty space and starts to transfer data stripe X1 to T1 after repositioning. The robotic arm exchanges T2 to the second drive. The third drive is idle.

3. The first drive starts to transfer the next data stripe X2. The second drive repositions T2 to an empty space and starts to transfer the data stripe X3 after repositioning. The robotic arm exchanges T3 to the third drive.

4. The first drive starts to transfer the next data stripe X4. The second drive starts to transfer the next data stripes X5. The third drive repositions T3 to an empty space and starts to transfer the data stripe X6 to T3 after repositioning. The robotic arm is idle.

5. The first drive starts to transfer the next data stripe X7. The second drive starts to transfer the next data stripe X8. The first drive starts to transfer the next data stripe X9. The robotic arm is idle.

6. After all the drives have completely transferred the data stripes, all four devices are released. The storage system can serve the next request.

Therefore, the object X is written in parallel with relaxed synchronization to the tapes.

Similarly, object Y is also distributed across the tapes T_1, T_2, and T_3. When object Z is stored, the three tapes T_1 to T_3 are full, and they cannot store any

Figure 12.5. Triangular placement

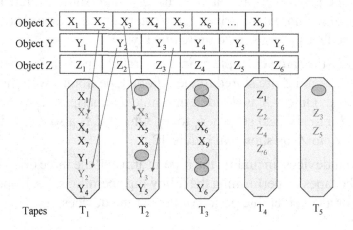

more objects. The object Z is written to the tapes by the following operations. The third drive is idle throughout the period.

1. The robotic arm exchanges the tape T4 to the first drive. The second drive is idle.

2. The first drive repositions T4 to an empty space and starts to transfer data stripe Z1 to T4 after repositioning. The robotic arm exchanges T5 to the second drive.

3. The first drive starts to transfer the next data stripe Z2. The second drive repositions T5 to an empty space and starts to transfer the data stripe Z3 after repositioning.

4. The first drive starts to transfer the next data stripe Z4. The second drive starts to transfer the next data stripes Z5. The robotic arm is idle.

5. The first drive starts to transfer the next data stripe Z6. The second drive is idle after it has completely transferred the data stripes Z5. The robotic arm is idle.

6. After the first drive has completely transferred the data stripe Z6, all four devices are released. The storage system can serve the next request.

Therefore, the object Z is written in parallel with relaxed synchronization to the tapes.

When objects are stored using the triangular placement, the drives access objects in parallel with relaxed synchronization. More data stripes are stored on the earlier exchanged tapes. It takes longer time to retrieve the stored data stripes. Thus, the tapes should always be exchanged in the same order.

When the object X is being retrieved, the four devices, including the robotic arm and the three drives, perform the following operations. Each operation below lasts for a considerable period of time at the devices.

1. The robotic arm exchanges the tape T1 to the first drive. The second and third drives are idle.

2. The first drive repositions T1 to the beginning of the data stripe X1 and starts to transfer X1 from T1 after repositioning. The robotic arm exchanges T2 to the second drive. The third drive is idle.

3.   The first drive repositions to the beginning of the next data stripe X2, if necessary, and starts to transfer X2 from T1 after repositioning. The second drive repositions T2 to the beginning of the data stripe X3 and starts to transfer X3 from T2 after repositioning. The robotic arm exchanges T3 to the third drive.

4.   The first drive repositions to the beginning of the next data stripe X4, if necessary, and starts to transfer X4 from T1 after repositioning. The second drive repositions T2 to the beginning of the data stripe X5, if necessary, and starts to transfer X5 from T2 after repositioning. The third drive starts to reposition T3 to the beginning of X6 and starts to transfer X6 from T3 after repositioning. The robotic arm is idle.

5.   The first drive repositions to the beginning of the next data stripe X7, if necessary, and starts to transfer X7 from T1 after repositioning. The second drive repositions T2 to the beginning of the data stripe X8, if necessary, and starts to transfer X8 from T2 after repositioning. The third drive starts to reposition T3 to the beginning of X9, if necessary, and starts to transfer X9 from T3 after repositioning. The robotic arm is idle.

6.   After the drives have completely transferred all data stripes of X from the tapes, all the drives and the robotic arm are released. The storage system can serve the next request.

The object Y and object Z are retrieved similarly. More details of how the objects are migrated will be described in the data migration part.

Performance of Triangular Placement

Similar to the parallel tape striping method, the drives access the objects in parallel. The time to perform the I/O operations overlaps with each other. The time to access an object is split among several drives. Apart from the reduced data transfer time, more time is available on the early exchanged drives. Thus, the triangular placement utilizes the usable bandwidth of the early exchanged drive.

In the example above, the objects are accessed in parallel with relaxed synchronization. When the object X is being accessed, the time when the drive exchanges, repositions, and transfers data stripes is illustrated in Figure 12.6. Let ω be the tape exchange time, α be the tape reposition time, and γ be the data transfer rate. Let X be the size of the object X being accessed without losing clarity. If the time to transfer a data stripe is equal to the time to exchange a tape, then

$$\omega = \frac{X_s}{\gamma}$$

$$\Leftrightarrow Xs = \omega\gamma$$

where X_s is the size of the data stripes X_1, X_2, and X_3. Thus, the amount of data that is transferred before the third drive starts to transfer data is:

$$= (2 + 1)X_s,$$
$$= 3\omega\gamma.$$

Thus, the time to access the object X from the tape library using triangular placement method is

$$= 3\omega + \alpha + \frac{X - 3\omega\gamma}{3\gamma}$$

$$= 2\omega + \alpha + \frac{X}{3\gamma}$$

Figure 12.6. Performance of triangular placement

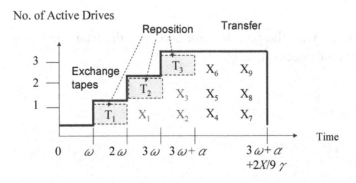

Compared with the parallel tape striping, the time to access the object X is reduced by

$$3\omega + \alpha + \frac{X}{3\gamma} - \left(2\omega + \alpha + \frac{X}{3\gamma}\right)$$

$$= \omega$$

In general, the time to access objects from the robotic tape library can be found similarly. If none of the tapes needed are already loaded to the tape drives, the time to access an object of size X using triangular placement is

$$= N*\omega + \alpha + \frac{X}{N*\gamma} - \frac{\omega*\left[(N-1)+(N-2)+...+2+1\right]}{N} \qquad (12.8)$$

where the object X is striped across N tapes.

After simplification, it becomes

$$= N*\omega + \alpha + \frac{X}{N*\gamma} - \frac{(N-1)*\omega}{2} \qquad (12.9)$$

$$= \left(N - \frac{N-1}{2}\right)*\omega + \alpha + \frac{X}{N*\gamma} \qquad (12.10)$$

$$= \frac{N+1}{2}*\omega + \alpha + \frac{X}{N*\gamma} \qquad (12.11)$$

Compared with the parallel tape striping, the triangular placement method reduces the access time by

$$= N*\omega + \alpha + \frac{X}{N*\gamma} - \left[\frac{N+1}{2}*\omega + \alpha + \frac{X}{N*\gamma}\right]$$

$$= \frac{(N-1)}{2}*\omega \qquad (12.12)$$

We could find the optimal number of striping tapes below. Let θ be the access time of the object. From equation (12.1), we have

$$\theta = \frac{N+1}{2}\omega + \alpha + \frac{X}{N*\gamma} \qquad (12.13)$$

The first order derivative of θ with respect to the number of striping tapes N is

$$\frac{d\theta}{dN} = \frac{\omega}{2} - \frac{X}{\gamma*N^2} \qquad (12.14)$$

Setting the first order derivative of θ to zero, we have

$$\frac{\omega}{2} - \frac{X}{\gamma*N^2} = 0$$

$$\Leftrightarrow \frac{\omega}{2} = \frac{X}{\gamma*N^2}$$

$$\Leftrightarrow N^2 = \frac{2X}{\omega*\gamma}$$

$$\Leftrightarrow N = \pm\sqrt{\frac{2X}{\omega*\gamma}} \qquad (12.15)$$

As N is greater than 1, we reject the negative value of N to get the optimal number of striping tapes as

$$N_{optimal} = +\sqrt{\frac{2X}{\omega*\gamma}} \qquad (12.16)$$

The second order derivative of θ with respect to N is

$$\frac{d^2\theta}{dN^2} = \frac{2X}{\gamma * N^3}$$

(12.17)

Since all the parameters X, γ, and N are all greater than 0, the second order derivative of θ is greater than zero. Therefore, the optimal access time is the minimum access time. The minimum access time is achieved when the object is striped across $+\sqrt{\dfrac{2X}{\omega * \gamma}}$ tapes.

If the value of $+\sqrt{\dfrac{2X}{\omega * \gamma}}$ is not an integer, then the floor function or the ceiling function may be applied to find the minimum access time. Thus, the optimal number of striping tapes is either equal to $\left\lfloor +\sqrt{\dfrac{2X}{\omega * \gamma}} \right\rfloor$ or $\left\lceil +\sqrt{\dfrac{2X}{\omega * \gamma}} \right\rceil$ depending on the actual access time when the floor function or ceiling function is applied.

The minimum access time and the optimal number of striping tapes of the triangular placement method are plotted in Figure 12.7. The nonstriping access time of the contiguous placement method and the striping access time of the parallel tape striping are also shown in the figure for comparison. The optimal number striping tapes of the triangular placement method is always more than that of the parallel tape striping method. Thus, more drives can be used together to transfer the object in parallel.

Similar to parallel tape striping, larger objects can be striped across more tapes to reduce the object access time. However, smaller objects should be striped across fewer tapes to avoid too much exchange overheads. The optimal number of striping tapes is equal to one only when the objects are very small. Thus, the small object should be stored on only one tape without striping. If the object is large, the optimal number of striping tapes may be more than the number of tape drives in the library. Since the tapes are accessed in parallel, the object should not be striped across more tapes than the number of tape drives.

Figure 12.7. Performance of triangular placement

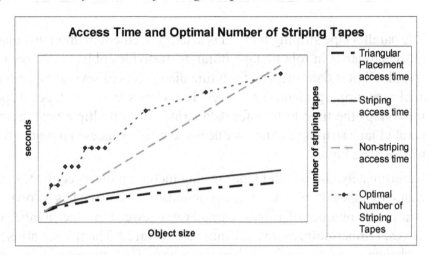

In addition, the optimal access time of the triangular placement method is always shorter than the access time of the parallel striping method and the access time of the nonstriping method. This is because some exchange time overlaps with some data transfer time. The triangular placement method reduces the time to access an object from the tape library.

Application Note: *Although the access time of the triangular placement method is always shorter than the access time of the parallel tape striping method, the triangular placement method relaxes the synchronization of individual operations. The storage system may need to create extra tasks to perform the operation on the drives. This increases the complexity in the controlling software.*

Furthermore, the tapes should always be exchanged in the same order. If the order in which tapes are exchanged is altered, the tape with more data stripes may be exchanged later. Such a tape would need more time to transfer an object than the others. Instead of reducing the access time, the time to access an object would be increased. Therefore, the order in which tapes are exchanged should be kept constant. Luckily, it is easy to implement this by assigning an order number to every tape. The robotic arm can exchange the striping tapes according to their order number.

Chapter Summary

The parallel tape striping method is a data placement method that places the objects to tapes in robotic tape libraries. It divides objects into data stripes and distributes data stripes of multimedia objects to several tapes. The parallel tape striping method accesses data stripes from the tapes in parallel. It overlaps the time to transfer data stripes from multiple tape drives. The parallel tape striping method reduces the time to access an object from the robotic tape library.

Unfortunately, the parallel tape striping method induces contentions on exchanging tapes. It may not cause problems if each drive has its own robotic arm or the number of robotic arms is not fewer than the number of tape drives. Furthermore, more exchanges are incurred. The robotic arms need to exchange several tapes for each object access. Thus, the parallel tape striping method increases the workload on the robotic arms.

The triangular placement method utilizes the usable bandwidth during the exchange time to reduce the data access time. A tape drive starts to reposition tapes and transfer data stripes while other drives are still waiting for exchanges. The triangular placement method further reduces the time to access objects from robotic tape libraries. It also increases the optimal number of striping drives.

References

Chiueh, T. C. (1995). Performance optimization for parallel tape arrays. In *Proceedings of the 9th ACM Conference on Supercomputing* (pp. 375-384).

Drapeau, A. L., & Katz, R. H. (1993). Striping in large tape libraries. In *Proceedings of the Conference on Supercomputing '93* (pp. 378-387).

Chapter XIII

Constraint Allocation on Hierarchical Storage Systems

Introduction

Multimedia objects are stored on hierarchical storage systems (HSS). The objects are large in size but the access latency of HSS is high. It is necessary to provide high throughput in delivering data from the storage system. In addition to the statistical placement and striping methods in the two previous chapters, constraint allocation can also improve the throughput of HSS.

Multimedia streams should be displayed with continuity. Depending on the data migration method, the whole object or only partial object is retrieved prior to the beginning of consumption. Thus, it may need to retrieve the parts of the object within guarantee times.

The maximum access time depends on the storage locations of the object. If the parts of the object are freely stored on any media units, it may take the longest exchange time to exchange a media unit. If the parts of the object are freely stored on any locations of the media units, it may take the longest reposition time to reposition the media unit. The maximum access time needs to include both the longest exchange time and the longest reposition time. As a result, the guarantee times should not be shorter than the maximum access time in the worst case. The long guarantee time results in a small number of acceptable streams to the hierarchical storage system.

The constraint allocation methods limit the freedom to place data on media units so that the worst case would never happen. They reduce the longest exchange time and/or the longest reposition time in accessing the objects. Two approaches to provide constraint allocations have been proposed on different types of media units. The interleaved contiguous placement limits the storage locations of data stripes on optical disks and it is described in the next section. The concurrent striping method that limits the storage locations of data stripes on tapes is described.

Interleaved Contiguous Placement

The interleaved contiguous placement method reduces the maximum over-heads in accessing the objects concurrently. It maintains the separation between consecutive data stripes so that the maximum reposition time and the maximum access time are bounded above.

Some multimedia streams have some correlations. These multimedia streams may be more likely to be played at similar times. The objects that are accessed by these streams are more likely to be accessed at similar times. For example, the audio data and video data of a movie may be created on separate objects. The multimedia stream that accesses one object would likely be initiated at the same time as the stream that accesses another object. These two objects thus have a high probability of being accessed together. The interleaved contiguous placement method stores these objects on the optical disk in a way that they can be accessed efficiently.

The interleaved contiguous placement method merges the data stripes of the objects that are likely to be accessed concurrently. It interleaves the data stripes on the same optical disk by maintaining the distance in separation between consecutive data stripes. Thus, the optical disk moves only the distance between consecutive data stripes to serve a request on the object. As

Figure 13.1. Interleaved contiguous placement

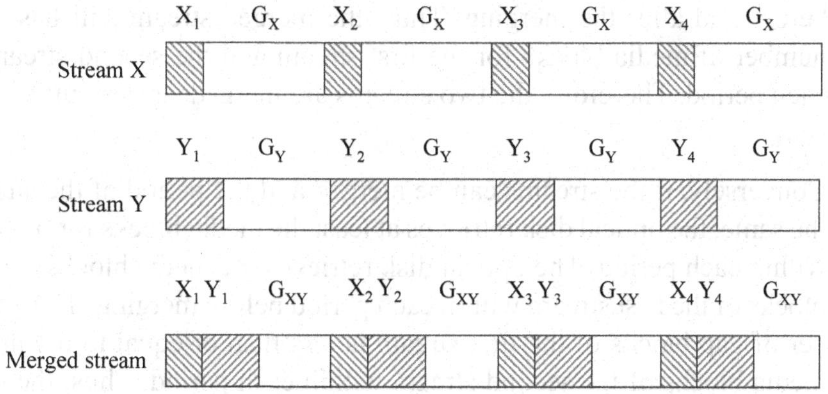

the separation distance between consecutive data stripes is limited, the time to access the next data stripe of the object is bounded above.

Each stored object is characterized by a storage pattern composing of two parameters M and G, where M is the number of data blocks of each data stripe, and G is the number of gap blocks between two consecutive data stripes of the stream.

Figure 13.1 shows the storage pattern of two homogeneous streams, stream X and stream Y. Stream X is divided into data stripes, X_1, X_2, X_3, X_4, and so on. The data stripes of stream X are placed on the storage media with some gap blocks. The gap blocks are indicated with G_X. The stream Y is divided into data stripes Y_1, Y_2, Y_3, Y_4, and so on. The data stripes of stream Y are placed on the storage media with gap blocks G_Y. When the two streams are merged, the media blocks of stream X are placed in the gap blocks of stream Y, and the media blocks of stream Y are placed in the gap blocks of stream X. The storage pattern of the merged streams shows that the data stripes of stream X and stream Y are placed on the storage media with a smaller gap G_{XY}.

Corollary 1. Two homogeneous streams can be merged if and only if the number of media blocks of the second stream is not more than the number of gap blocks of the first stream.

Proof. As optical disks store data in the constant linear velocity format, they access a fixed number of data blocks within a fixed period of time. If the number of media blocks of the second stream is not more than the number of gap blocks of the first stream, the media blocks can be placed within the gap blocks of the first stream. The period of the two streams remains the same before and after the merging. Thus, the merged stream still has the same number of media blocks for the first stream and the second stream within each period. Therefore, the two streams are merged successfully.

Conversely, if the streams can be merged and the period of the streams are the same, the optical disk retrieves at least the media blocks for both streams within each period. The optical disk retrieves the media blocks and the gap blocks of the first stream within each period before merging. Thus, the number of gap blocks of the first stream is less than or equal to the number of media blocks of the second stream within each period. Thus, the corollary is proved. The above merging condition of two homogeneous streams can be generalized to a number of homogeneous streams with the same period. The generalized merging condition is stated in Corollary 2.

Corollary 2. A number of homogeneous streams can be merged if and only if the total number of media blocks of the streams within a period of time is not more than the number of blocks that are retrieved within the same period of time.

Proof. As optical disks store data in the constant linear velocity format, they retrieve a fixed number of data blocks within a period of time. If this fixed number of data blocks is less than the total number of media blocks within the same period, some streams would not receive enough data blocks to display. Thus, the streams cannot be merged without violating the continuous display requirement.

Conversely, if the streams can be merged and the period of the streams are the same, the optical disk retrieves at least the media blocks for all streams within each period after merging. The optical disk retrieves the media blocks for every stream within each period before merging. Thus, the total number of media blocks of the streams within the period of time is not more than the number of blocks that are retrieved within the same period of time. Thus, Corollary 2 is proved.

For heterogeneous streams, the feasibility condition to merge the streams is not so simple. We shall show the feasibility conditions to merge heterogeneous streams later. Before that, we shall describe the continuous display requirement below. The storage pattern of an object can satisfy the continuous display requirement of the accessing stream if

$$\frac{M+G}{\rho} \leq \delta \tag{13.1}$$

where ρ is the optical disk retrieval bandwidth and δ is the display time for each data stripe of the stream.

The proof of equation (13.1) is as follows. If the storage pattern of a stream is maintained, the optical disk can linearly access all the data blocks. As the optical disks store data in the constant linear velocity format, the data blocks are delivered in the fixed data rate ρ. It takes an amount of time $= \frac{M+G}{\rho}$ to retrieve M data blocks belonging to the stream retrieved and G blocks not belonging to the stream. Thus, at least one data stripe is retrieved, and this data stripe can display for a time of δ. This access pattern is repeated to access all the data stripes, and each data stripe lasts for a time long enough for the retrieval of the next data stripe. Thus, the continuous display requirement of the stream is fulfilled.

The interleaved contiguous placement uses two policies to merge streams depending on whether the storage pattern of streams remains the same or not. The storage pattern preserving policy is described in the next section. After that, the storage pattern altering (SPA) policy is described.

Storage Pattern Preserving Policy

In the storage pattern preserving (SPP) policy, two streams are merged. The streams maintain their storage patterns before and after the merging (Yu, Sun, Bitton, Yang, Bruno, & Yus, 1989). We shall describe the feasibility condition to merge two streams in the paragraphs below. We then elaborate this feasibility condition with two examples. The limitations of the SPP policy are then analyzed.

The storage pattern preserving policy states that two media streams can be merged if and only if their greatest common divisor satisfies the feasibility condition,

$$M_1 + M_2 \leq \text{G.C.D.} (M_1 + G_1, M_2 + G_2), \tag{13.2}$$

where G.C.D.( ) is the greatest common divisor function.

In the first example, two streams S_1 and S_2 are stored on an optical disk. The storage pattern of stream S_1 is (1, 3) and the storage stream of stream S2 is (1, 5). That is, stream S1 stores one block in every data stripe and skips three blocks between two data stripes. The stream S2 also stores one block in every data stripe and skips five data blocks between two data stripes. Thus,

$$M_1 = 1, G_1 = 3, M_2 = 1, \text{and } G_2 = 5,$$
$$\Rightarrow \quad M_1 + M_2 = 2.$$

In addition, we have

$$M_1 + G_1 = 4 \text{ and } M_2 + G_2 = 6,$$
$$\Rightarrow \quad \text{G.C.D.}(M_1 + G_1, M_1 + G_1) = 2.$$

Thus, we have

$$M_1 + M_2 = \text{G.C.D.}(M_1 + G_1, M_1 + G_1).$$

The storage patterns of the two streams satisfy the equation (13.2). They can be merged using the SPP policy.

When the two streams are merged, the relative positions of the two streams are shown in Figure 13.2. The media data blocks are shown in colour, and the gap blocks are unshaded. Since we cannot store two media data blocks on the same block of the optical disk, we cannot merge the two streams at this relative position when the data blocks of stream S_2 is under the data blocks of stream S_1.

Since the smallest common multiple of 4 and 6 is equal to 12, the relative positions of the two streams repeat after every 12 data blocks as a cycle. Since the storage pattern of stream S_1 is (1, 3), the storage pattern of stream S_1 repeats after every four blocks. Thus, there are four relative positions of stream S_2 with respect to stream S_1.

The first row shows the positions of media data blocks and gap blocks of the stream S_1 on the data blocks of the optical disk. The second row shows the position of media data blocks and gap blocks of stream S_2. We can see that the first and the third data blocks of stream S_2 are under the data blocks of

Figure 13.2. Interleaved contiguous placement SPP example 1

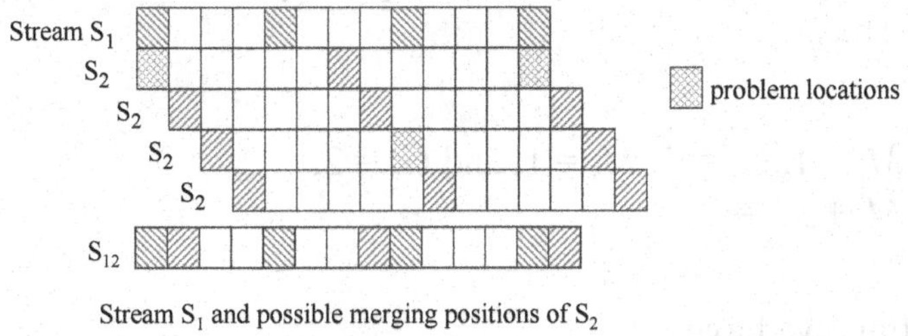

Stream S_1 and possible merging positions of S_2

stream S_1. Thus, the streams cannot be merged when the stream S_2 is at this position with respect to the stream S_1.

In the third row, the stream S_2 is shifted to the right by one data block. All the data blocks of stream S_2 come under the gap blocks of stream S_1. The data blocks of stream S_2 can be placed on the gap blocks of stream S_1. Thus, the two streams can be merged by storing the streams at this relative position on the optical disk.

In the fourth row, the stream S_2 is further shifted to the right by one data block. Similar to the second row, some media blocks of stream S_2 are under the media blocks of stream S_1. Thus, the streams cannot be merged when the stream S_2 is at this position with respect to the stream S_1.

In the fifth row, the stream S_2 is shifted further to the right by one data block. All the data blocks of stream S_2 come under the gap blocks of stream S_1. The data blocks of stream S_2 can be placed on the gap blocks of stream S_1. Thus, the two streams can be merged by storing the streams at this relative position on the optical disk.

If the stream S_2 is shifted to the right again, the relative positions of the two streams are the same as the second row. Therefore, we have exhausted all the relative positions of the merged streams.

The two streams can be merged if the stream S_2 is at the relative position of the third row or the fifth row with respect to stream S_1. The storage pattern of the merge stream S_{12} is also shown in Figure 13.2. We can see that the media blocks of the stream S_2 are placed at the gap blocks of stream S_1. Also, the media blocks of stream S_1 are placed at the gap blocks of stream S_2.

In the second example, two streams S_1 and S_3 are to be merged on an optical disk. The storage pattern of stream S_1 is (1, 3) and the storage stream of stream S_3 is (1, 2). That is, stream S_1 stores one block in every data stripe and skips three blocks between two data stripes. The stream S_2 also stores one block in every data stripe and skips only two blocks between two data stripes. Thus,

$$M_1 = 1, G_1 = 3, M_2 = 1, \text{ and } G_2 = 2,$$
$$\Rightarrow \quad M_1 + M_2 = 2.$$

In addition, we have

$$M_1 + G_1 = 4 \text{ and } M_2 + G_2 = 3,$$
$$\Rightarrow \quad \text{G.C.D.}(M_1 + G_1, M_1 + G_1) = 1.$$

Thus, we have

$$M_1 + M_2 > \text{G.C.D.}(M_1 + G_1, M_1 + G_1).$$

The storage patterns of the streams S_1 and S_3 do not satisfy the equation (13.2). They cannot be merged using SPP policy.

When the two streams are merged, the relative positions of the two streams are shown in Figure 13.3. Since the smallest common multiple of 4 and 3 is equal to 12, the relative positions of the two streams repeat after every 12 data blocks as a cycle. Since the storage pattern of stream S_1 is (1, 3), the storage pattern of stream S_1 repeats after every four blocks. Thus, there are four relative positions of stream S_3 with respect to stream S_1.

The first row shows the positions of media data blocks and gap blocks of the stream S_1 on the data blocks of the optical disk. The second row shows the position of media data blocks and gap blocks of stream S_3. We can see that the first data block of stream S_3 is under the data blocks of stream S_1. Thus, the streams cannot be merged when the stream S_3 is at this position with respect to the stream S_1.

In the third row, the stream S_3 is shifted to the right by one data block. The second media block of the stream S_3 comes under the media block of stream S_1. Thus, the streams cannot be merged when the stream S_3 is at this position with respect to the stream S_1.

In the fourth row, the stream S_3 is shifted further to the right by one data block. The third media block of the stream S_3 comes under the media block

Figure 13.3. Interleaved contiguous placement SPP example 2

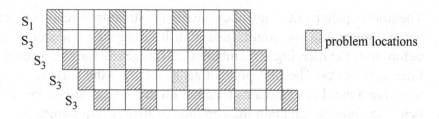

Problem locations exist in all possible merging positions of S_3

of stream S_1. Thus, the streams also cannot be merged when the stream S_3 is at this position with respect to the stream S_1.

In the fifth row, the stream S_3 is shifted further to the right by one data block. The fourth media block of the stream S_3 comes under the media block of stream S_1. Thus, the streams also cannot be merged when the stream S_3 is at this position with respect to the stream S_1.

If the stream S_3 is shifted to the right again, the relative positions of the two streams are the same as the second row. We have exhausted all the relative positions of the merged streams, and we have found that the two streams cannot be merged at any of the relative positions. Therefore, the two streams cannot be merged. If the streams are merged, there are problem locations no matter what is the relative position of the two streams as shown in Figure 13.3.

From the above examples, we can see that equation (13.2) provides a simple method to test if two streams can be merged on the optical disk. This simple equation can be evaluated quickly on every pair of objects to find out the pairs of streams that can be merged.

The storage pattern preserving policy does not change the storage patterns of individual streams that are involved in the merging. Thus, the continuous display requirements of the two streams can still be guaranteed.

Unfortunately, the merged stream cannot be described in the simple storage pattern as the streams before merging. Therefore, the merged stream cannot be further merged with other streams again. In addition, Equation (13.2) checks the feasibility to merge only two streams. The feasibility to merge a number of streams is not provided. In the next section on storage pattern altering policy, we shall see how the feasibility condition is generalized to merge more streams.

Storage Pattern Altering Policy

The storage pattern altering policy merges the streams by relaxing the storage pattern preserving constraint. Instead of keeping the same storage patterns before and after merging, it maintains the average storage pattern over a range time data blocks. The SPA policy thus generalizes the feasibility condition to merge a number of streams together on the optical disks. We shall show below the how to maintain the continuous display requirement of a stream even though its storage pattern is altered. After that, the feasibility condition to merge a number of streams is described.

The storage pattern altering policy changes the storage pattern of the streams after merging (Rangan & Vin, 1993). After the storage pattern of a stream is changed, the continuous display requirement of the stream in equation (13.1) must still be maintained. Since the storage pattern is changed, the number of media blocks and gap blocks would change. The media blocks can only be moved closer to the beginning of the object so that the data stripes would only be accessed at an earlier time. It makes sure that the data stripes would not be accessed at a later time that might violate the continuous display guarantee.

Although the SPA policy changes the storage pattern of the participating streams, the average number of gap blocks per media block remains the same. The storage system would retrieve the media blocks at the same average data rate. Thus, the buffers are filled at the same average rate as they are consumed so that buffer starvation would not occur. Buffer overflows can also be avoided simply by using more read-ahead buffers. By using extra buffers to maintain the continuous display requirements, the merging of streams can be generalized.

A number of multimedia data streams whose storage patterns are characterized by $(M_1, G_1), (M_2, G_2), ..., (M_k, G_k)$ can be merged if and only if

$$\frac{M_1}{M_1+G_1} + \frac{M_2}{M_2+G_2} + ... + \frac{M_k}{M_k+G_k} \leq 1 \qquad (13.3)$$

Consider the second example in the SPP policy again. Two streams S_1 and S_3 are to be merged on an optical disk. The storage pattern of stream S_1 is (1, 3) and the storage stream of stream S_3 is (1, 2). That is, stream S_1 stores one block in every data stripe and skips three blocks between two data stripes.

The stream S_3 also stores one block in every data stripe and skips only two blocks between two data stripes. Thus,

$M_1 = 1$, $G_1 = 3$, $M_2 = 1$, and $G_2 = 2$.

We substitute these values into equation (13.3) to get

$$\frac{M_1}{M_1 + G_1} + \frac{M_2}{M_2 + G_2} + \dots + \frac{M_k}{M_k + G_k}$$
$$= \frac{1}{1+3} + \frac{1}{1+2}$$
$$= \frac{7}{12} < 1$$

We can see that the two streams satisfy the feasibility condition. Thus, the two streams, stream S_1 and stream S_3, can be merged using the storage pattern altering policy of the interleaved contiguous placement method.

In Figure 13.4, we show that the two streams, stream S_1 and stream S_3, can be merged by altering the storage pattern of the stream S_3. The storage pattern of stream S_1 does not need to be altered. The second media block in every four media blocks of stream S_3 is moved towards the beginning of the object. Notice that the media blocks can only be moved towards the beginning of the object so that the moved blocks are retrieved earlier. If the media blocks of a stream are moved towards the end of the object, then the moved blocks are retrieved later than that of the original storage pattern leading to violations of the continuous display requirement.

Since the moved blocks are retrieved earlier than that of the original storage pattern, some extra buffers are needed to temporarily store the moved blocks when they are accessed. Thus, the buffer consumption seems to increase. Since the buffers are made available while the programs are waiting for the retrieval of the next data stripe, the buffer consumption is actually unchanged. Furthermore, some gaps exist between consecutive data stripes. The optical disk drive spends more time to access each individual data stripe. The interleaved contiguous placement retrieves data stripes at a short time before they are consumed. After the data in a buffer is consumed, the buffer may be released. Thus, the period of time between the filling and release of each

Figure 13.4. Interleaved contiguous placement SPA example

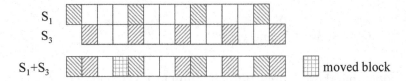

Problem locations are removed by moving some blocks of S_3

buffer is short. This leads to reduction of average buffer consumption.

Fortunately, more than one object can be accessed from the optical disk. When multiple interleaving objects are retrieved from the optical disk at the same time, the optical disk can use sequential reads to access the interleaving data stripes. The overheads which consist of seek and rotational latency in accessing the data stripes are shared among the concurrent streams. Thus, the overheads are low and the merged streams are served with high throughput. If the probability of several objects being concurrently served is high, then interleaving these objects could also raise the throughput.

In the extreme case when all the merged streams are concurrent, the optical disk may read all the blocks sequentially. The data stripes of the interleaving objects are accessed without need for seek actions. Thus, the storage system delivers the objects at the highest throughput. Hence, the interleaved contiguous placement method is very suitable for composite objects whose component objects must always be synchronized.

Concurrent Striping

The parallel tape striping method places data stripes of objects across tapes so that an object is retrieved in parallel from multiple tapes. The increase in exchange overheads however lowers the system throughput. The triangular placement method utilizes the usable bandwidth to further reduce the access time and increase the system throughput. Both methods reduce the time to access an object from the tapes. However, the exchange overhead is still heavy due to the synchronization of the parallel I/O operation.

The principle aim of the concurrent striping method is to increase the throughput of the hierarchical storage system (Tse, 1999; Tse & Leung, 1998, 2001, 2002). In particular, the concurrent striping method uses the following ideas:

1.   It desynchronizes all tape exchanges.
2.   It shares exchange overheads among concurrent streams.
3.   It supports efficient accesses for multiple concurrent streams.

The concurrent striping method desynchronizes the parallel I/O operation to avoid exchange contentions. That is, each individual I/O operation such as exchange, reposition, and transfer, on different drives does not need to be completed at the same time. Each device performs the I/O operations independently.

When multiple streams access objects concurrently, the overheads of switching tapes among the streams are heavy. The storage devices need to exchange the tapes unless the access data stripes reside on the same tape. The concurrent striping method places the data stripes of the concurrent streams on the same tape to avoid exchange overheads between services of concurrent streams. Thus, the exchange overheads are shared among concurrent streams.

The concurrent striping method assumes that the stored objects are accessed for normal display only. That is, the storage system does not need to support any interactive user functions. The system that uses concurrent striping method is a combination of five different components.

1.   Divide object into logical segment
2.   Distribute segments across all tapes
3.   Store in fixed order within tape
4.   Parallel stream controller
5.   Request scheduling

Each object is divided into a number of logical segments such that each logical segment is a logical starting point for consumption. The next segment is made available after the previous segment is accessed. A segment can start to display without the previous segment or it can display following the previous segment. For example, objects X, Y, and Z are divided into different number of logical segments as illustrated in Figure 13.5. Large objects are divided into many segments and small objects are divided into few segments.

In addition to dividing objects into logical segments, each logical segment may optionally be subdivided into slices or fixed length data stripes depending on the data migration method in use. If segments are divided into slices for pipelining as shown in Figure 13.6, the time to display the previous slice is longer than or equal to the time to retrieve the next slice.

When the size of a logical segment is X_i, the size of the first slice is approximately equal to

$$\approx X_i * (1 - \rho), \quad (13.4)$$

where ρ is the production consumption ratio of the tertiary storage devices. The production consumption ratio is defined as the ratio of tertiary bandwidth to the display bandwidth of the object.

Thus, the production consumption ratio is found as

$$\rho = \frac{\gamma}{\delta} \quad (13.5)$$

where γ is the tertiary bandwidth of the storage device, and δ is the display bandwidth of the object.

The size of the jth slice can be found as

$$\approx X_i * (1 - \rho) * \rho^j \quad (13.6)$$

More details of the sizes of the slices will be described in Chapter XVIII on the normal pipelining method.

The concurrent striping method distributes the segments across all tapes in the robotic tape library. The tapes are sorted into a fixed sequence. The objects are stored on the tapes according to this sequence with one segment on each tape. The segments of an object are stored in round robin cycles. The objects are stored in a fixed order on each tape. When an object is stored before another object on one tape, it is always stored before the other object on all other tapes. When object X is stored before object Y in tape T_1, object X is stored before object Y in all other tapes, T_2 to T_6, as shown in Figure 13.7.

Figure 13.5. Concurrent striping divides objects into logical segments

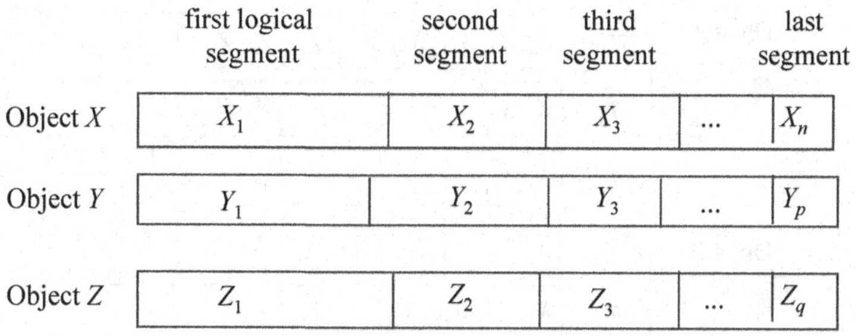

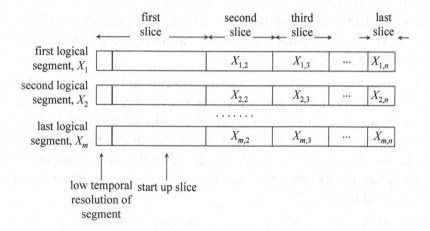

Figure 13.6. Concurrent striping subdivides an object into leaders and data strips

The concurrent striping method controls the delivery of the objects using a parallel stream controller. The parallel stream controller accepts requests for new streams. It creates a new "stream object" for each data object being accessed. The stream object is a software object in the storage system and it is different from the data objects. The stream object initially sends two requests to the service queue of each tertiary drive. The tertiary drive accesses segments for the requests on the tapes to the memory for display.

The tertiary drives serve all requests in currently loaded tapes before they serve the requests on other tapes that require switching. After all requests on the currently loaded tapes are served, the drive sends an exchange request to the robotic arm to exchange the next tape. After each request of a stream is served, the stream sends a new request that accesses the next segment from

Figure 13.7. Concurrent striping stores objects in fixed order on tapes

Drive 1					
	T_1	X_1, X_7, X_{13}, X_{19}	Y_3, Y_9	Z_4, Z_{10}	
	T_3	X_3, X_9, X_{15}, X_{21}	Y_5, Y_{11}	Z_6, Z_{12}	
	T_5	$X_5, X_{11}, X_{17}, X_{23}$	Y_1, Y_7, Y_{13}	Z_2, Z_8	
Drive 2	T_2	X_2, X_8, X_{14}, X_{20}	Y_4, Y_{10}	Z_5, Z_{11}	
	T_4	$X_4, X_{10}, X_{16}, X_{22}$	Y_6, Y_{12}	Z_1, Z_7	
	T_6	$X_6, X_{12}, X_{18}, X_{24}$	Y_2, Y_8, Y_{14}	Z_3, Z_9	

the tapes. After all the segments of an object are retrieved, the stream object sends a finish notification to the parallel stream controller before it destroys itself. The parallel stream controller can thus accept another new stream from its waiting queue.

The tertiary drives serve the requests in cycles and rounds. In each cycle, the drive exchanges a tape and serves one request per stream on the exchanged tape. Requests on the same tape are served in the order of the storage locations of the segments on the tape. Since the segments are stored in a fixed order on the tape, the streams are served in the same fixed order. In each round, the drive exchanges each tape once and serves the requests on the exchanged tapes.

Since each stream sends at least two requests to each tertiary drive, the tertiary drives have at least one outstanding request from each stream object. The drive exchanges one tape and serves one request of every stream in each cycle. As the drives do not perform the exchange operation in parallel, the requests for exchange are initiated at different times. The tape exchange operation is thus desynchronized. The drives do not waste bandwidth in the contention for the robotic arms. The throughput of the tertiary storage system remains high even when the objects are accessed in parallel.

As the drive serves one request for every stream after each exchange operation, the exchange overhead is shared among all concurrent streams. When many concurrent streams are served, the exchange overhead is shared among many concurrent streams. Thus, the exchange overhead per stream is light.

For example, two tertiary drives retrieve segments of three objects on six tapes as shown in Figure 13.8. Each drive exchanges a tape and retrieves one

Figure 13.8. Requests are scheduled in cycles and rounds

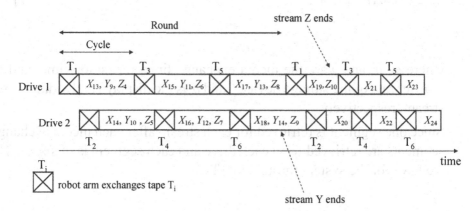

segment for each stream in each cycle. Drive 1 exchanges M_1 and retrieves segments X_{13}, Y_9, and Z_4 on M_1. Then, it exchanges M_3 and retrieves X_{15}, Y_{11}, and Z_6 on M_3. Afterwards, it exchanges M_5 and retrieves X_{17}, Y_{13}, and Z_8. It then exchanges M_1 again, but stream Y has finished. So, it retrieves X_{19} and Z_{10} from M_1 and so on. Drive 2 exchanges M_2 and retrieves segments X_{14}, Y_{10}, and Z_5 on M_2. Then, it exchanges M_4 and retrieves X_{16}, Y_{12}, and Z_7 on M_4. After that, M_6 is exchanged and X_{18}, Y_{14}, and Z_9 are retrieved. Drive 2 exchanges M_2 again, but stream Y has finished and stream Z is aborted. Thus, it retrieves X_{20} from M_2 only. Similarly, it exchanges M_4 and retrieves X_{22} and so on.

Performance Analysis

In order to display the streams continuously, the storage system must retrieve each segment before it is due for display. In the concurrent striping method, the maximum number of requests that can appear between two consecutive requests of the same stream is less than s, where s is the number of concurrent streams being accepted to the system.

If D drives are serving s streams that each stream accesses segments of size X, the time to display the previous segment should be longer than or equal to the time to retrieve the next segment. Thus, we have the continuous display requirement as

$$\frac{DX}{\delta_j} \geq \omega + s(\alpha + \frac{X}{\gamma}) \tag{13.7}$$

where ω, α, and γ are the media exchange time, reposition time, and data transfer rate of the storage devices, and δ_j is the display bandwidth of the jth stream, respectively.

Since one segment is retrieved for each stream after each media exchange, s segments are retrieved from each drive and each segment is of size X. Thus, we have for the system throughput (Tse, 1999)

$$= \frac{DsX}{\omega + s(\alpha + \frac{X}{\gamma})} \tag{13.8}$$

If data are migrated using the staging method, stage buffers on disks are needed to store data that are retrieved from tertiary storage on the disks. When the data are retrieved faster than they are consumed, the data stay on the staging buffer for a longer time. The average amount of buffer consumption is high. If the tertiary storage system delivers data at a rate just faster than the data consumption rate, the staging buffers are occupied for a short time. The average amount of staging buffer consumption becomes low.

When the time that the tertiary drives spend in serving each group of concurrent requests be E[B], the disk buffer size for the jth stream using the concurrency striping method is found as

$$= rX - \frac{r\delta_j}{D} E[B] \tag{13.9}$$

where r is the number of segments per object.

Since the concurrent striping method serves the streams concurrently, it takes longer time to deliver one segment for each individual stream. Thus, it uses smaller staging buffers on disks than the parallel tape striping method and other nonstriping methods.

Chapter Summary

Large multimedia objects are stored on hierarchical storage systems. The high access latency tertiary storage devices need to deliver the large multimedia objects at high throughput. Multimedia data of all objects must be retrieved from the tertiary storage devices to buffers on disks within the guarantee time in order to display the stream with continuity. Multimedia streams would have long waiting time if the objects are retrieved one by one. Heavy exchange overheads may be involved when streams are served concurrently.

The constraint allocation methods limit the storage locations of the objects on the storage media to reduce the longest exchange time and reposition time. They increase the system throughput when multiple streams are served concurrently.

The interleaved contiguous placement method maintains the separation between consecutive data stripes on an optical disk to provide an upper bound on the maximum access time of each data stripe. It chooses the highly correlated objects to be merged. The feasibility condition of merging homogeneous streams is easily determined. The storage pattern preserving policy provides the feasibility condition to merge two heterogeneous streams without changing their storage patterns. The storage pattern altering policy provides the feasibility condition to merge a number of heterogeneous streams by slightly changing the storage pattern of each stream.

The concurrent striping method desynchronizes the parallel I/O operation to avoid exchange contentions. It places the data stripes of the concurrent streams on the same tape to share the exchange overheads among concurrent streams. It divides multimedia objects into logical segments and distributes them across all tapes. The tertiary storage system stores segments in fixed order to maintain the continuous display guarantee of every stream. The concurrent striping method serves streams concurrently to reduce the start up latency. It improves the system throughput and reduces the buffer consumption.

References

Rangan, P.V., & Vin, H.M. (1993). Efficient storage techniques for digital continuous multimedia. *IEEE Transactions on Knowledge and Data Engineering, 5*(4), 564-573.

Tse, P. K. C. (1999). *Efficient storage and retrieval methods for multimedia information*. Doctoral dissertation, Victoria University, Melbourne, Australia.

Tse, P. K. C., & Leung, C. H. C. (1998). A low latency hierarchical storage organization for multimedia data retrieval. In *Proceedings of the IAPR International Workshop on Multimedia Information Analysis and Retrieval* (LNCS 1464, pp. 181-194). Springer-Verlag.

Tse, P. K. C., & Leung, C. H. C. (2001). Retrieving multimedia objects from hierarchical storage systems. In *Proceedings of the 18th IEEE Symposium on Mass Storage Systems and 9th NASA Goddard Conference on Mass Storage Systems and Technologies*, San Diego, CA (pp. 297-301).

Tse, P. K. C., & Leung, C. H. C. (2002). An efficient storage organization for multimedia databases. In *Proceedings of the 5th International Conference on Visual Information Systems*, HsinChu, Taiwan (pp. 152-162).

Yu, C., Sun, W., Bitton, D., Yang, Q., Bruno, R., & Yus, J. (1989). Efficient placement of audio data on optical disks for real-time applications. *Communications of the ACM, 7*, 862-871.

Summary to Section IIb

Data Placement on Hierarchical Storage Systems

The main objective of the tertiary storage level is to provide huge storage capacity at low cost. The tertiary storage devices in use include magnetic tapes, optical disks, and optical tapes. The media units are removable from the drive so that the storage capacity can be expanded by using more media units. The media units take the tape form so that the physical dimension of the media unit is small. Optical disks and tapes record data the laser beam to provide the highest recording density.

Large hierarchical storage systems may use robotic tape libraries to store many large objects. Robotic tape libraries use the robotic arms to exchange tapes automatically and quickly. When data are accessed from the tape drives, the drives spend much time in performing the mechanical steps. The drives have a minimum overhead to access data. The overheads are affected by the data placement method in use. It also takes a longer time to access large objects.

Similar to storage organizations on disks, there are many data placement methods being designed to improve the performance of HSS. These techniques use different strategies to optimize the HSS performance. We group these data placement methods according to the following four strategies:

1. Contiguous placement strategy
2. Statistical placement strategy
3. Striping strategy
4. Constraint allocation strategy

The contiguous placement method stores the whole object in the same media unit. It is simple and efficient when the objects are written and retrieved in their entirety. Unfortunately, it suffers from large staging buffer consumption and long response time.

The log structured placement is an efficient placement method for the back up and archival applications. It optimizes the writing performance by providing the append-only operations. However, the performance is not optimized due to the presence of reading requests that are present in multimedia storage systems.

We have explained the statistical placement method using the frequency based placement of objects on media units. The frequency based placement method places the objects to the media units according to the access frequency of the objects and the distance of the cell containing the media unit from the drive. The performance of the frequency based placement method is optimized when the objects are accessed independently and the objects are of the same size.

The parallel tape striping method is a data placement method that places the objects to tapes in robotic tape libraries. It divides objects into data stripes and distributes data stripes of multimedia objects to several tapes. The parallel tape striping method accesses data stripes from the tapes in parallel. It overlaps the time to transfer data stripes from multiple tape drives. The parallel tape striping method reduces the time to access an object from the robotic tape library. Unfortunately, the parallel tape striping method induces contentions on exchanging tapes. It may not cause problems if each drive has its own robotic arm or the number of robotic arms is not fewer than the number of tape drives. Furthermore, more exchanges are incurred. The robotic arms need to exchange several tapes for each object access. Thus, the parallel tape striping method increases the workload on the robotic arms.

The triangular placement method utilizes the usable bandwidth during the exchange time to reduce the data access time. A tape drive starts to reposition tapes and transfer data stripes while other drives are still waiting for exchanges. The triangular placement method further reduces the time to access objects from robotic tape libraries. It also increases the optimal number of striping drives.

Large multimedia objects are stored on the HSS. The high access latency tertiary storage devices need to deliver the large multimedia objects at high throughput. Multimedia data of all objects must be retrieved from the tertiary storage devices to buffers on disks within the guarantee time in order to display the stream with continuity. Multimedia streams would have long waiting time if the objects are retrieved one by one. Heavy exchange overheads may be involved when streams are served concurrently.

The constraint allocation methods limit the storage locations of the objects on the storage media to reduce the longest exchange time and reposition time. They increase the system throughput when multiple streams are served concurrently.

The interleaved contiguous placement method maintains the separation between consecutive data stripes on an optical disk to provide an upper bound on the maximum access time of each data stripe. It chooses the highly correlated objects to be merged. The feasibility condition of merging homogeneous streams is easily determined. The storage pattern preserving policy provides the feasibility condition to merge two heterogeneous streams without changing their storage patterns. The storage pattern altering policy provides the feasibility condition to merge a number of heterogeneous streams by slightly changing the storage pattern of each stream.

The concurrent striping method desynchronizes the parallel I/O operation to avoid exchange contentions. It places the data stripes of the concurrent streams on the same tape to share the exchange overheads among concurrent streams. It divides multimedia objects into logical segments and distributes them across all tapes. The tertiary storage system stores segments in fixed order to maintain the continuous display guarantee of every stream. The concurrent striping method serves streams concurrently to reduce the start up latency. It improves the system throughput and reduces the buffer consumption.

Section III

Disk Scheduling Methods

Introduction

In Part IIa and Part IIb, we have described how to improve the performance of storage systems using data placement methods. In this part, we shall describe how to improve the response time of requests using efficient disk scheduling methods.

Traditional computer systems only handle disk requests individually. Multimedia systems send multiple requests one after another to the disk system. These requests appear as a stream of requests to the storage system. These requests should be served with a proper scheduling method so that the streams can continue without any problems. Thus, new scheduling methods have been designed to serve streams of requests for multimedia data.

We shall describe the methods that arrange the order of disk requests in this section. First, we describe the scheduling methods for disk requests in Chapter XIV. After that, the feasibility conditions to accept streams by a storage system are presented in Chapter XV. Last, the scheduling methods that serve requests of multimedia streams are described in Chapter XVI.

Chapter XIV

Scheduling Methods
for Disk Requests

Introduction

Disk scheduling changes the sequence order to serve the requests that are waiting in the queue.

While data placement reduces the access time of a disk request, scheduling reduces the waiting time of a request. Thus, the response time is found as:

Response time = Waiting time + Access time

The longer the waiting queue, the more useful is the scheduling method. When there is no waiting queue, any scheduling methods perform the same. Expected waiting time and queue length can be found using queueing theory. The queueing theory is out of the scope of this book.

Figure 14.1. Disk scheduling policy

In general, a disk scheduling policy changes the service order of waiting requests. This can be illustrated using a modeling diagram as shown in Figure 14.1. A disk scheduling policy accepts the waiting requests and serves them in the new service sequence. Notice that the service sequence may or may not be the same as the incoming order of the waiting requests.

In this chapter, we shall describe two common disk scheduling methods. First, we shall describe the simple first-in-first-out method. After that, we shall describe the efficient SCAN algorithm in the following sections.

First-In-First-Out Method

The first-in-first-out (FIFO) method is also known as the first-come-first-serve (FCFS) method. The scheduling method serves requests in the queue according to the normal queue order. The requests are served in the incoming order of the requests. The request that has been waiting for the longest time is served first.

We shall model the FIFO scheduling policy as Figure 14.2. The service sequence is the same as the incoming order the requests. The FIFO scheduling method is very simple. New requests are entered into the end of the queue. The first one of the requests in the waiting queue is chosen to be served. Since the request that arrives earliest at the waiting queue is served first, the requests are being treated fairly. However, the accessed data may be randomly located. The disk head is jumping up and down the tracks, leading to long seek time. Thus, this scheduling method is not very efficient.

This scheduling method is also not suitable for multimedia systems. Since multimedia requests have deadlines, some requests may wait so long that their deadlines are passed before being served. Instead of being served after their deadlines, these requests should either be served earlier or removed from the waiting queue.

Figure 14.2. FIFO scheduling policy

The SCAN Algorithm

The FIFO method is too simple. More efficient scheduling methods are designed to serve disk requests. The SCAN algorithm is one of the most efficient scheduling methods (Gemmell & Christodoulakis, 1992).

In the SCAN algorithm, the disk heads traverse the surface from the innermost track to the outermost track and return. The requests for data from tracks that are nearest to the disk heads and in the current scanning direction will be served with priority. When there are no more requests in the current scanning direction, the disk head changes direction and serves requests on its way.

The SCAN algorithm is also called the elevator disk scheduling algorithm. It is analogous to a lift going from floor to floor picking up passengers on its way. A lift picks up some passengers on the ground floor. Some passengers push the button to initiate requests. Some passengers may wish to go to the top floor and some other passengers initiate requests to go to the middle floors. The lift stops at the middle floors to let passengers get off before it continues its way to the top floor. While the lift is moving from the top floor to the ground, it may receive requests for service from middle floors. The lift would stop in the middle floors to pick up passengers and move all passengers to the ground floor.

Let h be the current position of the disk heads in track number and let d be the current scanning direction. When the disk heads are moving in the outward direction, d is equal to +1. When the disk heads are moving in the inward direction, d is equal to -1.

Let t_i be the track number containing data that are accessed by the ith request in the queue. While the SCAN algorithm is moving in the outward direction, it compares all the waiting requests to find the request that has the smallest $(t_i - h)$, for all requests with $(t_i \geq h)$. If it cannot find any requests with $(t_i \geq h)$, then it changes direction by setting d to -1. While the SCAN algorithm is moving in the inward direction, it compares all the requests finds the request that has the smallest $(h - t_i)$, for all requests with $(t_i \leq h)$. If it cannot find any requests with $(t_i \leq h)$, then it changes direction by setting d to +1.

A tie condition may occur if more than one request access data from the same track. These requests should be served in the FIFO order. The disk heads first serve the request with the longest waiting time. Afterwards, the disk heads will be moved to the same track and serve other requests on this track as their distance from the disk heads position is equal to 0.

For example, the disk heads are staying at the outermost track near the rim of the disk. The tracks are numbered from the centre to the rim of the disk. Four requests are now waiting for their services (Figure 14.3). The requests arrive at the queue in the order A, B, C, and D. Let t_a, t_b, t_c, t_d be the track numbers of the tracks that are accessed by the requests A, B, C, and D, respectively. These requests access data on tracks with track numbers such that $h > t_a > t_c = t_d > t_b$ and $d = -1$.

According to the SCAN scheduling policy, which request is served first?

Since $h > t_a > t_c = t_d > t_b$ and $d = -1$, The storage systems find that the request A is accessing data from the track t_a that is the closest to its current position, h. The disk heads are then moved to t_a to serve request A as shown in Figure 14.4.

After the request A is served, which request is served next?

After the storage system has served request A, the disk heads are staying at the track containing data for request A. Now $h = t_a$. Since $t_a = h > t_c = t_d > t_b$ and $d = -1$, both request C and request D are accessing data from the tracks $t_c = t_d$ that are the closest to its current position t_a. Since request C arrives in the queue earlier than request D, request C is served next. The disk heads are then moved to t_c to serve request C as shown in Figure 14.5.

While request C is being served, a new request E has arrived at the waiting queue. Request E accesses data from track t_e such that $t_a > t_e > t_c$. After the request C is served, which request is served next?

After the storage system has served request C, the disk heads are staying at the track containing data for request C. Now $h = t_c$. Request E is excluded as $t_e > h$. Since $t_c = h = t_d > t_b$ and $d = -1$, request D is accessing data from the tracks

Figure 14.3. SCAN algorithm 1

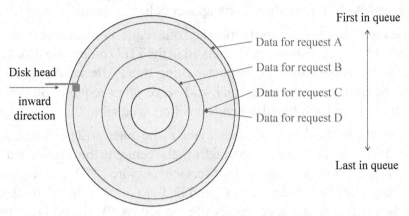

Figure 14.4. SCAN algorithm 2

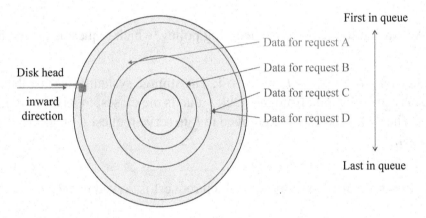

Figure 14.5. SCAN algorithm 3

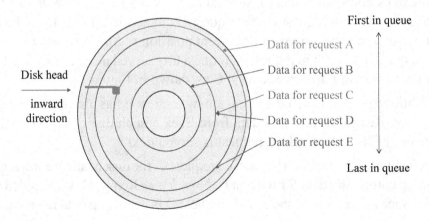

$t_d = h$ that are the closest to its current position. The disk heads then stay at its current track position to serve request D as shown in Figure 14.6.

After the request D is served, which request is served next?

After the storage system has served request D, the disk heads are staying at the track containing data for request D. Now $h = t_d$. Request E is excluded as $t_e > h$. Since request B is the only request whose track number is less than or equal to h, the disk heads is then moved to track number t_b to serve request B as shown in Figure 14.7.

Figure 14.6. SCAN algorithm 4

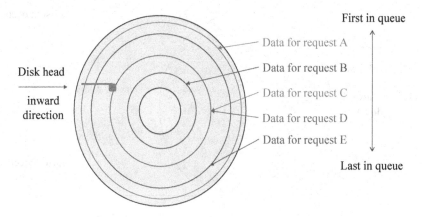

Figure 14.7. SCAN algorithm 5

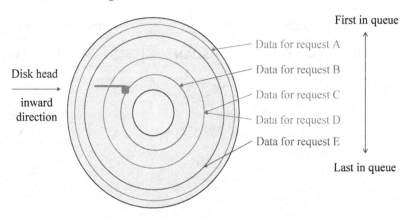

After the storage system has served request B, $h = t_b$. All the requests do not satisfy track number less than or equal to h. The storage system then changes to the outward direction and set d to +1. As request E is the only request, the disk heads are thus moved to track t_e to serve request E as shown in Figure 14.8.

Therefore, the requests are served in the order of A, C, D, B, and E using the SCAN scheduling policy. The request B is served after the requests C and D because request B accesses data from the tracks far away from the disk heads. Request E is served after request B since it arrives at the waiting queue after the disk heads pass the track from which it accesses data.

In principle, the SCAN scheduling policy is a scheduling policy that aligns the waiting requests in the order of their accessing track locations. The order

Figure 14.8. SCAN algorithm 6

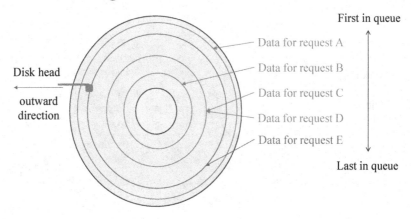

Figure 14.9. SCAN scheduling policy

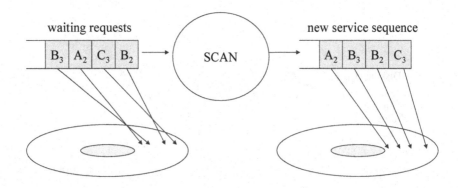

of the requests in the waiting queue is thus changed into the sequence of their physical track numbers. After the waiting requests are reordered, these waiting requests are thus served in their physical track number order.

The SCAN scheduling policy increases the efficiency in serving requests. The disk heads are moved to serve waiting requests at short seek distances before they serve other requests at long seek distance. The heavy seek time overheads in serving long seeks are thus shared among the requests that access data in-between the disk head and the destination track of the long seeks. The average seek distance and average seek time are reduced significantly. Therefore, the SCAN scheduling policy is a very efficient disk scheduling policy.

Although the SCAN scheduling policy does not increase or decrease the priority in serving requests, it is unfavourable to some requests. As the disk heads move from one end of the tracks to another end, the requests that access data from the far end are served with later than the requests that access data from the middle of the tracks. The requests that access data from the middle of the tracks have a shorter waiting time to be served. In addition, the disk heads do not consider requests that access data from in the reverse of its moving direction. The requests that access data from the two ends have a longer time to be excluded. Thus, the SCAN scheduling policy is unfair to the requests that access data near the centre or the rim of the disk platters.

In order to serve all requests fairly, the unidirectional SCAN was designed. The unidirectional SCAN policy serves requests only when the disk heads are moving in one of the two directions. After the disk heads reach the last track, they are swung back to the farthest track being accessed. Then, it starts to serve this request and other requests in the same direction.

Consider another example. The disk heads serve requests when they move in the inward direction. They are staying at the outermost track near the rim of the disk. Three requests which have arrived at the waiting queue in the order A, B, and C are now waiting for their services as shown in Figure 14.10. These requests access data on tracks with radii in the decreasing order as A, C, and B. Let t_a, t_b, and t_c be the track numbers of the tracks being accessed by the requests A, B, and C, respectively. That is, $h > t_a > t_c > t_b$ and $d = -1$.

According to the unidirectional SCAN scheduling policy, which request is served first?

Since $h > t_a > t_c > t_b$ and $d = -1$, the storage system finds that the request A is accessing data from the track t_a that is the closest to its current position, h. The disk heads are then moved to t_a to serve request A as shown in Figure 14.11.

Figure 14.10. Unidirectional SCAN algorithm 1

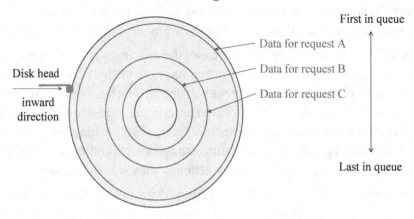

Figure 14.11. Unidirectional SCAN algorithm 2

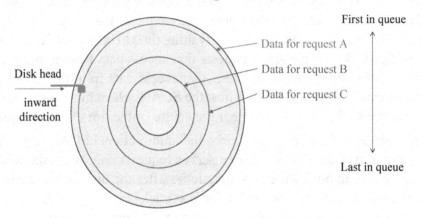

Figure 14.12. Unidirectional SCAN algorithm 3

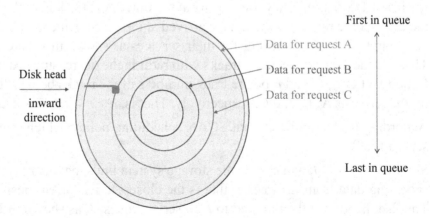

After the request A is served, which request is served next?

After the storage system has served request A, the disk heads are staying at the track containing data for request A. Since $t_a = h > t_c > t_b$, request C is accessing data from the track t_c that is the closest to its current position t_a. The disk heads are then moved to t_c to serve request C as shown in Figure 14.12.

After the storage system has served request C, the disk heads are staying at the track t_c. Since request B is the only request in the waiting queue. The disk heads are then moved to track number t_b to serve request B as shown in Figure 14.13.

While request B is being served, two new requests D and E have arrived at the waiting queue. They access data from track t_d and t_e such that $t_e > t_d$. After the request B is served, which request is served next?

After the storage system has served request B, the disk heads are staying at the track containing data for request B. Now $h = t_b$. All the requests do not satisfy track number less than or equal to h. The storage system then swings the disk head to the rim of the disk. Since $h > t_e > t_d$, request E is accessing data from the track t_e that is the closest to its current position. The disk heads are then moved to t_e to serve request E as shown in Figure 14.14.

After the storage system has served request E, $h = t_e$. The storage system then moved to track t_d to serve request D as shown in Figure 14.15.

The unidirectional SCAN scheduling policy serves all requests in only one direction. After the disk heads have passed the tracks that are accessed by a request, the request needs to wait for the requests to be served in a cycle. Thus, all requests are treated fairly.

Although the requests are served fairly, the efficiency of the storage system is traded off. Since the disk heads are swung to the other end after serving all requests in one direction, this imposes a fixed overhead on swinging the disk heads. Thus, the unidirectional SCAN scheduling method is less efficient than the bidirectional SCAN scheduling method.

Multimedia storage systems deliver data stripes to the clients for display. While the clients are displaying a stream, the data stripes of this stream must arrive before they are due for display. Otherwise, the stream undesirably starves. Thus, a deadline is associated with every data stripe and the requests that access it. If the request is served after the deadline has passed, the returned data stripe is no longer used. Therefore, the multimedia storage

Figure 14.13. Unidirectional SCAN algorithm 4

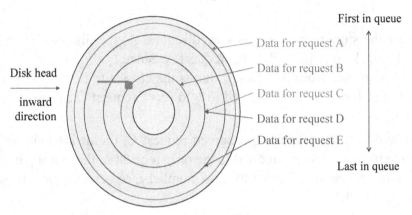

Figure 14.14. Unidirectional SCAN algorithm 5

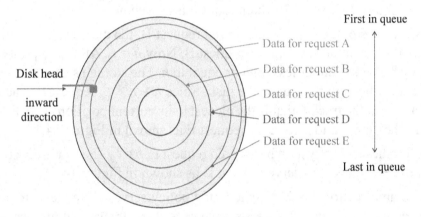

Figure 14.15. Unidirectional SCAN algorithm 6

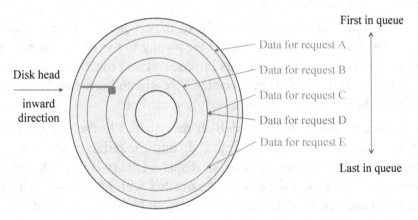

system should be aware of the deadlines of requests and serves them at some time before the deadline.

Chapter Summary

The first-in-first-out scheduling method serves requests according to their incoming order. It is simple and fair, but not efficient. Disk requests in multimedia storage systems should be served before their deadlines are passed. Thus, the FIFO scheduling method is not suitable for scheduling requests of multimedia streams.

The SCAN scheduling method serves the waiting requests in the order of their accessing physical track locations. The disk heads traverse the disk surface and serve requests that access data on the tracks in its path. The heavy seek time overheads of the long seeks are shared among these requests. The average seek distance and average seek time are reduced. The storage system thus serves requests efficiently.

Although the bidirectional SCAN scheduling policy is unfair to the requests that access data near the centre or the rim of the disk platters, the unidirectional SCAN scheduling method can serve all requests fairly. However, the efficiency of the storage system is slightly traded off.

References

Gemmell, D. J., & Christodoulakis, S. (1992). Principles of delay-sensitive multimedia data storage and retrieval. *ACM Transactions on Information Systems, 10*(1), 51-90.

Chapter XV

Feasibility Conditions of Concurrent Streams

Introduction

Multimedia storage systems store data objects and receive streams of requests from the multimedia server. When a client wishes to display an object, it sends a new object request for the multimedia object to the multimedia server as shown in Figure 15.1. The multimedia server checks to see if this new stream can be accepted. If accepted, the server sends a data request to the storage system to retrieve the first data stripe. The storage system returns the data stripe to the server. The server then encapsulates the data stripe as data packets and sends the data packets to the client. The client extracts the data stripe from the data packets. Afterwards, the server sends data requests periodically to the storage system. Each of these data requests has a deadline associated with it. If the request cannot be served before the deadline, the client program does not have any more data to display. The stream thus will be suspended or aborted. Therefore, every request of a stream, except the first one, must be served within the deadline to ensure continuity of the stream. Before we consider the scheduling methods for request streams in the next chapter, we describe the feasibility to accept concurrent streams in this chapter.

Consider a stream that accesses object A from the storage system. The stream is composed of a number of requests A_1, A_2, ... , and A_n. Each request will arrive at the storage system at different times as illustrated in Figure 15.2. The requests are then served by the storage system.

The server may send multiple requests to the storage system so that the waiting times of the requests may overlap with each other. It needs to allocate separate memory buffers to store the data stripes being accessed. The storage system may not serve a request before the next request arrives. Thus, there may be more than one request in the waiting queue of the storage system. If the requests are in the waiting queue, the storage system would serve them one by one.

Figure 15.1. Multimedia stream of requests

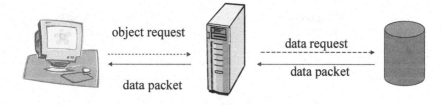

Figure 15.2. A stream of requests

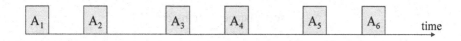

If the disk serves the request in the first-in-first-out scheduling method, it serves the requests one by one, from A_1 to A_3 as shown in Figure 15.3. It gets request A_1 from the waiting queue and retrieves the data stripe for it. During the service of request A_1, a new request A_6 may have arrived at the waiting queue. Then, the disk gets the second request A_2 from the waiting queue and retrieves the data stripe for it. During the service of request A_2, a new request A_7 may have arrived at the waiting queue. Afterwards, the disk gets request A_3 from the waiting queue and retrieves the data stripe for it, and so on.

The stream can start to display only after the first data stripe is received. If the waiting time and service time of the first request of a stream is long, the

Figure 15.3. Service of individual request of a stream

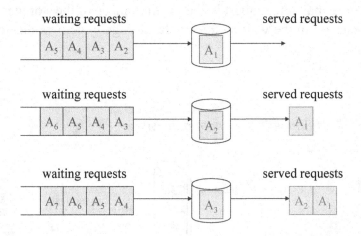

Figure 15.4. Response time of a stream

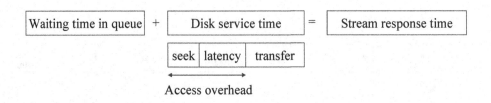

response time of the stream is long. The response time of a stream, R_s, can be found as

$$R_s = W_1 + S_1,$$

where W_1 is the waiting time of the first request and S_1 is the service time of the first request as shown in Figure 15.4.

The service time of the first request is actually the access time of the first data stripe from the disk. From Chapter III, the disk access time is mainly composed of the seek time, rotational latency, and data transfer time. Both the seek time and rotational latency are access overheads in serving a request.

If the stream is not accepted by the server, the client may try to initiate the stream again. The actual response time of the stream is further raised by these retry times before the stream is accepted. The stream can continue to display only after the data stripe containing the multimedia data of the object is received. The response time of a request is composed of the waiting time in queue and the service time of the requests. The response time of the ith request, R_i, can be found as

$$R_i = W_i + S_i,$$

where W_i is the waiting time of the ith request and S_i is the service time of the ith request. The service time of each request is actually the access time of the data stripe from the disk. The disk access time is mainly composed of the seek time, rotational latency, and data transfer time. Both the seek time and rotational latency are access overheads in serving a request.

The time that a request is sent plus the response time should be earlier than the deadline as illustrated in Figure 15.5. If the waiting time is long, the deadline may have passed. It would be too late to serve the request. As a result, the stream starves and the client does not have the necessary data to display. The stream has to suspend or abort.

From the above discussion, we can see that the waiting time in queue is a significant component of the response time of streams. It has a very significant impact on the response time and the continuity of the streams. We first describe the feasibility conditions for a storage device to accept new streams in the next section. Then, we will prove the feasibility conditions for a storage

Figure 15.5. Response time of individual requests of a stream

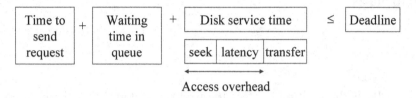

device to accept homogeneous streams. After that, the feasibility conditions for a storage device to accept heterogeneous streams are proved. Before summarizing this chapter, we prove the more general feasibility conditions for a number of storage devices to accept heterogeneous streams.

Feasibility Condition for a Storage Device to Accept New Streams

Multimedia systems accept new object requests from clients. If it accepts a stream request, it needs to retrieve the data stripes of the object from the storage system and deliver them as a data stream to the client. The multimedia system does not accept all incoming streams. It checks its own storage system's workload whether the data stripes can be retrieved and delivered on time. This feasibility condition can be found in several methods:

1.   Check the number of accepted streams
2.   Trial and error
3.   Check the current workload condition

The feasibility condition may be found by checking the maximum number of streams that can be accepted. If the number of accepted streams is already equal to the maximum number of acceptable streams, any new streams are rejected until some streams have finished. The multimedia system needs to find out beforehand how many streams it can accept. This may not be too difficult if all the streams are homogeneous. However, the maximum number of streams needs to assume the worst case when the streams are heterogeneous. The dynamic workload of the system may also allow more streams to be accepted. Thus, the utilization of the multimedia system would be low.

Table 15.1. Notations in feasibility conditions

Parameter	Meaning
M	transfer time
δ	display time
S	access overheads
G	gap time

The feasibility condition may be dynamically established by trial-and-error. The multimedia system may try to accept the stream and deliver the data stripes. If the storage system becomes overloaded, it then stops a stream until the storage system no longer overloads. This method is simple, but the quality of service of the stopped streams becomes low.

The feasibility condition may be found by checking the workload of the system. The storage system should check its own workload to determine whether new streams can be accepted. We shall describe how to check whether the streams would overload the storage devices. Using this method, the feasibility condition to accept new streams can easily be found.

The objective of the feasibility condition is to check whether the streams would overload the storage devices. The feasibility condition is checked on the temporal domain. It can be applied on general storage organizations and arbitrary scheduling methods. It considers variable data transfer rates over the gaps so that performance characteristics of general storage devices can be included. The parameters in Table 15.1 are used in this model.

The data transfer time and the display time depend on the size of each data stripe. Both of them are needed to specify the characteristics of a stream. Data on magnetic disks are stored in tracks. The disk heads move across the tracks at a seek time that increases with the seek distance. Hence, data on storage devices are accessed with an overhead which depends on the data placement method. When the access overhead of each data stripe of a stream is long, the storage device only has short gap time to serve other concurrent streams. Thus, both the access overheads and the gap time are considered to find the feasibility condition.

We assume that each stream seeks an overhead of S seconds, and each data stripe is transferred in M seconds. After that, the stream suspends data retrieval for G seconds. Each data stripe can display for δ seconds. This is illustrated in Figure 15.6. A multimedia stream (S, M, δ) is acceptable if and only if it satisfies the continuous display requirement:

Figure 15.6. Feasibility condition of a single stream

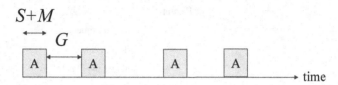

$$S + M \leq \delta. \tag{15.1}$$

This continuous display requirement must be maintained over a period of time. The requirement may temporarily be violated by satisfying requests in advance. The data stripes that are retrieved in advance are kept in read-ahead buffers. The average ratio of transfer time to display time must however be maintained over a finite period of time.

Feasibility of Homogeneous Streams

Multimedia streams are considered homogeneous if all streams have similar display time period δ. Let n streams be characterized by (M_1, δ), (M_2, δ), to (M_n, δ). Let S_i be the access overhead times in serving the ith stream and G_i be the gap time of the ith stream, for $i = 1$ to n. The gap time of a stream is the period of time that a storage system may serve other concurrent streams. By this definition (Tse & Leung, 2002), we have

$$G_i \leq \delta - (S_i + M_i). \tag{15.2}$$

Corollary 1: n streams can be concurrent if and only if

$$S_1 + M_1 + S_2 + M_2 + \ldots + S_n + M_n \leq \delta. \tag{15.3}$$

Proof: In order to be able to accept n streams concurrent, requests of any stream are served during the time gap of other streams. The continuous display requirement necessitates that k requests are served within a continuous time period $k\delta$ for finite value of k.

If n streams are concurrent, then these n streams are served in turn over a finite time period $k\delta$ such that k requests of each stream are served within the time gap of other stream. Hence, we have

$$\sum_{j=1, j\neq i}^{n} k\left(S_j + M_j\right) \leq kG_i \qquad i = 1, 2, ..., n.$$

This implies that

$$\sum_{j=1, j\neq i}^{n} \left(S_j + M_j\right) \leq G_i \qquad i = 1, 2, ..., n. \tag{15.4}$$

Summing equation (15.4) for all streams, we have

$$\sum_{i=1}^{n} \sum_{j=1, j\neq i}^{n} \left(S_j + M_j\right) \leq \sum_{i=1}^{n} G_i \qquad \bullet$$

which implies

$$(n-1)\sum_{j=1}^{n} \left(S_j + M_j\right) \leq \sum_{i=1}^{n} G_i$$

Substituting G_i from equation (5.2), this becomes

$$(n-1)\sum_{j=1}^{n} \left(S_j + M_j\right) \leq \sum_{i=1}^{n} \left(\delta - S_i - M_i\right)$$

which implies

$$(n-1)\sum_{j=1}^{n} \left(S_j + M_j\right) \leq n\delta - \sum_{i=1}^{n} \left(S_i + M_i\right) \tag{15.5}$$

Changing the subscript of the left hand side in equation (15.5) from j to i, we have

$$(n-1)\sum_{i=1}^{n}\left(S_i + M_i\right) \leq n\delta - \sum_{i=1}^{n}\left(S_i + M_i\right)$$

which implies

$$n\sum_{i=1}^{n}\left(S_i + M_i\right) \leq n\delta$$

$$\Rightarrow \sum_{i=1}^{n}\left(S_i + M_i\right) \leq \delta$$

Therefore, we have

$$S_1 + M_1 + S_2 + M_2 + ... + S_n + M_n \leq \delta$$

which is the necessary condition. Conversely, we have

$$S_1 + M_1 + S_2 + M_2 + ... + S_n + M_n \leq \delta$$

Since all terms are positive, we have

$$S_i + M_i \leq \delta, \forall i = 1, 2, ..., n$$

Hence, the continuous display requirement of all streams is fulfilled. Therefore, the n streams can be concurrently served.

As the corollary is true, the streams that satisfy the feasibility condition may be concurrently served by interleaving their requests. As shown in Figure 15.7, requests of stream A are served in the gap time of stream B and requests of stream B are served in the gap time of stream A.

Figure 15.7. Feasibility of homogeneous streams

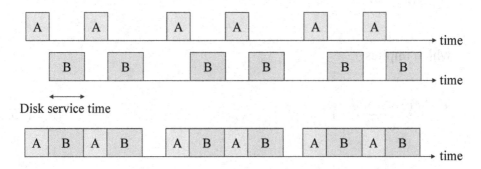

Feasibility Condition of Heterogeneous Streams

Multimedia streams are heterogeneous streams when their time periods are different (Tse & Leung, 2002). Let n streams be characterized by $(M_1, \delta_1), (M_2, \delta_2)$, to (M_n, δ_n) such that not all δ_i are the same. Let S_i be the access overhead time in serving the ith stream and G_i be the gap time of the ith stream.

Corollary 2: A group of n streams (S_i, M_i, δ_i) can be concurrent if and only if

$$\frac{S_1 + M_1}{\delta_1} + \frac{S_2 + M_2}{\delta_2} + ... + \frac{S_n + M_n}{\delta_n} \le 1$$

(15.6)

Proof: If n streams are concurrent, then there exists a finite time period δ that k_j requests of the jth streams are served. By the continuous display requirement, this time period does not exceed the display time of each stream. We have

$$\delta \le k_j \delta_j, \qquad j = 1, 2, ..., n,$$

$$\Rightarrow \frac{1}{\delta_j} \le \frac{k_j}{\delta}, \quad j = 1, 2, ..., n.$$

(15.7)

Since the time period δ is the retrieval time of all requests, we have

$$\sum_{i=1}^{n} k_j \left(S_j + M_j \right) = \delta$$

which implies

$$\sum_{j=1}^{n} \frac{k_j \left(S_j + M_j \right)}{\delta} = 1 \tag{15.8}$$

Substituting $\dfrac{1}{\delta_j} \leq \dfrac{k_j}{\delta}$ from equation (15.7), we obtain

$$\sum_{j=1}^{n} \frac{\left(S_j + M_j \right)}{\delta_j} \leq 1$$

which is the necessary condition. Conversely, we let

$$\delta = \delta_1 \delta_2 \delta_3 ... \delta_n$$

and let $k_j \in \Re$ such that

$$k_j = \frac{\delta}{\delta_j}, \qquad j = 1, 2, ..., n,$$

which gives

$$\frac{k_j}{\delta} = \frac{1}{\delta_j}, \qquad j = 1, 2, ..., n. \tag{15.9}$$

From the necessary condition, we have

$$\frac{S_1 + M_1}{\delta_1} + \frac{S_2 + M_2}{\delta_2} + ... + \frac{S_n + M_n}{\delta_n} \leq 1$$

This implies

$$\sum_{j=1}^{n} \frac{\left(S_j + M_j\right)}{\delta_j} \leq 1$$

Substituting from equation (15.9), we obtain

$$\sum_{j=1}^{n} \frac{k_j \left(S_j + M_j\right)}{\delta} \leq 1$$

which implies

$$\sum_{j=1}^{n} k_j \left(S_j + M_j\right) \leq \delta \qquad\qquad (15.10)$$

Hence, we obtain

$$k_i \left(S_i + M_i\right) + \sum_{j=1, j \neq i}^{n} k_j \left(S_j + M_j\right) \leq k_i \delta_i, \qquad i = 1, 2, ..., n. \qquad (15.11)$$

Since all terms are positive, we can take away the term from the left hand side of the inequality. Hence, we have

$$k_i(S_i + M_i) \leq k_i \delta_i, \qquad \forall i, i = 1, 2, ..., n,$$

which implies

$$S_i + M_i \leq \delta_i, \qquad \forall i, i = 1, 2, ..., n.$$

The continuous display requirement of each stream can be fulfilled over a finite period of time. Hence, the n streams can be concurrently served.

Figure 15.8. Feasibility of heterogeneous streams

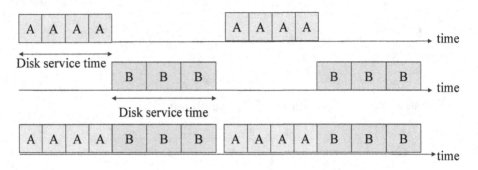

When the feasibility condition in Corollary 2 is satisfied, the streams may be concurrently served by interleaving their requests in groups. As shown in Figure 15.8, a group of requests belonging to stream A are served in the gap time of stream B and a group of requests belonging to stream B are served in the gap time of stream A.

Feasibility of Heterogeneous Streams Over Multiple Storage Devices

A multimedia storage system may have several storage devices, like a disk farm. When multiple storage devices are available, the storage devices may serve the streams independently or in parallel. When the streams are served in parallel, the above inequality for a single drive with different access overheads and transfer rate may be used. When the streams are served independently, one request is served by one storage device each time. We may consider each storage device using the above feasibility condition for each storage device. Alternatively, we may distribute the requests evenly to the devices and serve them accordingly. Otherwise, some storage devices may be overloaded while others are underutilized. Thus, we assume that the requests are evenly distributed to p devices in establishing the following feasibility condition.

Let n streams be characterized by (M_1, δ_1), (M_2, δ_2), to (M_n, δ_n). Let S_i be the access overhead time in serving the ith stream and G_i be the gap time of the ith stream.

Corollary 3: A group of n streams (S_i, M_i, δ_i) can be concurrently served on p independent devices if

$$\frac{S_1 + M_1}{\delta_1} + \frac{S_2 + M_2}{\delta_2} + \ldots + \frac{S_n + M_n}{\delta_n} \leq p$$

(15.12)

and the workload is evenly distributed among p devices.

Proof: If n streams are concurrently served by p devices, then there exist a finite time period δ such that k_j requests of the jth streams are served by p devices. By the continuous display requirement, this time period should not exceed the display time of each stream. We have

$$\delta \leq k_j \delta_j, \qquad j = 1, 2, \ldots, n$$

which implies

$$\frac{1}{\delta_j} \leq \frac{k_j}{\delta}, \qquad j = 1, 2, \ldots, n$$

(15.13)

Since the total retrieval time of all requests must be less than the service time of the p devices over the time period δ, we have

$$\sum_{i=1}^{n} k_j \left(S_j + M_j \right) \leq p\delta$$

which implies

$$\sum_{j=1}^{n} \frac{k_j \left(S_j + M_j \right)}{\delta} \leq p$$

(15.14)

Substituting $\dfrac{1}{\delta_j} \leq \dfrac{k_j}{\delta}$ from equation (15.7), we obtain

$$\sum_{j=1}^{n} \frac{\left(S_j + M_j\right)}{\delta_j} \leq p$$

Hence, the necessary part is proved. Conversely, we let

$$\delta = \delta_1 \delta_2 \delta_3 ... \delta_n$$

and let $k_j \in \Re$ such that

$$k_j = \frac{\delta}{\delta_j}, \qquad j = 1, 2, ..., n,$$

which implies

$$\frac{k_j}{\delta} = \frac{1}{\delta_j}, \qquad j = 1, 2, ..., n. \tag{15.15}$$

Substituting from Equation (15.15) to the necessity condition, we have

$$\sum_{j=1}^{n} \frac{k_j \left(S_j + M_j\right)}{\delta} \leq p$$

which implies

$$\sum_{j=1}^{n} k_j \left(S_j + M_j\right) \leq p\delta \tag{15.16}$$

Since all terms are positive, we can take away all except the ith term from. Hence, we obtain

$$k_i(Si + M_i) \leq pk_i\delta_i, \qquad i = 1, 2, ..., n,$$

which implies

$$(S_i + M_i) \leq p\delta_i, \qquad i = 1, 2, ..., n. \tag{15.17}$$

That is, requests of the ith stream can be served within time period δ_i by p devices. As long as the requests are distributed evenly to the devices, the continuous display requirement of all streams is fulfilled. Therefore, the n streams can be accepted to be served concurrently.

Therefore, the feasibility condition to concurrently serve a group of n streams (S_i, M_i, δ_i) on p independent storage devices if

$$\frac{S_1 + M_1}{\delta_1} + \frac{S_2 + M_2}{\delta_2} + ... + \frac{S_n + M_n}{\delta_n} \leq p \tag{15.18}$$

and the workload is evenly distributed among p devices.

When a new stream arrives at the multimedia storage system, the storage system can directly calculate the feasibility to serve all streams including the new stream according to their data transfer time, display time, and access overhead. If the feasibility condition is satisfied, then the new stream is accepted. Otherwise, the new stream should be rejected.

Chapter Summary

We have shown that the multimedia streams have real-time continuous display requirements. The storage system should only accept streams that can be served without violating their continuous display requirements. Thus, the feasibility conditions to check whether new streams should be accepted are investigated.

We have first shown the feasibility conditions to accept homogeneous streams on a storage system with only one storage device. After that, we have proved that heterogeneous streams can be accepted when their streams accessing patterns satisfies the feasibility conditions. Last, we have proved the general feasibility condition to accept heterogeneous streams over multiple storage devices.

References

Tse, P. K. C., & Leung, C. H. C. (2002). An efficient storage organization for multimedia databases. *Proceedings of the Recent Advances in Visual Information Systems 5th International Conference, VISUAL 2002*, Hsin Chu, Taiwan (LNCS 2314, pp. 152-162). Springer-Verlag.

Chapter XVI

Scheduling Methods for Request Streams

Introduction

In the previous chapter, we have presented the feasibility condition to serve request streams concurrently. In this chapter, we describe the efficient methods to schedule the requests to avoid missing their deadlines. Multimedia requests, except the first request, of a stream need to be served before their deadlines (Anderson, Osawa, & Govindan, 1992; Gemmell, Beaton, & Christodoulakis, 1994; Gemmell & Christodoulakis, 1992). Thus, the scheduling algorithm should consider the deadline so that the requests do not miss their deadlines. In the next section, we describe the EDF-SCAN algorithm. After that, we shall describe the group sweeping scheduling (GSS) method.

Earliest Deadline First Scheduling

The earliest deadline first (EDF) method is fully aware of the deadlines of the requests. It assigns priorities to requests and serves the request according to the time of their deadlines (Freeman & DeWitt, 1995). The deadlines of the requests in the waiting queue are compared. The requests with the earliest deadline are served first. That is, the urgent requests are served with priority. Other requests that can wait will be served later. When a tie occurs among several requests having the same deadline, these requests are served according to the first-in-first-out (FIFO) scheduling method.

For example, four requests A, B, C, and D arrive at the storage device.

1. Request A should be served before 09.000 seconds.
2. Request B should be served before 09.300 seconds.
3. Request C should be served before 09.150 seconds.
4. Request D should be served before 09.150 seconds.

These requests may belong to the same or different streams. The requests A, B, C, and D should be served before their deadlines at 9.000 seconds, 9.300 seconds, 9.150 seconds, and 9.150 seconds, respectively.

The storage system compares their deadlines and finds that the deadline of request A is the earliest. Thus, it serves the request A first. After it has finished serving request A, it finds that both request C and request D have the earliest deadline. Since request C arrives at the waiting queue before request D, it serves request C first. Afterwards, it serves request D. Finally, request B is served unless some new incoming requests with an earlier deadline have arrived. Therefore, the requests are served in the order of A, C, D, and B.

The EDF scheduling policy can be described with a model that changes the order of the waiting requests according to their deadline time. The deadlines of the waiting requests may point at different times that are not in sequence. After the EDF scheduling, the requests are aligned with the increasing order of their deadlines.

The earliest deadline first scheduling method serves all requests according to their deadlines. Thus, urgent requests are served with priority. It is likely that most requests would not miss their deadlines while waiting for service.

Figure 16.1. EDF scheduling policy

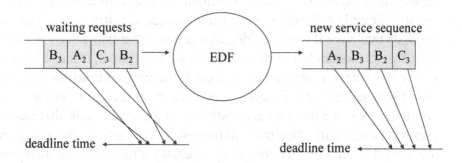

Some streams may send their requests early in time with a longer deadline. Other streams may send their requests close to their deadlines. However, the requests with short deadlines are served with priority. This is however unfair to the well behaving streams that schedule their requests ahead of time.

Although this strict EDF method is optimal for CPU scheduling, it should not be applied directly on disk scheduling. The EDF scheduling method does not consider the storage locations of the data stripes being accessed by the requests. The disk heads would randomly traverse across the disk surfaces to serve the most urgent request. Thus, the EDF scheduling is inefficient due to excessive seek time overheads.

The SCAN-EDF Scheduling Method

The EDF method is inefficient since it incurs heavy overheads in long seeks to serve more urgent requests that are far away. More efficient scheduling method should serve requests with short seeks while the urgent requests can still wait. The SCAN-EDF scheduling method strikes a balance between efficiency and urgency.

The SCAN-EDF scheduling method combines the seek optimization of the SCAN method and the real-time guarantees of the EDF method (Reddy & Wyllie, 1993, 1994). Since the deadlines of the requests should not be missed, the waiting request with the earliest deadline is always served first. Among waiting requests with the same deadline, the one that is first according to the scan direction is served first.

The storage system selects requests according to the SCAN-EDF algorithm as shown in Figure 16.2. First, it compares the deadlines of the waiting requests. The earliest deadline of the waiting requests is first found. The waiting requests that have the earliest deadline are inserted into a set T in Step 1. It then checks the number of request in the set T in Step 2. If the set T contains only one request, it serves this request. Otherwise, it finds the first request with the smallest seek distance in one scanning direction and serves it. It continues to serve the next requests with the shortest seek distance in the current scanning direction until all requests in the current scanning direction are served. If the set T is not empty, it changes the scanning direction and serves all requests in the new direction similarly. Afterwards, it goes back to Step 1 to fill the set T again.

We explain the SCAN-EDF algorithm using an example. Five requests A, B, C, D, and E arrive at the storage device.

1. Request A reads track number 0 and it should be served before 09.000 seconds.

2. Request B reads track number 400 and it should be served before 09.300 seconds.

3. Request C reads track number 350 and it should be served before 09.150 seconds.

4. Request D reads track number 950 and it should be served before 09.150 seconds.

5. Request E reads track number 550 and it should be served before 09.150 seconds.

These requests may belong to the same or different streams. The request A, B, C, D, and E should be served before their deadlines at 9.000 seconds, 9.300 seconds, 9.150 seconds, 9.150 seconds, and 9.150 seconds, respectively. The request A, B, C, D, and E reads from track number 0, 400, 350, 950, and 550, respectively.

The storage system first compares the requests' deadlines and finds that the earliest deadline is 09.000 seconds. Thus, it fills the set T in Step 1 with request A only. In Step 2, it finds that the set T only has one request. It then serves request A. After it finishes the service of request A, it goes back to Step 1.

Figure 16.2. The SCAN-EDF algorithm

- Step 1: Let T= set of tasks with the earliest deadline
- Step 2: if n(T) = 1, (there is only a single request in T),

    serve that request.

  else

    let t_1 be the first task in T in scan direction,
        serve t_1.

  go to Step 1.

The storage system then compares the requests' deadlines and finds that the earliest deadline is 09.150 seconds. It fills the set T in Step 1 with requests C, D, and E. In Step 2, it finds that the set T has more than one request. The disk heads are now staying at track number 0. The storage system finds that request C is the request in set T with the shortest seek distance in the outward direction. It thus moves the disk heads to track number 350 to serve request C. After it has served request C, it finds that request E is the request in set T with the shortest seek distance in the outward direction. It thus moves the disk heads to track number 550 to serve request E. After it has served request E, it finds that request D is the remaining request in set T. It then serves request E. After it has served request E, it goes back to Step 1.

The storage system now compares the requests' deadlines and finds that the earliest deadline is 09.300 seconds. Thus, it fills the set T in Step 1 with request B only. In Step 2, it finds that the set T only has one request. It then serves request B. After it has finished serving request B, it goes back to Step 1 to continue serving any new requests. Therefore, the requests are served in the order A, C, E, D, and B.

Notice that the SCAN-EDF algorithm is not preemptive. While a group of requests in set T are being served, it will not stop even if some urgent requests with an earlier deadline arrive at the storage system. The algorithm only rebuilds the set T after all the requests in the set T have been served.

The SCAN-EDF scheduling policy can be described as a method that aligns the waiting requests into an order based on two criteria as shown in Figure 16.3. The first one of the ordering criteria is the deadline time. All the requests are served according to their deadlines. Urgent requests are served with priority. The second one of the ordering criteria is the track location of the data stripes being accessed by the requests. The requests with the same deadline are served according to their accessing track locations.

Figure 16.3. SCAN-EDF scheduling policy

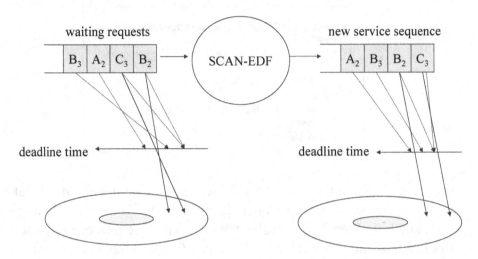

The SCAN-EDF scheduling method has some overheads in creating the set T and serving the requests in set T using the SCAN algorithm. This increases the complexity of the algorithm. If unidirectional SCAN scheduling is used instead of the bidirectional SCAN scheduling, the SCAN-EDF algorithm can be simplified by slightly modifying the EDF scheduling method.

Let D_i be the deadline of the ith waiting request and let T_i be the track number of the data stripe being accessed by the ith waiting request. The deadline of the ith waiting request can be modified to

$$= D_i + f(Ti) \qquad (16.1)$$

where the function $f(.)$ converts track number of the ith request into a small negative value. Thus, the deadlines of the requests are slightly moved ahead. The requests with the same deadline will be differentiated by their track numbers such that the requests are served in the unidirectional SCAN order.

Many functions can be chosen as $f(.)$ to modify the deadlines. The modified deadlines of the ith and the jth waiting requests should be served in the unidirectional SCAN order if $D_i = D_j$. If tracks with small track numbers are served first, then

$$f(Ti) < f(Tj) \text{ if } (T_i < T_j), \qquad \forall i,j \qquad (16.2)$$

In addition, the value of $f(T_i)$ has to be small enough so that the modified deadlines would not swap the service order of any two requests with different deadlines. That is,

$$D_i + f(Ti) < D_j + f(T_j) \text{ if } (D_i < D_j), \quad \forall i,j \qquad (16.3)$$

Thus, the requests are served according to their deadlines if their deadlines are different.

For example, the deadlines are originally specified to the number of seconds. The storage system chooses the modification function as

$$f(T_i) = \frac{T_i}{T_{max}} - 1 \qquad (16.4)$$

where $0 \leq T_i < T_{max}$ and $T_{max} = 1000$. Four requests A, B, C, and D have arrived and they are waiting in the queue.

1. Request A reads track number 347 and it should be served before 09.000 seconds.
2. Request B reads track number 113 and it should be served before 09.000 seconds.
3. Request C reads track number 256 and it should be served before 10.000 seconds.
4. Request D reads track number 851 and it should be served before 09.000 seconds.

The deadlines are modified as follows:

1. For request A, the function f(Ti) = -0.653 sec. Thus, the new deadline is 08.347 seconds.
2. For request B, the function f(Ti) = -0.887 sec. Thus, the new deadline is 08.113 seconds.
3. For request C, the function f(Ti) = -0.744 sec. Thus, the new deadline is 09.256 seconds.

4. For request D, the function $f(Ti) = -0.149$ sec. Thus, the new deadline is 08.851 seconds.

The requests with their new deadlines are then scheduled using the simpler EDF policy. Thus, the requests are served in the SCAN-EDF order of B, A, D, and C. Thus, the SCAN-EDF scheduling order is achieved with a simpler implementation.

The SCAN-EDF scheduling method serves the requests according to their deadlines first. If all requests have different deadlines, the SCAN-EDF scheduling method becomes the same as the EDF scheduling method. If all requests have the same deadlines or they do not have any deadlines, the SCAN-EDF scheduling method is the same as the SCAN scheduling method.

Application Note: *The efficiency of the SCAN-EDF method depends on the number of requests with the same deadline being served together using the SCAN scheduling. In order for the SCAN-EDF scheduling method to be efficient, some requests need to have the same deadline to be grouped together. Two options may be used to increase the number of requests that are served together as a group using the SCAN scheduling.*

First, the deadlines may be specified with a coarser granularity to increase the chance that requests have the same deadline. If the deadlines are specified at fine granularity, it is unlikely that the deadlines would be the same. When the granularity of the deadlines is coarse, similar deadlines would become the same deadline. As a result, more requests would have the same deadline. However, the granularity of the deadlines should not be too coarse since the deadlines may not be easily met. Therefore, the deadlines should be specified at medium granularity to strike a good balance between efficiency and continuity guarantee.

Second, the deadlines of the requests may be moved in advance. Some requests with early deadlines may be advanced with shorter times, while other requests with later deadlines may be advanced with longer times. If the storage system can serve all these requests with the new advanced deadline, these requests can thus be served more efficiently according to the storage location of their accessing data stripe. The SCAN-EDF scheduling method can move the requests' deadlines dynamically according to the number of waiting requests.

Similar to the EDF scheduling method, the SCAN-EDF serves requests with short deadlines with priority. Thus, it is also unfair to the well behaving streams that schedule their requests ahead of time.

Group Sweeping Scheduling

Multimedia streams send requests to the storage system. These requests belonging to different concurrent streams wait for service in the waiting queue of the storage system. Each request has its own deadline. The storage system should serve the concurrent streams efficiently and fairly. Homogeneous streams send requests in the same period of time. The storage system can serve one request of each stream in every period. The homogeneous concurrent streams are treated fairly when they are served in this interleaving manner.

The group sweeping scheduling method considers streams that are strongly periodic and strongly regular. These requests access the data stripes of the same size from the storage system. Instead of specifying deadlines to requests, it uses a smoothing buffer to assure the continuity of streams.

The GSS method divides the set of concurrent streams into a number of groups. Each group consists of a number of requests. The groups are served in round robin cycles. A stream is assigned to the same group until the stream ends. When a group of requests is being served, the storage system serves individual requests within a group consecutively. To achieve high efficiency, the requests within a group are served according to the SCAN algorithm (Chen, Kandlur, & Yu, 1993).

The groups are served in fixed cycles. The order of groups being served is thus fixed. The requests within a group are not served in fixed order. In the previous cycle, the request belonging to a stream may be served first. In the next cycle, the request belonging to the same stream may be served last.

Let n be the number of concurrent streams and let g be the number of groups. The set of n streams are divided into g groups. There are two particular cases for the number of groups.

1. When $g = 1$, all the concurrent streams are assigned to the same group. Thus, the GSS method schedules requests into the order as the SCAN algorithm.

Figure 16.4. The delay and buffering due to the first-in-first-out scheduling

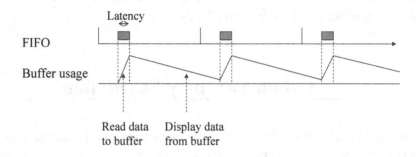

2. When g = n, each stream is assigned to a different group. Thus, all the streams are served in round robin cycles. Thus, the GSS method schedules stream requests in the fixed round robin cycles.

Depending on the scheduling method in use, the stream may not be able to respond immediately after the first data stripe is received. For some scheduling methods, it may need to wait for an additional delay. This delay is called the start-up latency. When the requests are served and the data stripes are accessed, the scheduling method needs to store the data stripes in the smoothing buffers. The smoothing buffer usage also increases when the start-up latency increases.

If the first-in-first-out scheduling method is used, the requests are served according to the time of arrival in the waiting queue. Since homogeneous streams send requests using the same period of time, the same number of requests are received in the same period of time. Thus, the streams are served in the fixed round robin cycles. One request is served within a regular period of time as shown in Figure 16.4. Each stream will expect to receive one data stripe after every *n* data stripes are accessed by the storage system. Thus, the time interval between the consecutive requests belonging to the same stream is fixed. After the first data stripe is received, each stream can expect to receive the next data stripe after a fixed period of time. Therefore, a stream may start immediately after the first data stripe is retrieved.

Requests belonging to the same stream may store the data stripes in the same buffer. After a data stripe is accessed, it is stored in the buffer for consumption. The buffer usage increases when the request is served and it decreases slowly until the next request is served as shown in Figure 16.4. The buffer

Figure 16.5. The delay and buffering due to the SCAN scheduling

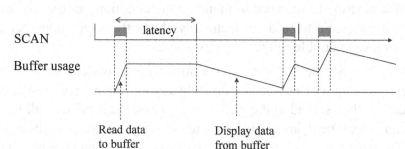

Figure 16.6. The delay and buffering due to the group sweeping scheduling

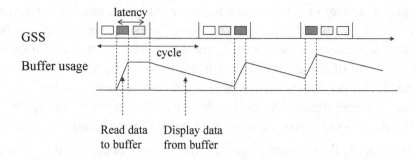

should not be empty before the next data stripe is accessed to maintain the continuity of the stream.

If the SCAN scheduling method is used, the homogeneous streams still send requests using the same period of time. But the storage system does not serve the requests following the time that the requests arrive at the waiting queue. It serves requests in scanning cycles. Within each scanning cycle, the disk heads traverse the disk surface once in each direction. The second request of a stream may be served as the last request in the new cycle even though the first request of the stream is served as the first request in the previous cycle. Thus, the stream can only expect one request to be served before the end of the scanning cycle as shown in Figure 16.5. After receiving the first data stripe, the stream waits for the end of a scanning cycle before it can start.

Requests belonging to the same stream may store the data stripes in the same buffer. After the first data stripe is accessed, it is stored in the buffer. Thus, the buffer usage increases when the request is served. It stays at the same level until the end of the scanning cycle as shown in Figure 16.5. After the stream has started to display, it decreases slowly. When the next request is served, the buffer usage increases again. The buffer should not be empty before the next data stripe is accessed to maintain the continuity of the stream. If two data stripes are retrieved consecutively, the buffer usage may increase to a level close to double of the data stripe size.

When the GSS method is used, the streams are divided into groups. If the previous request of a stream is served in a group, the next request of the same stream will be served in the same group. Thus, the service of all requests of a stream may be delayed until the end of the group that the stream belongs as shown in Figure 16.6. The streams can expect to receive one data stripe from the storage system within each service of the same group. After receiving the first data stripe, the stream waits for the completion of a group before it can start.

Requests belonging to the same stream may store the data stripes in the same buffer. After the first data stripe is accessed, it is stored in the buffer. Thus, the buffer usage increases when the request is served. It stays at the same level until the end of the group as shown in Figure 16.6. After the stream starts to display, it decreases slowly. When the next request is served, the buffer usage increases again. The buffer should not be empty before the next data stripe is accessed to maintain the continuity of the stream.

Depending on the number of groups, the start-up latency and the buffer size are affected. We shall find the optimal number of groups below. The smoothing buffer should be large enough to store one data stripe for each stream and the data stripes accessed by one group of request. Thus, the size of the smoothing buffer in the GSS method, B_b, is found as

$$B_b = \left(n + \left\lceil \frac{n}{g} \right\rceil \right) k B_m$$

(16.5)

Table 16.1. Parameters in GSS

Parameter	Description
T	Disk rotation time
s_g	Seek time across groups
s_r	Seek time of requests within a group
Δ	Playback time of one block of data
B	Number of blocks in a track

where k is the size (in number of blocks) of each data stripe and B_m is the size (in bytes) of a block.

Since the group of requests is served using the SCAN scheduling method, the request within a group can be served with a short seek time, s_r. Each request transfers k blocks of data and each track stores b blocks. Thus, each request transfers $\left\lceil \dfrac{k}{b} \right\rceil$ tracks of data. Assuming that data are transferred in tracks, the rotational latency and the data transfer time of each request is found as

$$= \left(\left\lceil \frac{k}{b} \right\rceil + l \right) T$$

where l is a small correction term for the extra overheads and l is between 0 and 1. Since the first and the last blocks of a data stripe may cross the track boundary, the number of disk rotations could be increased by one.

The access time of each request is thus equal to

$$= s_r + \left(\left\lceil \frac{k}{b} \right\rceil + l \right) T$$

The first request in each group is served with a different seek time. Thus, the seek time of the first request of each group is s_g. The cycle time to serve n requests in g groups, T_c, can be found as

$$T_c = n \left(\left\lceil \frac{k}{b} \right\rceil + l \right) T + n s_r + g s_g$$

Since the playback time of each stream should be longer than or equal to the cycle time, we have

$$k\delta \geq T_c$$

$$\Leftrightarrow k\delta \geq n\left(\left\lceil \frac{k}{b} \right\rceil + l\right)T + ns_r + gs_g$$

If $l = 0$, k is multiple of b, and $(b\delta\text{-}nT) > 0$, we can solve for k to get

$$k \geq b\left\lceil \frac{ns_r + gs_g}{b\delta - nT} \right\rceil$$

From the above equation, we can see that the buffer size, B_b, increases with the data stripe size, k, in number of blocks. The data stripe size should be reduced to its smallest value so that the smoothing buffer is the smallest. An optimal value of data stripe size, k, can be found using the optimal data stripe size algorithm below.

Optimal Data Stripe Size Algorithm

1.   Initially setting k to $= b\left\lceil \dfrac{ns_r + gs_g}{b\delta - nT} \right\rceil$.
2.   If $(k - 1)$ satisfies the timing constraint, set $k = k - 1$ and repeat this step.
3.   Otherwise, the optimal k is reached.

In addition, the optimal number of groups can be found using the optimal groups algorithm below.

Optimal Groups Algorithm

1.   For g =1 to n, repeat the above algorithm to find the optimal k and its corresponding Bb.
2.   Compare all these buffer sizes to find the optimal group size.

Figure 16.7. Group sweeping scheduling policy

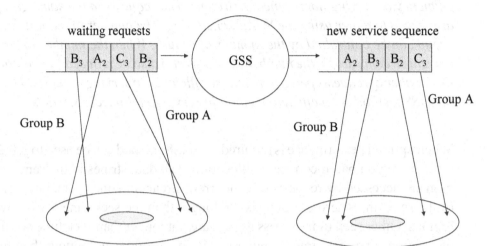

The group sweeping scheduling policy can be described in the model as shown in Figure 16.7. The waiting requests are first grouped into service groups. The waiting requests within each group are scheduled. The service order of these requests is aligned according to the track locations of the accessing data stripes.

The group sweeping scheduling method is designed for the homogeneous streams. Since heterogeneous streams have different display periods, a periodic fill policy would be required to change the period of the streams so that all concurrent streams can become homogeneous. The periodic fill policy accepts requests of the original period and outputs new requests according to the period of the other streams. These new requests at the new period would access more or less data stripes than the old requests at the original period. The heterogeneous streams can thus be served using the GSS policy.

The group sweeping scheduling method does not use the deadline to provide real-time continuity guarantees. It serves the streams in an interleaving manner to provide continuous data supply to the streams. The storage system serves one request of each stream in each cycle. As long as the cycle time is not longer than the playback time of each data stripe, the continuity requirement of the streams are not violated. Thus, the GSS method can provide real-time continuity guarantee to the multimedia streams.

Application Note: *The group sweeping scheduling method improves the efficiency of serving homogeneous streams. The requests in the same group are served together using the SCAN scheduling. The number of requests in a group can be controlled by the number of groups. When the number of concurrent streams drops, the number of groups can also be reduced to maintain the number of requests per group and the efficiency in serving requests. Thus, the GSS method is an efficient method in serving multimedia streams.*

When optimal performance is required, the GSS method can be used together with the region based constraint allocation. The data stripes in the same region are accessed by requests of concurrent streams in one cycle. Only one of the seek times across groups is not longer than the seek time across two regions. Other seek times across groups are not longer than seek time within one region. The seek time of requests within a group is not longer than the seek time within one region. Therefore, seek times are short and the GSS becomes very efficient.

Chapter Summary

The scheduling methods for multimedia streams are described in this chapter. These scheduling methods use either serve requests according to their deadline or serve the stream in round robin cycle in order to provide real-time continuity guarantee. They all use the SCAN scheduling method to improve the efficiency in serving requests. These scheduling methods include the earliest deadline first method, the SCAN-EDF method, and the group sweeping scheduling method.

The earliest deadline first scheduling method serves requests according to their deadlines so that the requests would not wait too long and miss their deadlines. Thus, the requests with short deadlines are served with priority. This is however unfair to the well behaving streams that send their requests ahead of time.

The SCAN-EDF scheduling method serves requests with the same deadline in the SCAN order. It improves the efficiency of the storage system using the EDF scheduling method. However, it is still unfair to the well behaving streams that send their streams ahead of time. The SCAN-EDF method using unidirectional SCAN can be simplified by adjusting the deadlines of the waiting requests.

The group sweeping scheduling method serves groups of streams in round-robin cycles and serves requests within each group in the SCAN order. It improves the efficiency of the storage system and provides real-time continuity guarantees to the streams. It is fair to all the streams by serving one request of every stream in each cycle. However, it increases the start-up latency and the smoothing buffer in order to implement the scheduling method.

References

Anderson, D. P., Osawa, Y., & Govindan, R. (1992). A file system for continuous media. *ACM Transactions on Computer Systems, 10*(4), 311-337.

Chen, M. S., Kandlur, D. D., & Yu, P. (1993). Optimization of the grouped sweeping scheduling (GSS) with heterogeneous multimedia streams. In *Proceedings of the ACM Multimedia Conference* (pp. 235-241).

Freeman, C. S., & DeWitt, D. J. (1995). The SPIFFI scalable video-on-demand system. In *Proceedings of the ACM SIGMOD International Conference on Management of Data* (pp. 352-363).

Gemmell, D. J., Beaton, R. J., & Christodoulakis, S. (1994). Delay-sensitive multimedia on disks. *IEEE Multimedia, 1*(4), 56-67.

Gemmell, D. J., & Christodoulakis, S. (1992). Principles of delay-sensitive multimedia data storage and retrieval. *ACM Transactions on Information Systems, 10*(1), 51-90.

Reddy, A. L. N., & Wyllie, J. C. (1993). Disk scheduling in a multimedia I/O system. In *Proceedings of the 1st ACM Conference on Multimedia* (pp. 225-233).

Reddy, A. L. N., & Wyllie, J. C. (1994). I/O issues in a multimedia system. *IEEE Computer, 27*(3), 69-74.

Summary to Section III

Disk Scheduling

Traditional computer systems only handle disk requests individually. Multimedia systems send multiple requests one after another to the disk system. These requests appear as a stream of requests to the storage system. These requests should be served with proper scheduling method so that the streams can continue without any problems. Thus, new scheduling methods have been designed to serve streams of requests for multimedia data.

The first-in-first-out scheduling method serves requests according to their incoming order. It is simple and fair, but not efficient. Disk requests in multimedia storage systems should be served before their deadlines are passed. Thus, the FIFO scheduling method is not suitable for scheduling requests of multimedia streams.

The SCAN scheduling method serves the waiting requests in the order of their accessing physical track locations. The disk heads traverse the disk surface and serve requests that access data on the tracks in its path. The heavy seek time overheads of the long seeks are shared among these requests. The average seek distance and average seek time are reduced. The storage system thus serves requests efficiently.

Although the bidirectional SCAN scheduling policy is unfair to the requests that access data near the centre or the rim of the disk platters, the unidirectional SCAN scheduling method can serve all requests fairly. However, the efficiency of the storage system is slightly traded off.

We have shown that the multimedia streams have real-time continuous display requirements. The storage system should only accept streams that can be served without violating their continuous display requirements. Thus, the feasibility conditions to check whether new streams should be accepted are investigated.

We have first shown the feasibility conditions to accept homogeneous streams on a storage system with only one storage device. After that, we have proved that heterogeneous streams can be accepted when their streams accessing patterns satisfy the feasibility conditions. Last, we have proved the general feasibility condition to accept heterogeneous streams over multiple storage devices.

The scheduling methods for multimedia streams are described in this chapter. These scheduling methods use either serve requests according to their deadline or serve the stream in round robin cycle in order to provide a real-time continuity guarantee. They all use the SCAN scheduling method to improve the efficiency in serving requests. These scheduling methods include the earliest deadline first method, the SCAN-EDF method, and the droup sweeping scheduling method.

The earliest deadline first scheduling method serves requests according to their deadlines so that the requests would not wait too long and miss their deadlines. Thus, the requests with short deadlines are served with priority. This is however unfair to the well behaving streams that send their requests ahead of time.

The SCAN-EDF scheduling method serves requests with the same deadline in the SCAN order. It improves the efficiency of the storage system using the EDF scheduling method. However, it is still unfair to the well behaving streams that send their streams ahead of time. The SCAN-EDF method using unidirectional SCAN can be simplified by adjusting the deadlines of the waiting requests.

The group sweeping scheduling method serves groups of streams in round-robin cycles and serves requests within each group in the SCAN order. It improves the efficiency of the storage system and provides real-time continuity guarantees to the streams. It is fair to all the streams by serving one request of every stream in each cycle. However, it increases the start-up latency and the smoothing buffer in order to implement the scheduling method.

Section IV

Data Migration

Introduction

Storage system stores data objects on different storage devices. When these storage devices are of the same type, the objects may be stored and retrieved with similar access latency. When these storage devices are of different types, the objects may be stored and retrieved with different access latencies. Thus, the type of storage devices that contain the stored object affects the access latency in an accessed stored object.

A common method to arrange the storage devices of different types is the hierarchical storage systems (HSS). All or most objects are stored on the storage devices with longer access latency. When these data objects are accessed, the objects are moved from these storage devices with longer access latency to the storage devices with shorter access latency. This is called data migration. Similar to the chapters on disk scheduling of Part III, data migration on HSS also improves the performance of HSS, especially at the response time of request streams.

In hierarchical storage systems, data migration is the process of moving data from tertiary storage devices to secondary storage devices. There are three approaches to migrate multimedia data objects across the storage levels. These methods are:

1. Staging
2. Time slicing
3. Pipelining

Three pipelining methods are used to reduce the start up latency and staging buffer size. They include:

1. Normal pipelining
2. Space efficient pipelining
3. Segmented pipelining

We shall explain the simple staging method which migrate data across the storage levels prior to using them in Chapter XVII. After that, we describe the time-slicing method in Chapter XVIII for low latency tertiary storage devices. Afterwards, we describe the pipelining methods for slow tertiary storage devices. The normal pipelining method is described in Chapter XIX. In the normal pipelining method, the sizes of the slices are minimized to maximize the overlapping between the displaying time and the retrieval time of the slices. Then, the space efficient pipelining method is described in Chapter XX. In the space efficient pipelining methods, the buffer size in accessing the slices is minimized. After that, the segmented pipelining method is presented in Chapter XXI. In the segmented pipelining method, the latency in serving interactive requests is reduced.

Chapter XVII

Staging Methods

Introduction

When data are stored in the tertiary storage devices, the tape drives shall read them from the tapes using the input/output (I/O) operations. Due to the long delay in exchanging tapes, it is inconvenient to exchange a tape for each read/write access operation. Thus, the entire object or file is accessed from the tape drives well before they are being used (Federighi & Rowe, 1994; Kienzle, 1995; Pang, 1997). These accessed objects are temporarily stored in the magnetic hard disks as secondary storage level.

Staging Method

The simplest method to migrate data from the tertiary storage devices is the staging method. This method accesses an object using two stages. In the first stage, the entire file or object is migrated from tapes to the staging buffers in the disks. In the second stage, the file or object is consumed from the staging buffers.

Before we start stage one, the stage buffer is checked to make sure it still contains the object being accessed. If the object does not exist in the stage buffers, the stage one is executed to migrate the object from its permanent storage in the tertiary storage devices. During the stage one, the file or object is migrated from its permanent storage on the tertiary storage device to the staging buffers the secondary storage devices. This copy action is illustrated in Figure 17.1 and performed in four steps:

1. Exchange
2. Reposition
3. Transfer from tape to disk via memory
4. Wrap up

First, the tape drive exchanges the tape to the drive. The tape is moved from the cell containing the tape to a drive. If there is an existing tape in the drive, the old tape is first removed using the robotic arm. Then, the new tape is inserted in the drive using another robotic arm. We have assumed that there are two robotic arms in the exchange device. In the case that there is only one robotic arm, the robotic arm will first remove the old tape from the drive before it can fetch the new tape from the tape cell.

Second, the tape drive will reposition the tape to the first data block of the file or object. This may take a very long time depending on the position of the required file or object within the tape.

Third, the tape drive will then transfer the data blocks from the tape to the memory. The drive reads a data block from the tape, transfers it via the I/O bus, the I/O processor, and the system bus to the memory. The data blocks in the memory are written to the *stage buffers* or *staging buffers* in the disks. The staging buffers are checked to see if enough space is available. If the staging buffers are full, some objects are deleted from the staging buffers to

Figure 17.1. The first stage in the staging method

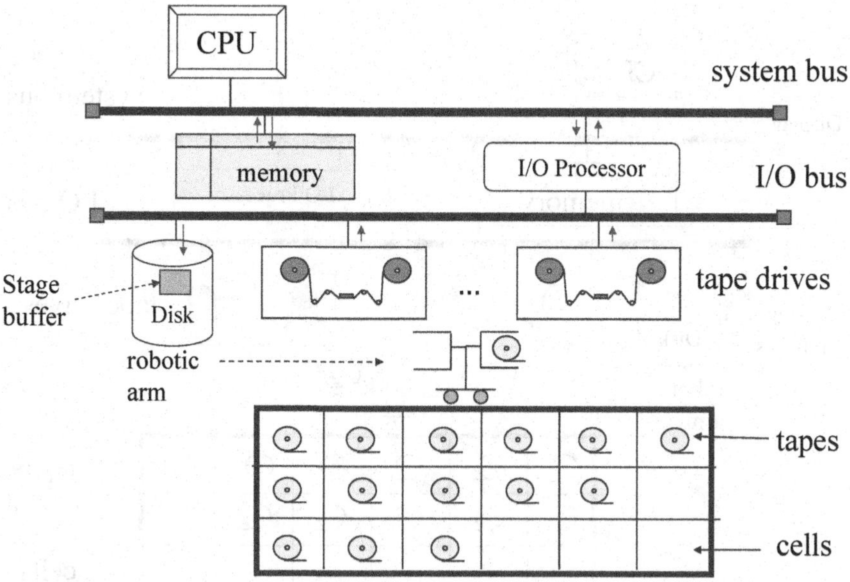

release space. The program then sends I/O requests to the disk to write the data block to the staging buffers. The data blocks in the staging buffers are prevented from being deleted until they are accessed in the second stage. This step is repeated until all the data blocks of the object are copied to the staging buffers.

Last, the data blocks in the memory are erased, and the tape drive is released. The allocated memory or used memory buffer is released. The tape drive is released, and it may be used by other programs. The tapes in the drive may then be unloaded to load other tapes. Stage one has now completed, and the accessed object has been migrated from its permanent storage on the tertiary storage devices to the staging buffers on the secondary storage devices.

In the first stage, the object is migrated from its permanent storage on the tertiary storage devices to the staging buffers on the secondary storage devices. During the second stage, the required blocks of data are copied from the staging buffers to the memory for consumption. The second stage is shown in Figure 17.2, and it is done in two steps:

1. Read from staging buffers
2. Consume from memory

Figure 17.2. The second stage in the staging method

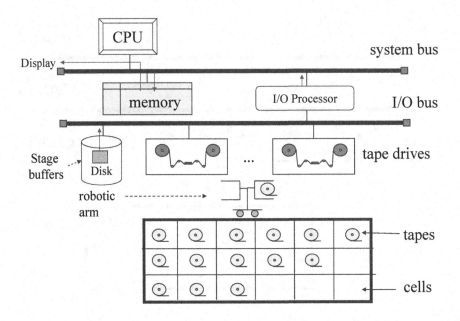

First, the data in the memory are read from the staging buffers in the disks. The staging buffers are checked for the location of the stored object. If the object is found, then I/O requests are sent to the disk to read the required data blocks from the staging buffers. Second, the data blocks in the memory are consumed. After the first step, the data migration is completed. The user program can thus consume data blocks from the memory.

The second stage continues until all data blocks are consumed. After the entire object is consumed and its data blocks are no longer required, the object in the staging buffers may then be deleted so that it could be deleted to release space.

Note that the two stages access data using two different granularities. The first stage accesses data at a coarse granularity, and the second stage accesses data at a fine granularity. In the first stage, the entire object is accessed as a migration unit. This is to achieve an object based transfer from the tertiary storage devices so that the number of exchanges can be small. If the entire object is stored on a single media unit, only one exchange is needed to access the entire object.

In the second stage, the objects are accessed in an unit of data block. This can reduce the amount of memory usage during the consumption period. Since the storage space on the memory is more expensive than the storage space on the disks, the disk space should be used in place of the memory space if possible. In addition, local disks can often deliver data at higher data rate than the stream consumption data rate. The data blocks can stay on the staging buffers until the object is no longer required.

When tertiary storage devices are used, the multimedia objects are accessed only once from the tertiary storage devices. They go through the disks twice, once for writing to the staging buffers and once for reading back from the staging buffers. They go through the memory and the system bus four times, the first time when the object is read from the tertiary storage devices, the second time when the object is writing to the staging buffers, the third time when the object is read from the staging buffers, and the fourth time when the object is being consumed. The multimedia objects also pass through the I/O processor and the I/O bus three times. Apart from the high latency of the tertiary storage devices, the workloads on the disks, the memory, the system bus, the I/O bus, and the I/O processor could become the bottleneck of the storage system that limits its maximum throughput.

Performance of the Staging Method

In order to understand the performance of the staging method, we use the performance model of the tape drives in the previous chapter. That is, the access time to access an object from the tape drive is

$$= \omega + \alpha + \frac{X}{\gamma}$$

where ω is the exchange time, α is the reposition time, γ is the tape transfer rate, and X is the data size.

The two stages are considered together along the time line as illustrated in Figure 17.3. In a double buffers arrangement, the tape drive can start to transfer the next data block while the disk is writing the previous data block. After the first data block is accessed from the tape to memory in memory buffer Mem_1, the tape drive can start to read the second data block into memory buffer Mem_2 while the disk is writing the first data block from Mem_1. Since

Figure 17.3. The two stages in transferring data using the staging method

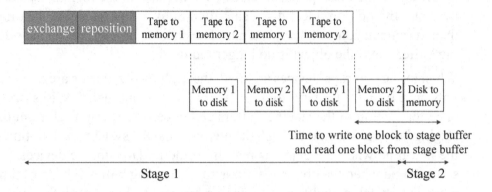

the access latency of the tapes is higher than the access latency of the disks, the access time of each disk access is shorter than the access time of a tape access. When the access time of the disks is occasionally long, more memory buffers may be used to cater for the variations in access time.

The time to write the first data block to disks is thus hidden within the time to read the second data block from tape. Similarly, the time to write the second data block to disks is hidden within the time to read the third data block from tape, and so on. After the last data block is accessed from tape, the disk writes the last data block. The access time of this data block is thus revealed as part of the time to complete stage one.

After stage one is completed, the data are retrieved from the staging buffers to memory in stage two. At least one data block must be retrieved from the staging buffers before the object stream can start to display. Thus, the start-up latency in using the staging method is

$$= \omega + \alpha + \frac{X}{\gamma} + 2 * \left(s + L + \frac{B_m}{\beta} \right)$$

$$(17.1)$$

where s is the seek time, L is the rotational latency, B_m is the media block size, and β is the data transfer rate of the disks.

Since the time to write one data block to the disks is much shorter than the time to read an object from the tape, the access time of the two data blocks to/from the disks can be ignored. The time spent in the second stage is comparatively short, and it also overlaps with the playback time of the object.

Therefore, the access time is dominated by the time spent reading the object from the tape in stage one. Therefore, the access time of an object from the tape drive is approximately equal to

$$= \omega + \alpha + \frac{X}{\gamma}$$

For example, consider an object of 1GB on tape with transfer rate 5 MB/s and exchange using 10 seconds. Assume that the object is at the position of the head after loading. If the contiguous method is used to store the objects and the first object on the tape is being accessed, the access time of the object is

= 10 + 0 + 1*1024/5 seconds
= 214.8 seconds.

The access time is thus longer than 3 minutes.

Alternatively, if the object is striped over four tape drives, it takes longer time to exchange all four tapes for four drives. The access time is

= 10*4 + 0 + 1*1024/4/5 seconds
= 91.2 seconds.

The required time is now more than 1.5 minutes.

If the object is spread over four drives using the triangular placement method. During the first 40 seconds of exchange time, the four drives will perform the following actions:

1. The first drive may transfer 30 seconds of data after exchanging.
2. The second drive waits for 10 seconds while the robotic arms are serving the first drive. Then, it can transfer 20 seconds of data after exchanging.
3. The third drive waits for 20 seconds while the robotic arms are serving the first and second drives. Then, it can transfer 10 seconds of data after exchanging.

4.   The fourth drive waits for 30 seconds while the robotic arms are serving the other drives. It does not have any time to transfer data.

The amount of data that can be transferred within the first 40 seconds is

= 30 + 20 + 10
= 60 seconds of transfer time.

Therefore, there are 5 * 60 = 300 MB of data being transferred within the first 40 seconds. The remaining data are transferred by all four drives in parallel. Thus, the access time is

= 10*4 + 0 + (1024-300)/4/5
= 76.2 seconds.

Therefore, the access time is slightly above one minute using the triangular placement method.

Chapter Summary

The staging method is simple. Using the staging method, the entire object is available after staging. The program can freely access any part of the required object after waiting for the time required to migrate the object to the staging buffers. The staging method is also flexible. The access time from tertiary storage is completely separated. This is suitable for any type of data on any tertiary storage systems.

Unfortunately, the time spent in waiting for stage one to complete can be very long. This leads to a very slow response to even the simplest request. Since the entire object is stored on the staging buffers during the complete consumption time period, this wastes disk space for a considerably long time. In addition, the entire object is written to and read back from the disks, and it may unnecessarily waste disk bandwidth in migrating unused data.

References

Federighi, C., & Rowe, L. A. (1994). A distributed hierarchical storage manager for a video-on-demand system. In *Proceedings of SPIE Conference on Storage and Retrieval for Image and Video Databases II* (Vol. 2185, pp. 185-195).

Kienzle, M. G., Dan, A., Sitaram, D., & Tetzlaff, W. (1995). Using tertiary storage in video-on-demand servers. In *Proceedings of IEEE COMPCON* (pp. 225-233).

Pang, H. H. (1997). Tertiary storage in multimedia systems: Staging or direct access. *ACM Multimedia Systems, 5*, 386-399.

Chapter XVIII

Time Slicing Method

Introduction

Tertiary storage devices provide huge storage capacity at low cost. Multimedia objects stored on the tertiary storage devices are accessed with high latency. Despite the high access latency, some tertiary storage devices are able to deliver data at high throughput.

The time slicing method is designed to reduce the start-up latency in accessing multimedia objects from tertiary storage devices. The start-up latency is lowered by reducing the amount of data being migrated in stage one of the staging method being described in the last chapter.

In order to support the time-slicing method, the tertiary storage devices should have the ability to deliver data at high throughput. The tertiary storage devices that cannot deliver data at sufficiently high throughput; the start-up latency cannot be reduced.

Time Slicing Method

The time slicing method assumes that data of an object is consumed from the beginning to the end. The object is divided into time slice units such that each time slice is a continuous segment of the object. Each time slice is consumed for a period of time. The later slices are not required while the earlier slices are being consumed. Thus, the later slices can be retrieved from the tertiary storage later after the early slices are being displayed.

When an object is being accessed, the object request is split into several tasks. The number of tasks is equal to the number of time slices of the object. Each task accesses a time slice of the object. The first task accesses the first time slice. The second task accesses the second time slice, and so on. The entire object is thus accessed by the tasks.

After the first time slice is migrated to the staging buffers on disks, the object can start to display the first slice. As long as the second time slice is retrieved before the first time slice has finished displaying, the object can continue to display. If the tertiary storage device changes the tape to serve another object while the first time slice is being displayed, the storage system can start to serve the other object at an earlier time (Lau, Lui, & Wong, 1995).

Consider that the object streams are homogeneous and the tape drive bandwidth is between m to $m+1$ times of the data consumption rate of the objects, where $m > 1$. The tertiary storage device can serve the n object requests in fixed round robin cycles, where $n \leq m$. Each object request is split into m tasks such that every task accesses only one time slice for every object.

Unlike the staging method, the streams start to display after the first time slice of the object is accessed. The second time slice should be retrieved before the first time slice has finished displaying. The third time slice should be retrieved before the second time slice has finished displaying and so on. Thus, the later parts of the objects are retrieved from the tertiary storage devices while the earlier parts of the objects are being consumed.

Since the tape drive bandwidth is at least m times of the data consumption rate of the objects, the tape drive can access m time slices before each object has displayed one time slice. Since the tasks are served in round robin cycles, there are at most n-1 tasks between two tasks of the same object request. These other tasks access the time slices of other objects. The tertiary storage system thus serves one task in every n tasks being served. It accesses one time slice of an object in every n time slices being accessed.

For example, we consider two objects X and Y are stored on the tapes of a tertiary storage system. The storage system has only one tape drive. The tape drive bandwidth is more than twice the data consumption rate of each object. The object X is divided into time slices X_1 and X_2 such that X_1 can display for half of the display time of object X. Similarly, the object Y is divided into time slices Y_1 and Y_2 such that Y_1 can display for half of the display time of object Y.

Two requests for X and Y have arrived at the waiting queue of the storage system. The request for each object is divided into two tasks. Request for object X is divided into two tasks such that the first task accesses time slice X_1, and the second task accesses time slice X_2. Similarly, the request for object Y is divided into two tasks such that the first task accesses time slice Y_1 and the second task accesses time slice Y_2.

The storage system accesses both objects X and Y in an interleaving manner as illustrated in Figure 18.1. It first serves the first task of object X to access the time slice X_1. After the first task of object X has completed, the storage system serves the first task of object Y to access the time slice Y_1. After the first task of object Y has completed, the storage system serves the second task of object X to access the time slice X_2. After the second task of object X has completed, the storage system serves the second task of object Y to access the time slice Y_2.

After the first time slice of object X is accessed, the stream of object X starts to display. After the first time slice of object Y is accessed, the stream of object Y starts to display. Since the tape drive bandwidth is more than twice of the data consumption rate of each object, the displaying time of X_1 should

Figure 18.1. Time slicing method

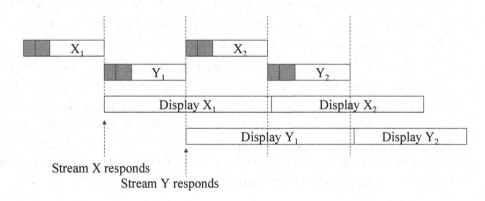

be longer than the retrieval time of the time slices Y_1.and X_2. For the same reason, the displaying time of Y_1 should be longer than the retrieval time of the time slices X_2.and Y_2. Therefore, both streams can the necessary data to display continuously.

Performance

The main improvement of the time slicing method is the start-up latency of streams or the stream response times. Each stream starts to display after the first time slice of the stream is accessed from the tertiary storage system. Thus, the stream starts to respond with shorter time. We compare the start-up latency of the time slicing method with the start-up latency of the staging method.

Consider the scenario that n homogeneous streams arrive at an idle system and each stream is divided into m slices, where $n \leq m$. The start-up latency of the ith stream is the time to retrieve i time slices from the tertiary storage system. Thus, the start-up latency of the ith stream using the time slicing method is

$$= i\left(\omega + \alpha + \frac{S}{m\gamma}\right)$$

(18.1)

where $i=1, \ldots, n$ and S is size of each object. The start-up latency of the ith stream using the staging method is

$$= i\left(\omega + \alpha + \frac{S}{\gamma}\right)$$

(18.2)

Comparing the start up latency of the two methods, the time slicing method reduces the response time of the ith stream by

$$= \frac{i(m-1)S}{m\gamma}$$

(18.3)

In the above example, stream X starts to display object X after retrieving X_1 only and the stream Y starts to display object Y after retrieving Y_1 only. If both streams X and Y arrive at an idle system, then the start-up latency of stream X using the staging method is

$$= \omega + \alpha + \frac{S_x}{\gamma}$$

where S_x is the size of object X. The start-up latency of stream X using the time slicing method is

$$= \omega + \alpha + \frac{S_x}{2\gamma}$$

Thus, the start-up latency of stream X is reduced by

$$= \frac{S_x}{2\gamma}$$

In addition, the start-up latency of stream Y using the staging method is

$$= 2\omega + 2\alpha + \frac{S_x + S_y}{\gamma}$$

where S_y is the size of object Y. The start-up latency of stream Y using the time slicing method is

$$= 2\omega + 2\alpha + \frac{S_x + S_y}{2\gamma}$$

Thus, the start-up latency of stream Y is reduced by

$$= \frac{S_x + S_y}{2\gamma}$$

Since the tape drives need to access objects from concurrent streams, the exchanger would switch tapes when a different slice is accessed. Thus, the number of tape switches increases from once per object to once per slice. The extra tape switching overheads are incurred except when both objects reside on the same tape.

Using the time slicing method, the tape drive uses more time in serving each request. The service time of n streams increases. The access time to serve n streams in the staging method is

$$= n\left(\omega + \alpha + \frac{S}{\gamma} \right)$$

However, the access time to serve n streams in the time slicing method is

$$= m * n * \left(\omega + \alpha + \frac{S}{m\gamma} \right)$$

Thus, the access time to serve n streams is increased by

$$= (m-1) * n * (\omega + \alpha)$$

In the above example, the service time of the two streams X and Y in the staging method is the time to access both objects X and Y. This is also equal to the start-up latency of stream Y. Thus, the total service time of the two object requests in the staging method is

$$= 2\omega + 2\alpha + \frac{S_x + S_y}{\gamma}$$

The total service time of the two object requests using the time slicing method is

$$= 2 * \left(\omega + \alpha + \frac{S_x}{2\gamma} \right) + 2 * \left(\omega + \alpha + \frac{S_y}{2\gamma} \right)$$

$$= 4\omega + 4\alpha + \frac{S_x + S_y}{\gamma}$$

Thus, the total service time of the two object requests is increased by

$$= 2\omega + 2\alpha$$

In the time slicing method, only the beginning part of the objects is accessed prior to consumption. If a stream is canceled in the middle of consumption, the access stream is removed. The tape library no longer retrieves the rest of the objects. Thus, the time slicing method may save workloads on the tertiary storage system in such situations.

Application Note: *The time slicing method is a method to reduce the response time of staging. This method is applicable only when the tape drive bandwidth is at least twice of the data consumption rates of objects. That is, time to retrieve two objects is shorter than the time to display each object. The time slice method has been designed for homogeneous streams only. It is necessary to expand it to the heterogeneous streams environment for more flexible and practical systems.*

Chapter Summary

The time slicing method accesses objects at the unit of slices instead of objects. It reduces the start-up latency in accessing objects from the tertiary storage devices. Streams can start to respond at an earlier time. It also saves tape drive bandwidth if some streams are canceled when objects are canceled in the middle of consumption. Unfortunately, extra tape switching overheads are incurred unless all concurrent objects reside on the same tape. The service time in accessing objects is however increased.

References

Lau, S. W., Lui, J., & Wong, P. C. (1995). A cost-effective near-line storage server for multimedia systems. In *Proceedings of the 11th International Conference over Data Engineering* (pp. 449-456).

Chapter XIX

Normal Pipelining

Introduction

Multimedia objects can be stored on tertiary storage devices to provide large storage capacity at low cost. The staging method retrieves the whole objects to the staging buffers prior to consumption. Thus, the start-up latency is high. The time slice method being described in the last chapter reduces the start-up latency only when the tertiary storage bandwidth is higher than double of the displaying data rate of the object.

However, if the tertiary storage bandwidth is below double of the data consumption rate of the object, then we can only stage the object prior to using it. The pipelining methods aim at minimizing the start-up latency when the tertiary storage bandwidth is not higher than the data consumption rate of the objects. The pipelining methods are used to reduce the start-up latency and staging buffer size.

In the normal pipelining method, the sizes of the slices are minimized to maximize the overlapping between the displaying time and the retrieval time of the slices. In the space efficient pipelining methods, the buffer size in accessing the slices is minimized. In the segmented pipelining method, the latency in serving interactive requests is reduced.

The normal pipelining method is described in this chapter. The space efficient pipelining method and the segmented pipelining method are presented in the following two chapters.

We shall describe the objective of the normal pipelining method. Then, the bounds on the sizes of the slices are shown. After that, the start-up latency and the minimum size of the first slice are shown. The reduction in the start-up latency using the normal pipelining method is presented.

The Normal Pipelining Method

The normal pipelining method splits the objects and retrieves the objects while displaying the object. Its objective is to maximize the overlapping time between the retrieval time and the displaying time. Its approach is to retrieve only sufficiently large front part of the object to start the stream, and overlap the retrieval time of the rest with the displaying time of the object (Wang, Hua, & Young, 1996).

The normal pipelining method considers the condition that the data transfer rate of the tertiary storage device is lower than the displaying rate of the object. It assumes that the data of the object are consumed at linearly with the displaying of the object. Since each object is considered separately, the streams can be heterogeneous.

The normal pipelining method divides each object into a sequence of $n+1$ slices $S_0, S_1, \ldots, S_n$. Its idea is to control the size of each slice so that the display time of a slice S_i is longer than the time to retrieve the next slice S_{i+1}, where $0 \leq i \leq n-1$. The normal pipelining method retrieves and displays the object as shown in Figure 19.1. The tertiary storage device first retrieves S_0. The stream starts to display the object after the slice S_0 is retrieved. Then, it retrieves S_1 during the time that the stream is displaying S_0. The tertiary storage device should have retrieved the next slice S_1 before the stream has finished displaying S_0. After the tertiary storage device has retrieved S_1, it continues to retrieve the next slice S_2. When the stream has displayed S_0, the

Figure 19.1. Overlapping time in retrieving and displaying slices of a stream

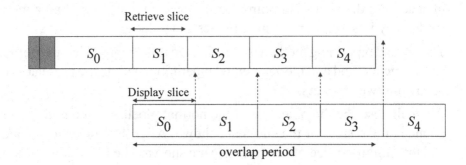

next slice S_1 is ready. Thus, the stream can continue to display the slice S_1 and so on. Thus, the stream is supplied with slices of data so that it can display the entire stream continuously.

Let γ be the data transfer rate of the tertiary storage device and δ be the data consumption rate of the objects. The production consumption rate (PCR) is defined as the ratio between the transfer rate of the tertiary storage device and the data consumption rate of the object. Let ρ be the production consumption rate of an object stored on a tertiary storage device. Thus, we get

$$\rho = \frac{\gamma}{\delta} \tag{19.1}$$

As the transfer bandwidth of the tertiary storage device is lower than the data consumption rate of the objects, we have

$$\gamma \le \delta$$
$$\Rightarrow \rho \le 1 \tag{19.2}$$

Let X_i be the size of the ith slice, S_i, where $0 \le i \le n$. The time to access the first slice, S_0, is

$$= \omega + \alpha + \frac{X_0}{\gamma} \tag{19.3}$$

where ω is the exchange time and α is the reposition time.

When the object is stored contiguously on the same media unit, the time to access the ith slice, S_i, is

$$= \frac{X_i}{\gamma}, \qquad i = 1, 2, ..., n$$

(19.4)

The time to display the ith slice, S_i, is

$$= \frac{X_i}{\delta}, \qquad i = 0, 1, 2, ..., n$$

(19.5)

Since the time to display the ith slice is longer than the time to retrieve the $(i+1)$th slice, we have

$$\frac{X_i}{\gamma} \leq \frac{X_{i-1}}{\delta} \qquad i = 1, 2, ..., n-1$$

$$\Leftrightarrow X_i \leq \frac{\gamma}{\delta} * X_{i-1} \qquad i = 1, 2, ..., n-1$$

$$\Leftrightarrow X_i \leq \rho * X_{i-1} \qquad i = 1, 2, ..., n-1$$

(19.6)

We substitute the value of X_{i-1} into the equation of X_i to get

$$X_i \leq \rho * X_{i-1} \leq \rho * \left(\rho * X_{i-2}\right)$$

$$\Rightarrow X_i \leq \rho^2 * X_{i-2}$$

(19.7)

Repeating the above substitutions, we get

$$X_i \leq \rho * X_{i-1} \leq \rho^2 * X_{i-2} \leq ... \leq \rho^{i-1} * X_1 \leq \rho^i * X_0$$

$$\Rightarrow X_i \leq \rho^i * X_0 \qquad \text{for} \quad i = 1, 2, ..., n$$

(19.8)

Therefore, the sizes of the slices are bounded above by the size of the first slice. Conversely, the size of the first slice is also bounded below by the size of other slices. Thus, we get

$$X_0 \geq \frac{X_i}{\rho^i}, \quad \text{for} \quad i = 1, 2, ..., n$$

(19.9)

From the above two equations, we can see that if ρ is less than 1, the sizes of the slices decrease monotonically. If ρ is equal to 1, the sizes of all slices may decrease monotonically or they may be the same.

When we sum over all values of i from 0 to n, we get

$$\sum_{i=1}^{n-1} X_i \leq \sum_{i=1}^{n-1} \rho^i * X_0$$

$$\Leftrightarrow \sum_{i=1}^{n} X_i \leq X_0 \sum_{i=1}^{n} \rho^i$$

(19.10)

We add the term X_0 to both sides of the inequality to get,

$$X_0 + \sum_{i=1}^{n} X_i \leq X_0 + X_0 \sum_{i=1}^{n} \rho^i$$

$$\Leftrightarrow \sum_{i=0}^{n} X_i \leq X_0 \sum_{i=0}^{n} \rho^i$$

$$\Leftrightarrow \sum_{i=0}^{n} X_i \leq X_0 \left(1 + \rho + ... + \rho^n \right)$$

(19.11)

The left hand side of the inequality is the total sum of the slice sizes. It is thus equal to the size of the object. The right hand side of the inequality is the sum of a geometric series. If ρ is less than or equal to 1, then we get

$$X \leq X_0 \left(\frac{1-\rho^{n+1}}{1-\rho} \right)$$

(19.12)

or

$$X_0 \geq X \left(\frac{1-\rho}{1-\rho^{n+1}} \right)$$

(19.13)

where X is the size of the object.

In addition, if the production consumption ratio, ρ, is greater than or equal to 1, then the tape transfer rate is higher than the data consumption rate. As the data block's displaying time is longer than its retrieval time, we may just use the same size to all the slices. In order to minimize the start-up latency, this size should be set to the size of one data block. Thus, we have established a lower bound on the size of the first slice, X_0, based on the size of the object, the number of slices, and the production consumption ratio when the production consumption ratio is less than 1.

As shown in Figure 19.2, the retrieval time of the second slice to the last slice overlaps with the displaying time of all except the last slice. The non-overlapping time consists of the retrieval time of the first slice, S_0, and the displaying time of the last slice, S_n. Thus, it is necessary to minimize the size of the first slice and the size of the last slice to optimize the benefits of the normal pipelining method.

In order to supply the data with continuity, the time to display the sequence $\{ S_0, S_1, \ldots, S_{i-2}, S_{i-1} \}$ should be longer than the time to materialize the sequence $\{ S_1, S_2, \ldots, S_{i-1}, S_i \}$, for $i = 1, 2, \ldots, n$. Thus, we have

$$\frac{X_0}{\delta} + \frac{X_1}{\delta} + \ldots + \frac{X_{i-1}}{\delta} + \geq \frac{X_1}{\gamma} + \frac{X_2}{\gamma} + \ldots + \frac{X_i}{\gamma}, \qquad i = 1, 2, \ldots, n$$

$$\Leftrightarrow \frac{X_0 + X_1 + \ldots + X_{i-1}}{\delta} \geq \frac{X_1 + X_2 + \ldots + X_i}{\gamma}, \qquad i = 1, 2, \ldots, n.$$

Figure 19.2. Reducing slice sizes in the normal pipelining method

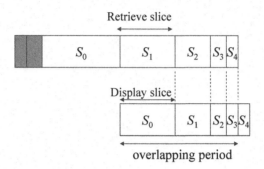

In particular, when $i = n$, the data consumption time of the sequence $\{S_1, S_2, \ldots, S_n\}$ is longer than the displaying time of $\{S_0, S_1, \ldots, S_{n-1}\}$. It is equivalent to say that the data consumption of all but the first slice eclipses the displaying time of all but the last slice. Thus, we have

$$\frac{X_0 + X_1 + \ldots + X_{n-1}}{\delta} \geq \frac{X_1 + X_2 + \ldots + X_n}{\gamma}$$

$$\Leftrightarrow \frac{X - X_n}{\delta} \geq \frac{X - X_0}{\gamma}$$

$$\Leftrightarrow \frac{\gamma}{\delta}\left(X - X_n\right) \geq X - X_0$$

$$\Leftrightarrow X - X_0 \leq \rho\left(X - X_n\right)$$

$$\Leftrightarrow X - \rho\left(X - X_n\right) \leq X_0$$

$$\Leftrightarrow X_0 \geq X - \rho\left(X - X_n\right)$$

$$\Leftrightarrow X_0 \geq X\left(1 - \rho\right) + \rho X_n. \tag{19.14}$$

The size of the first slice is bounded below by a function of the object's size, the production consumption ratio, and the size of the last slice.

The start-up latency to display the object using the normal pipelining method is the time to retrieve the first slice, X_0, and it is equal to

$$= \omega + \alpha + \frac{X_0}{\gamma} \tag{19.15}$$

Thus, the reduction in the start-up latency using the pipelining method is

$$= \frac{X - X_0}{\gamma} \tag{19.16}$$

To optimize the start-up latency of the normal pipelining method, the size of the first slice should be minimized. Thus, the size of S_0 needs to be as small as possible. To achieve this, the last slice, S_n, must be as small as possible.

As the slices are retrieved from the tertiary storage devices in integral number of data blocks, the smallest size of a slice is one data block. Thus, we have

$$X_0 \geq X(1-\rho) + \rho \tag{19.17}$$

Therefore, the minimum size of the first slice is approximately equal to

$$\approx X(1-\rho) \tag{19.18}$$

The start-up latency to display the object using the staging method is

$$= \omega + \alpha + \frac{X_0}{\gamma}$$

The start-up latency to display the object using the normal pipelining method is the time to retrieve the first slice, X_0, and it is equal to

$$= \omega + \alpha + \frac{X_0}{\gamma} \tag{19.19}$$

Therefore, the normal pipelining method minimizes the start-up latency and the start-up latency is reduced by

$$= \frac{X - X_0}{\gamma} \qquad\qquad (19.20)$$

The normal pipelining method copies only the minimally sufficient size of the object prior to consuming it. When the sufficiently large fraction of the object is copied, the stream can start to display the object while the tertiary storage device continues to retrieve the rest of the object. Therefore, the normal pipelining method minimizes the start-up latency in the low tertiary bandwidth environments.

Application Note: *A limitation of the normal pipelining method is that only the retrieved portion of the object can be consumed before the entire object is copied to the staging buffer. The object is copied to the staging buffers similar to the staging method. The object could stay on the staging buffers for a period of time so that the object can be reused or displayed again from the staging buffers.*

Chapter Summary

The normal pipelining method has been explained in this chapter. The normal pipelining method finds the minimum fraction of the object before the stream can start to display it. It minimizes the start-up latency for the tertiary storage devices whose data transfer rate is lower than the data consumption rate of the objects. The formula to find minimum size of the first slices is explained in this chapter. We have also described the start-up latency in using the normal pipelining method.

References

Wang, J. Z., Hua, K. A., & Young, H. C. (1996). SEP: A space efficient pipelining technique for managing disk buffers in multimedia servers. In *Proceedings of IEEE Multimedia'96* (pp. 598-607).

Chapter XX

Space Efficient Pipelining

Introduction

Multimedia objects that are stored on tertiary storage devices enjoy the large storage capacity at low cost. These objects may be retrieved using staging, time slicing, or pipelining. The staging method retrieves the whole objects to the staging buffers prior to consumption at the cost of high start-up latency. The time slice method reduces the start-up latency at the cost of heavy switching overheads. The pipelining methods aim at minimizing the start-up latency when the tertiary storage bandwidth is not higher than the data consumption rate of the objects. Three pipelining methods are used to reduce the start-up latency and staging buffer size:

1. Normal pipelining
2. Space efficient pipelining
3. Segmented pipelining

In the normal pipelining method, the sizes of the slices are minimized to maximize the overlapping between the displaying time and the retrieval time of the slices. In the space efficient pipelining (SEP) methods, the buffer size in accessing the slices is minimized. In the segmented pipelining method, the latency in serving interactive requests is reduced.

We have described the normal pipelining method in the previous chapter. The space efficient pipelining method is explained in this chapter. The segmented pipelining method is presented in the next chapter. In this chapter, the basic space efficient pipelining algorithm is first described in the next section. Next, the buffer replacement policies are explained before this chapter is summarized.

The Basic Space Efficient Pipelining Algorithm

The space efficient pipelining method has two objectives:

1. Reduce staging buffer size
2. Hide the start-up latency

The space efficient pipelining algorithm reduces the start-up latency by caching the beginning part of the objects on the secondary storage. It reduces the stage buffer size by re-cycling the disk space (Wang, Hua, & Young, 1996).

The space efficient pipelining method can be used in the following conditions:

1. Objects are stored on tapes or CD with low bandwidth.
2. Disk space is available to store temporary data.
3. Objects are retrieved for display purpose only.

Similar to the normal pipelining method, the space efficient pipelining method divides each object into a sequence of $n+1$ slices, $\{S_0, S_1, \dots, S_n\}$. The first slice, S_0, of an object is called the head of the object and other slices, including S_1, S_2, to S_n, of the object are called the tail of the object (Wang et al., 1996).

The head of objects is stored on the resident disk that can be accessed with low latency as shown in Figure 20.1. The head of objects is accessed from the disk storage directly to the memory buffer for display. If the storage space of the disks is insufficient to store the head of all objects, the objects with high popularity may be chosen to be stored. The head of other objects may be stored on the tertiary storage devices and accessed on demand.

The tail of the objects is stored on magnetic tapes or optical disks which have large storage capacity and low cost. The tail of objects is loaded on demand via a circular buffer on disks. Similar to the staging buffer, the circular disk temporarily stores the data retrieved from the tertiary storage devices. The name "circular disk buffer" does not mean that the disk space has any shape. It only indicates that the disk buffer space is allocated and it uses two pointers to indicate the starting position of the used area and the starting position of the vacant area. The buffer space switches between the "used" and "free" status in cycles.

As shown in Figure 20.1, the new data of the objects on the tertiary storage devices are read to the circular disk buffer. The free space of the circular disk buffer is used when data from the tertiary storage devices are stored. Data on the circular disk buffer are then read to the memory buffer for consumption. Although the circular disk buffer and the disk cache are drawn separately on Figure 20.1, they may reside on the same disk or separate disks.

Figure 20.1. Space efficient pipelining

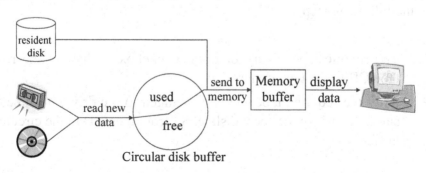

When an object is being accessed, the storage system retrieves the object from both the resident disks and the tertiary storage devices. The storage system serves the object request and accesses the objects as illustrated in Figure 20.2, Figure 20.3, and Figure 20.4.

After a new stream is accepted, the storage system starts to retrieve the object by performing the following actions in parallel:

1.   It retrieves the head, S_0, of objects from the resident disks to memory.
2.   It retrieves the tail of the object from tertiary storage devices to the circular buffer.
3.   It retrieves the tail of the object from the circular disk buffer to memory.

Although a user program only runs sequentially from the beginning to the end, a program may initiate several threads or tasks to run in parallel. These threads could check for synchronization points when necessary. In addition, the stream displays the object continuously when the necessary slices are ready. It also runs in parallel with the storage system.

The first thread accesses the head of the object directly from the resident disk to the memory as shown in Figure 20.2. The stream uses a memory buffer to control the variations in disk bandwidth. The size of the memory buffer is only a few data blocks and it may be much smaller than the size of the head. The stream starts to display after the memory buffer is filled. The stream continues to display the object while the head of the object is being retrieved from the resident disks to the memory buffer.

The second thread retrieves the tail of the object from the tertiary storage devices to the memory buffer via the circular disk buffer as shown in Figure 20.3. The second slice of the object should be ready at the memory buffer before the head of the object has been consumed completely. It is retrieved in the following steps:

1.   The robotic tape library or optical jukebox exchanges the required tape/CD to the tape/optical drive.
2.   After the required tape/CD is exchanged to the drive, it immediately starts to retrieve the second slice, S_1, from tape/CD to the circular disk buffer.

Figure 20.2. The space efficient pipelining method retrieves the head of object from resident disks to memory before displaying the object.

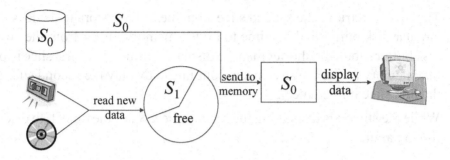

Figure 20.3. The space efficient pipelining method retrieves the second slice from tape or CD to memory via the circular disk buffer.

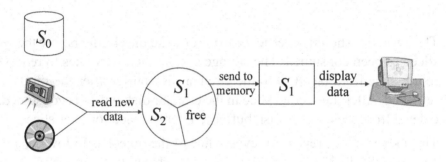

Figure 20.4. The space efficient pipelining method retrieves and displays the slices from tape or CD via the circular disk buffer.

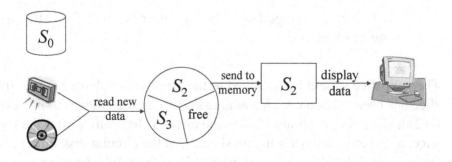

The third thread waits until the first slice of the object, S_0, is completely retrieved to the memory buffer. It then retrieves the second slice from the circular disk buffer to fill the memory.

The time to retrieve the second slice from the tertiary storage devices to the circular disk buffer and the time to fill the memory buffer from the circular disk buffer should be shorter than the displaying time of the first slice in order that memory buffer the stream can continue to display the second slice after the first slice immediately.

While the stream is displaying the second slice, S_1, of the object, two actions run in parallel:

1. The second slice is retrieved from the circular disk buffer to the memory buffer.
2. The tertiary storage device retrieves the third slice, S_2, to the circular disk buffer.

The third slice should be retrieved to the circular disk buffer before the second slice has been consumed. The storage system then continues to retrieve the fourth slice from tape/CD to the circular disk buffer after the third slice is retrieved. After the second slice in the circular disk buffer is consumed, it is deleted from the circular disk buffer to release space for later slices.

The above actions repeat for every slice of the object as follows. While the stream is displaying the ith slice, S_i, of the object, two actions run in parallel:

1. The ith slice, S_i, is retrieved from the circular disk buffer to the memory buffer.
2. The tertiary storage device retrieves the next slice, S_{i+1}, to the circular disk buffer.

The next slice should be retrieved to the circular disk buffer before the ith slice has been consumed. The storage system then continues to retrieve the $(i+2)$th slice, S_{i+2}, from tape/CD to the circular disk buffer after the $(i+1)$th slice, S_i, is retrieved. After the ith slice, S_i, in the circular disk buffer is consumed, it is deleted from the circular disk buffer to release space.

Therefore, the circular disk buffer contains at least two slices. While the storage system is retrieving the ith slice from and storing the $(i+1)$th slice, S_{i+1}, to the circular disk buffer, the circular disk buffer contains the ith and the $(i+1)$th slices, that is S_i and S_{i+1}. We shall find the size of the circular disk buffer and the start-up latency in the next section.

Circular Buffer Size and Start-Up Latency

Let X_i be the size of the ith slice, S_i. The storage space on the resident disks for an object is

$$= X_0.$$

From last chapter, we have

$$X_0 \geq X(1 - \rho) + \rho \tag{20.1}$$

and

$$X_0 \approx X(1 - \rho) \tag{20.2}$$

where X is the size of the object and ρ is the production consumption ratio of the object on the tertiary storage devices. Therefore, the minimum size amount of storage space on the resident disks for an object is approximately equal to

$$\approx X(1 - \rho) \tag{20.3}$$

The circular disk buffer needs to contain the two consecutive largest slices. If the production consumption ratio, ρ, is less than or equal to 1, the circular disk buffer is the largest when it is storing the two slices, S_1 and S_2. Thus, the size of the circular disk buffer is found as

$$= X_1 + X_2$$

Since $X_i \leq \rho^i * X_0$ and the overlapping is maximized when

$$X_i = \rho^i * X_0 \tag{20.4}$$

Thus, the size of the circular disk buffer is

$$
\begin{aligned}
&= \rho X_0 + \rho^2 X_0 \\
&= \rho(1 + \rho)X_0 \\
&\approx \rho(1 + \rho)(1 - \rho)X \\
&\approx \rho(1 - \rho^2)X
\end{aligned}
\tag{20.5}
$$

Therefore, the size of the circular disk buffer is approximately equal to $\rho(1-\rho^2)X$.

Since the stream starts to display immediately after the head of the object is copied to the memory buffer, this is very small when compared to the start-up latency in the staging method or the normal pipelining method. Thus, it hides the start-up latency by keeping the head of the object resident on disks.

Buffer Replacement Policies

There are three buffer replacement policies available for the space efficient pipelining method (Wang et al., 1996). They are:

- The basic policy
- The shrinking buffer policy
- The space stealing policy

The basic policy uses the largest circular buffer until display finishes. It reuses the circular buffer to store the tail part of the objects. The shrinking buffer policy reduces the circular buffer size after a slice is displayed. It will use the buffer space more efficiently. This is particularly useful when the buffer constraint is tight.

While the storage system is retrieving the ith slice from and storing the $(i+1)$th slice, S_{i+1}, to the circular disk buffer, the circular disk buffer contains the ith and the $(i+1)$th slices, that is S_i and S_{i+1}. If the ith slice, S_i, and the $(i+1)$th slice, S_{i+1}, are stored on the circular disk buffer, the size of the circular disk buffer is

$$
\begin{aligned}
&= X_i + X_{i+1} \\
&= \rho^i X_0 + \rho^{i+1} X_0 \\
&\approx \rho^i (1 + \rho)(1 - \rho) X \\
&\approx \rho^i (1 - \rho^2) X
\end{aligned}
\tag{20.6}
$$

The space stealing policy uses the space containing the head part of the object as part of the circular buffer to reduce the space requirement. Since the head part of the object is not required when the tail part is being displayed, this policy can significantly reduce the circular disk buffer space requirement.

As the size of the first slice is larger than the size of all other slices when the production consumption ratio is less than or equal to 1, the circular disk buffer is the largest when the second slice is being retrieved from the tape or CD. Thus, the size of the circular disk buffer is

$$
\begin{aligned}
&= X_1 \\
&= \rho X_0 \\
&\approx \rho (1 - \rho) X
\end{aligned}
\tag{20.7}
$$

Thus, the total size of object on the resident disk and the circular disk buffer is

$$
\begin{aligned}
&= X_0 + X_1 \\
&\approx (1 - \rho^2) X
\end{aligned}
\tag{20.8}
$$

Application Note: *Since the storage space containing the head part is modified, the head part should be restored after the entire object is displayed. Thus, the space stealing policy will increase the workload in retrieving objects from hierarchical storage systems.*

Chapter Summary

The space efficient pipelining method is designed for pipelining objects from low bandwidth storage devices for display. It retrieves data at a rate lower than the data consumption rate. It keeps the front part of objects resident on disk cache to start a new stream at disk latency. It uses the disk space efficiently to handle more streams.

The basic policy reuses the circular buffer to store the later slices of the objects. Thus, the circular disk buffer only contains the second and the third slices. The shrinking buffer policy reduces the circular buffer size after a slice is displayed. It is particularly useful when the circular disk buffer constraint is tight. The space stealing policy reuses the storage space containing the head of the object as part of the circular buffer. However, the head of the object should be restored after the object is displayed and this leads to increased workloads.

References

Wang, J. Z., Hua, K. A., & Young, H. C. (1996). SEP: SEP: A space efficient pipelining technique for managing disk buffers in multimedia servers. In *Proceedings of IEEE Multimedia '96* (pp. 598-607).

Chapter XXI

Segmented Pipelining

Introduction

The robotic tape library and optical jukebox provide huge and cheap capacity for the storage of multimedia objects. The stored objects may be retrieved using staging, time slicing, or pipelining. The staging method retrieves the whole objects to the staging buffers prior to consumption at the cost of high start-up latency. The time slice method reduces the start-up latency at the cost of heavy switching overheads. The pipelining methods aim at minimizing the start-up latency.

In the normal pipelining method, the sizes of the slices are minimized to maximize the overlapping between the displaying time and the retrieval time of the slices. In space efficient pipelining methods, the buffer size in accessing the slices is minimized. We have already described the normal pipelining and the space efficient pipelining methods in the two previous chapters. The segmented pipelining method to reduce the latency in serving interactive requests is presented in this chapter.

Multimedia objects are usually displayed from the beginning to the end in video on demand systems. Interactive video-on-demand systems support VCR-like functions, including fast forward, rewind, pause, and resume functions. Large video systems store many objects. The video systems should allow some searching to allow users find the desired objects. When searching is required, the video-on-demand system would need to provide browsing, jump, keyword, and content based searching.

Unless the staging method is used, the multimedia storage system cannot support any VCR-like operations. The segmented pipelining method is designed to provide efficient retrieval of multimedia objects with supporting of previews.

In this chapter, the segmented pipelining method is first described in the next section. The performance of the segmented pipelining method is then described and analyzed before this chapter is summarized.

Segmented Pipelining

The segmented pipelining method has three objectives:

1. It supports efficient pipelining at limited disk bandwidth.
2. It supports browsing of objects by previews.
3. It supports jumping operations to start at any segments.

The segment pipelining method uses the following techniques to store and retrieve the objects:

1. The object is divided into a number of independent logical segments. Each segment is divided into time slices according to pipelining.
2. The first slice of every segment is stored on disks to hide the start-up latency. The initial part of the first slice of every segment together forms the preview files. The remaining part of the first slice of every segment forms the preload data.

3.   All other slices of every segment are stored on tertiary storage devices and they are migrated while the object is being displayed. Each slice is accessed from the tertiary storage devices to the disks while the previous slice is being displayed.

In the segmented pipelining method, multimedia objects are divided into independent logical segments (Tse & Leung, 1998). Each segment can start to display without dependence on the previous or later segments. If the object is compressed using the MPEG compression method, the first frame should be an I-frame. Logical segments are logical divisions of a video. Two logical segments have different logical meanings such that each logical segment expresses a different meaning to the users. For example, a logical segment may indicate a camera shot or a scene. The breaking points are suitable positions to start viewing a video without losing important information.

Each logical segment is divided into time slices as shown in Figure 21.1. Similar to the pipelining method, the time to display a slice is longer than the time to retrieve the next slice from the tertiary storage device. Thus, the slices are retrieved continuously from the tertiary storage device when the stream is displaying. We have changed the granularity for pipelining from the objects to logical segments. The granularity is coarse when each object is divided into slices for pipelining. The granularity is fine when each segment

Figure 21.1. Video segmentation

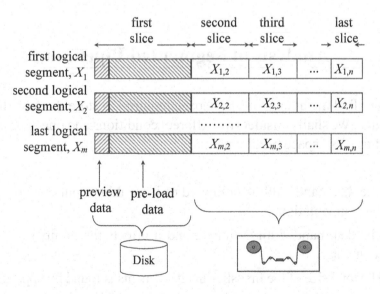

is divided into slices for pipelining. The change in granularity of pipelining affects the total percentage of objects being included in the first slices.

The first slice of every segment is stored on disks to hide the start-up latency. The first slice of each segment is further divided into an initial part and a remaining part. The initial part of the first slice of every segment is placed together to form the preview file of the object. This preview file is kept resident on disks to allow previewing quickly. Since the initial part of the first slice of different segments comes from different segments of the object, the user can view these initial parts from the disks to preview the object before actually viewing it. If the user is satisfied that this object should be viewed, the actual object will be pipelined from the tertiary storage devices.

The remaining part of the first slice of every segment is the preload data of the object. These preload data may reside on the disks similar to the preview file. When the amount of disk space is insufficient to store the first slices of all segments, the preload data of some cold objects may be loaded on demand from the tertiary storage devices.

All other slices of every segment should be stored on tertiary storage devices and they are migrated while the object is being displayed. While the user is displaying the first slice of a segment, the second slice of the same segment is being retrieved from the tertiary storage device. The second slice should have been retrieved before the first slice has finished displaying. The third slice is retrieved while the second slice is being displayed. Each slice is retrieved while the previous slice of the same segment is being displayed.

Analysis of Segmented Pipelining

We shall find the amount of disk space required to store the first slice of all segments. We shall consider two different conditions and one approximation to find the disk space requirement:

1.   The disk bandwidth is unlimited or it would not put any constraint on the segmentation.
2.   The disk bandwidth is limited and it affects the number of slices per segments.
3.   The total size of the first slice in all segments is found by approximation.

Afterwards, the reposition latency to serve jumping requests is found.

In these analyses, we use these notations. Let ω be the exchange time, α be the reposition time, and γ be the tape transfer rate of tertiary storage device. An object of size X is divided into m segments such that the size of the ith segment is X_i, for $i = 1, 2, \ldots, m$. Let δ be the data consumption rate and ρ be the production consumption ratio of the object. The ith segment is divided into n slices such that $X_{i,j}$ is the size of the jth slice of the ith segment.

Unlimited Disk Bandwidth

In the first condition, the preload data of the first slice reside on the disks with sufficient bandwidth to deliver the object without any bandwidth constraints and the logical segments can be as long as possible. The size of the slices can easily be found below.

Since the segment is pipelined from the tertiary storage devices, we apply equation (19.17) to find the size of the first slice as

$$X_{i,1} \geq X_i(1 - \rho) + \rho \qquad (21.1)$$

The size of the jth slice of the ith segment can be found as

$$X_{i,j} \leq \rho^{j-1} X_{i,1} \qquad (21.2)$$

The total disk space being consumed for the first slices of all segments is

$$\sum_{i=1}^{m} X_{i,1} \geq \sum_{i=1}^{m} \left[X_i (1 - \rho) + \rho \right]$$

$$\Rightarrow \sum_{i=1}^{m} X_{i,1} \geq m\rho + (1 - \rho) \sum_{i=1}^{m} X_i$$

$$\Rightarrow \sum_{i=1}^{m} X_{i,1} \geq m\rho + (1 - \rho) X \qquad (21.3)$$

Limited Disk Bandwidth

In the second condition, the preload data may not reside on the same disk containing the staging buffers. When the disk bandwidth to retrieve the preload data is insufficient or the preload data are loaded from slower disks than the staging buffers, we need to consider the disk bandwidth in serving requests on accessing the preload data of the first slice of segments in order to ensure stream continuity. The first slice of the next segment is retrieved from disk while the last slice of the previous segment is displaying.

To simplify the analysis, we assume that all segments are divided into the same number of slices. In order to ensure that the multimedia object can be displayed continuously, the display time of the first slice of each segment should be longer than the access time of the second slice of the same segment. Since the second slice of a segment is the first slice of the segment being accessed, the access time should include the exchange time, reposition time, and the transfer time. Thus, we have

$$\frac{X_{i,1}}{\delta} \geq \omega + \alpha + \frac{X_{i,2}}{\gamma}, \quad \text{for } i, \ 0 < i < m. \tag{21.4}$$

In addition, the display time of each slice should be longer than the transfer time of the next slice. Thus, we get

$$\frac{X_{i,j}}{\delta} \geq \frac{X_{i,j+1}}{\gamma}, \quad \text{for } 1 < j < n \text{ and } 0 < i < m. \tag{21.5}$$

Since the display time of the last slice of a segment is longer than the retrieval time of the first slice of the next segment, we have

$$\frac{X_{i,n}}{\delta} \geq \frac{X_{i+1,1}}{\beta}, \quad \text{for } 0 < i < m. \tag{21.6}$$

where β is the disk bandwidth. The disk bandwidth can be found as the average of data size divided by the access time.

Since the segment sizes and slice sizes can be very different, we use the mean segment size and the mean slice size. Letting be the mean size of all logical segments and $\overline{X_j}$ be the mean size of the jth slices of segments, we have

$$\overline{X} = \frac{X}{m}$$

(21.7)

and

$$\overline{X_j} = \frac{1}{m} \sum_{i=1}^{m} X_{i,j}$$

(21.8)

We apply the mean average to equations (21.4) to (21.6) to get

$$\frac{\overline{X_1}}{\delta} \geq \omega + \alpha + \frac{\overline{X_2}}{\gamma}$$

(21.9)

$$\frac{\overline{X_j}}{\delta} \geq \frac{\overline{X_{j+1}}}{\gamma} \ , \quad \text{for } 1 < j < n,$$

(21.10)

and

$$\frac{\overline{X_n}}{\delta} \geq \frac{\overline{X_1}}{\beta}$$

(21.11)

When more slices are created in each segment, the pipeline method is more efficient. The continuous display requirements however impose limitations on the maximum number of slices per segment and the size of the slices. We apply equation (21.10) repeatedly to get

$$\overline{X_n} \leq \frac{\gamma}{\delta} \overline{X_{n-1}} \leq \cdots \leq (\frac{\gamma}{\delta})^{n-2} \overline{X_2},$$

$$\Rightarrow \overline{X_j} \geq \left(\frac{\delta}{\gamma}\right)^{n-j} \overline{X_n}, \quad \text{for } 1 < j < n.$$

(21.12)

From equation (21.9), we have

$$\Rightarrow \overline{X_1} \geq (\omega + \alpha)\delta + \left(\frac{\delta}{\gamma}\right)^{n-1} \overline{X_n}$$

(21.13)

We combine the two equations (21.12) and (21.13) above to get both the lower and upper bounds on the first slice

$$(\omega + \alpha)\delta + \left(\frac{\delta}{\gamma}\right)^{n-1}\overline{X_n} \le \overline{X_1} \le \frac{\beta}{\delta}\overline{X_n} \qquad (21.14)$$

Thus, we get

$$(\omega + \alpha)\delta + \left(\frac{\delta}{\gamma}\right)^{n-1}\overline{X_n} \le \frac{\beta}{\delta}\overline{X_n} \qquad (21.15)$$

Since the ω, α, δ, and $\overline{X_n}$ all have positive values, we get

$$\left(\frac{\delta}{\gamma}\right)^{n-1}\overline{X_n} < \frac{\beta}{\delta}\overline{X_n}$$

$$\Rightarrow \frac{\beta}{\delta} > \left(\frac{\delta}{\gamma}\right)^{n-1}$$

$$\Rightarrow \log\left(\frac{\beta}{\delta}\right) > (n-1)\log\left(\frac{\delta}{\gamma}\right)$$

$$\Rightarrow n < \frac{\log(\beta) - \log(\delta)}{\log(\delta) - \log(\gamma)} + 1 \qquad (21.16)$$

We have arrived at an upper bound on the number of slices per segment. In order to achieve the maximum pipeline efficiency, we should divide each segment into the maximum number of slices. Since n is an integer, we may use the floor function to get

$$n = \left\lfloor \frac{\log(\beta/\delta)}{\log(\delta/\gamma)} \right\rfloor + 1 \qquad (21.17)$$

This is the maximum number of slices per segment according to the disk bandwidth, tertiary bandwidth, and the data consumption rate. For short logical segments, the number of slices in these short segments could be less. For long logical segments, the number of slices is bounded by this maximum number of slices per segment. The long segments may be handled one of two ways below:

1. The sizes of all slices are increased proportionally.
2. The long segments are broken down into multiple short segments.

When the sizes of the slices are increased proportionally, the sizes of the slices depend on the number of slices per segment. However, the slices could become very large when $\frac{\beta}{\delta} - \left(\frac{\delta}{\gamma}\right)^{n-1}$ is close to zero. In such a condition, only a few segments are created. The size of the first slice also increases proportionally. The first slice becomes large leading to high user latency. The data segmentation method becomes ineffective. Therefore, the pipeline efficiency should be slightly traded off for effective data segmentation by slightly reducing the number of slices being used.

Instead of increasing the sizes of all slices, long logical segments should be divided into shorter segments such that the number of slices in this segment does not exceed this maximum number of slices per segment. We shall establish the length of each segment below.

Since the size of each slice should be at least one media block, the size of the last slice is at least one media block. Thus, we have

$$\overline{X_n} \geq M \tag{21.18}$$

where M is the size of one media block.

From equation (21.5) above, we also get

$$\frac{X_{i,j}}{\delta} \geq \frac{X_{i,j+1}}{\gamma}, \quad \text{for } 1 < j < n \text{ and } 0 < i < m,$$

$$\Rightarrow X_{i,j} \geq \left(\frac{\delta}{\gamma}\right) X_{i,j+1} \geq \left(\frac{\delta}{\gamma}\right)^2 X_{i,j+2} \geq \ldots \geq \left(\frac{\delta}{\gamma}\right)^{n-j} X_{i,n}, \text{ for } 1 < j < n \text{ and } 0 < i < m,$$

$$\Rightarrow X_{i,j} \geq \left(\frac{\delta}{\gamma}\right)^{n-j} M, \text{ for } 1 < j < n \text{ and } 0 < i < m.$$

$$(21.19)$$

In particular, when $j = 2$,

$$X_{i,2} \geq \left(\frac{\delta}{\gamma}\right)^{n-2} M, \quad i, 0 < i < m.$$

$$(21.20)$$

From Equation (21.4), we get

$$\frac{X_{i,1}}{\delta} \geq \omega + \alpha + \frac{X_{i,2}}{\gamma}, \quad i, 0 < i < m,$$

$$\Rightarrow \frac{X_{i,1}}{\delta} \geq \omega + \alpha + \frac{1}{\gamma}\left(\frac{\delta}{\gamma}\right)^{n-2} M, \quad i, 0 < i < m,$$

$$\Rightarrow X_{i,1} \geq (\omega + \alpha)\delta + \left(\frac{\delta}{\gamma}\right)^{n-1} M, \quad i, 0 < i < m,$$

$$(21.21)$$

We sum over all values of j from 1 to n and we get

$$\sum_{j=1}^{n} X_{i,j} \geq (\omega + \alpha)\delta + \sum_{j=1}^{n}\left(\frac{\delta}{\gamma}\right)^{n-j} M, \quad \text{for } 0 < i < m,$$

$$\Rightarrow \sum_{j=1}^{n} X_{i,j} \geq (\omega + \alpha)\delta + M\left[\left(\frac{\delta}{\gamma}\right)^{n-1} + \left(\frac{\delta}{\gamma}\right)^{n-2} + \ldots + 1\right], \quad \text{for } 0 < i < m,$$

$$\Rightarrow X_i \geq (\omega + \alpha)\delta + M \frac{\left(\dfrac{\delta}{\gamma}\right)^n - 1}{\left(\dfrac{\delta}{\gamma}\right) - 1}, \quad \text{for } 0 < i < m.$$

(21.22)

The size of the ith segment that has the maximum number of slices per segment is

$$X_i \geq (\omega + \alpha)\delta + \frac{\left(\dfrac{1}{\rho}\right)^n - 1}{\left(\dfrac{1}{\rho}\right) - 1} M, \quad \text{for } 0 < i < m,$$

$$\Rightarrow X_i \geq (\omega + \alpha)\delta + \frac{\left(1 - \rho^n\right)}{\rho^{n-1}\left(1 - \rho\right)} M, \quad \text{for } 0 < i < m,$$

(21.23)

A logical segment whose length is equal to this lower bound will optimize the pipelining efficiency. The slices are delivered with the maximum overlapping and the first slice is at its minimum size. Therefore, the logical segments are classified as long segments or short segments depending on whether its length exceeds

$$(\omega + \alpha)\delta + \frac{\left(1 - \rho^n\right)}{\rho^{n-1}\left(1 - \rho\right)} M$$

(21.24)

Long logical segments can be split into shorter segments of this length so that each segment can have the maximum number of slices and these segments can be pipelined at the highest efficiency.

If we divide all segments longer than this length into shorter segments, then all the segments have an upper bound on their segment length. In addition, the average segment length also has an upper bound as

$$\overline{X} \le (\omega + \alpha)\delta + \frac{(1-\rho^n)}{\rho^{n-1}(1-\rho)} M$$

(21.25)

where $\overline{X}$ is the mean segment length of the object. The object should be divided into a minimum number of segments such that

$$m\overline{X} \le m\left[(\omega + \alpha)\delta + \frac{(1-\rho^n)}{\rho^{n-1}(1-\rho)} M\right]$$

(21.26)

$$\Rightarrow X \le m\left[(\omega + \alpha)\delta + \frac{(1-\rho^n)}{\rho^{n-1}(1-\rho)} M\right]$$

(21.27)

$$\Rightarrow m \ge \frac{X}{\left[(\omega + \alpha)\delta + \frac{(1-\rho^n)}{\rho^{n-1}(1-\rho)} M\right]}$$

(21.28)

Therefore, each object should be split into the minimum number of segments as shown above.

Since the first slice of all segments should reside on disks permanently, the total size of first slice of all segments can be found as

$$\sum_{i=1}^{m} X_{i,1}$$

$$\Rightarrow \sum_{i=1}^{m} X_{i,1} \ge \sum_{i=1}^{m}\left[(\omega + \alpha)\delta + \left(\frac{\delta}{\gamma}\right)^{n-1} M\right]$$

$$\Rightarrow \sum_{i=1}^{m} X_{i,1} \ge m\left[(\omega + \alpha)\delta + \left(\frac{\delta}{\gamma}\right)^{n-1} M\right]$$

We substitute the lower bound of m to get

$$\sum_{i=1}^{m} X_{i,1} \geq \frac{X\left[(\omega+\alpha)\delta+\left(\dfrac{\delta}{\gamma}\right)^{n-1}M\right]}{\left[(\omega+\alpha)\delta+\dfrac{(1-\rho^n)}{\rho^{n-1}(1-\rho)}M\right]}$$

$$\Rightarrow \sum_{i=1}^{m} X_{i,1} \geq \frac{X\left[(\omega+\alpha)\delta+\dfrac{M}{\rho^{n-1}}\right]}{\left[(\omega+\alpha)\delta+\dfrac{(1-\rho^n)}{\rho^{n-1}(1-\rho)}M\right]}$$

$$\Rightarrow \sum_{i=1}^{m} X_{i,1} \geq \frac{X(1-\rho)\left[(\omega+\alpha)\delta\rho^{n-1}+M\right]}{\left[(\omega+\alpha)\delta\rho^{n-1}(1-\rho)+(1-\rho^n)M\right]}$$

$$(21.29)$$

Therefore, we have found the amount of disk space required to store the first slice of all segments.

Approximation of Disk Space

In the third approach, we find the approximate amount of disk space required. When the number of segments is not many, approximately the same percentage of the object is considered as the first slice of the object. We wish to show that the total size of all first slices is increased by less than m data blocks when m segments are created.

Since the segment is pipelined from the tertiary storage device, we apply equation (19.14) to get

$$X_{i,1} \geq X_i(1-\rho)+\rho X_{i,n}, \quad \text{for } i = 1, 2, \&, m. \qquad (21.30)$$

Summing over all values of i, we get

$$\sum_{i=1}^{m} X_{i,1} \geq \sum_{i=1}^{m} \left[X_i (1-\rho) + \rho X_{i,n} \right]$$

$$\Rightarrow \sum_{i=1}^{m} X_{i,1} \geq (1-\rho) \sum_{i=1}^{m} X_i + \rho \sum_{i=1}^{m} X_{i,n_i}$$

(21.31)

Since the last slice of each segment should not be smaller than one media data block, we have

$$\sum_{i=1}^{m} X_{i,1} \geq (1-\rho) \sum_{i=1}^{m} X_i + \rho * m * M$$

$$\Leftrightarrow \sum_{i=1}^{m} X_{i,1} \geq (1-\rho) X + \rho * m * M$$

(21.32)

Therefore, the difference between the lower bounds in the total size of the first slices due to the change in granularity is

$$= (m-1) * \rho * M$$

(21.33)

Since the production consumption ratio, ρ, is less than 1, the total size of the first slices due to the change in granularity is

$$< (m-1) * M$$

(21.34)

Therefore, the additional number of data blocks in the total size of all first slices is less than one data block for every new segment. This cost is low when the number of logical segments is small. For example, if the production consumption ratio, ρ, of an object in a tertiary storage device is equal to 0.8 and the size of the object is X, then the size of the first slice is approximately equal to

$X*(1 - 0.8)$
$= 0.2X.$

If the object is divided into four segments such that each segment is one quarter of the object, the size of each segment is equal to $X/4$. Thus, the size of each segment is

$$= \frac{X}{4} * (1 - 0.8)$$
$$= 0.05 * X.$$

As there are four segments, the total size of all first slices is equal to

$$= 4 * 0.05 * X$$
$$= 0.2X.$$

Thus, approximately the same percentage of the object is divided as the first slice of the object. Therefore, the change in granularity of pipelining only slightly affects the percentage of an object being included in its first slice.

Reposition Latency

While the stream is displaying, the user may wish to change the current displaying position. The user issues a jump request and the stream starts to access the segment of the object at the new position. The storage system serves these requests and accesses the object at the new position. The segmented pipelining method can serve these interactive requests efficiently. We find the amount of necessary data to retrieve from tertiary storage device for pipelining and the start-up latency to wait prior to display below. We shall find the amount of necessary data under three conditions:

1. The new displaying position is at the beginning of a segment.
2. The new displaying position is inside the first slice of a segment.
3. The new displaying position is within the second to the last slice of a segment.

Afterwards, the reposition latency is found.

If the new displaying position is at the beginning of a segment, the first slice of this segment can be accessed immediately from the disks and subsequent slices can be accessed from the tertiary storage devices. Thus, the reposition latency is the same as disk latency.

If the new displaying position is inside the first slice of a segment, the stream waits for a short time to retrieve some data from the tertiary storage devices before responding to the stream request. Let Y be the new displaying position from the beginning of the segment in number of data blocks.

The size of the ith segment from the new displaying position to the end of the segment is found as

$$= X_i - Y \tag{21.35}$$

The minimum amount of data to start pipelining

$$= (1 - \rho)(X_i - Y) \tag{21.36}$$

As the first slice is already residing on the disks, then the amount of data already available on disks from the new displaying position is

$$
\begin{aligned}
&= (X_{i,1} - Y) \\
&= (1 - \rho) X_i - Y
\end{aligned}
\tag{21.37}
$$

Thus, the amount of extra data to be retrieved from tertiary storage devices prior to displaying is

$$
\begin{aligned}
&= (1 - \rho)(X_i - Y) - ((1 - \rho) X_i - Y) \\
&= -Y(1 - \rho) + Y \\
&= \rho Y
\end{aligned}
\tag{21.38}
$$

After retrieving ρY blocks of the second to the last slices from the tertiary storage device, there are already enough data on the disks to pipeline the segment.

If the new position is inside other slices of the segment, the minimum amount of data to start pipelining is

$$= (1 - \rho)\,(X_i - Y) \tag{21.39}$$

This is also the amount of data blocks that should be retrieved from tertiary storage devices prior to displaying. We can simply substitute the segment size by the object size to find the necessary amount of data in the normal pipelining method. In all three cases, the amount of necessary data in segmented pipelining is less than that in the normal pipelining method.

We have found the necessary amount of data that should be retrieved for pipelining. The reposition latency is the just start-up latency to retrieve the required amount of data for pipelining prior to display. As the required media units are already loaded to the drive, the exchange operation is not necessary. Let Z be the amount of data blocks to be retrieved for pipelining prior to displaying. Thus, the reposition latency is

$$= \alpha + \frac{Z}{\gamma} \tag{21.40}$$

Therefore, we have found the reposition latency that depends on the position of the jumping destination inside the segment. Due to less data being retrieved, the reposition latency in the segmented pipelining method is much smaller than the reposition latency in the normal pipelining method.

Performance of Segmented Pipelining

The reposition latency is the start-up latency to change the current viewing position of a stream. When the current viewing position of a stream is changed, the normal pipelining method needs to start a new stream by considering the data from the new destination displaying position to the end of the original object as a new object. The new first slice is then calculated to find the amount of data being retrieved prior to displaying. However, the start-up latency cannot be hidden since all the data that need to be displayed are not accessed from disks. If the new jump to position is near the end of the object, the start-up latency is low. If the new jump to position is near the beginning of the object, the start-up latency is high.

In segmented pipelining, the performance is much better. Since the object is already divided into segments and the first slice of each segment is resident on the disk, the later part of object also has some data resident on disks. Any segments can be displayed in a pipeline manner. Thus, the reposition latency is consistently low.

The reposition latency of the multimedia object is much lower than the reposition latency in normal pipelining. The reposition latency is compared against the latency in fast forward function using a two phase service model. The two phase service model is a method to deliver data over low bandwidth networks. It also supports some VCR-like functions. The reposition latency using the segmented pipelining method is consistently lower than the other method. Therefore, the segmented pipelining method supports interactive multimedia streams from tertiary storage devices efficiently.

The amount of disk space required in segmented pipelining has been compared against the size of the first slice in the normal pipelining method. The size of the head in space efficient pipelining is the same as the size of the first slice in the pipelining method. The amount of disk space required decreases with an increase in the tertiary bandwidth increases. This is because more data are included in the first slice when the data consumption ratio is low. The segmented pipelining method uses a small amount of extra disk space to support efficient interactive functions.

Discussion

The segmented pipelining method has four main advantages:

1. It supports efficient pipelining and hides the start-up latency.
2. It efficiently supports the jumping operations to start at any segments.
3. It provides browsing of objects from the preview data on disks.
4. The amount of preload data on disks can be adjusted according to the availability of disk space.

First, the segmented pipelining method supports efficient pipelining. After dividing the object into segments, the first slice of the segments is stored on disks to hide the start-up latency and to support stream continuity. The entire object is thus pipelined from the tertiary storage devices at disk latency.

Second, the segmented pipelining method overcomes one of the main limitations of tertiary storage devices. It supports the interactive functions from the tertiary storage devices at low latency. When the user jumps to the starting position of any segments, the storage system can immediately reposition the stream to start displaying. Thus, the latency is very low. The user can also jump to any positions with shorter latency than the normal pipelining method. In addition, the reposition latency stays consistently at a very low level under different tertiary bandwidth conditions.

Third, the segmented pipelining method separates the beginning part of all logical segment to form the preview file. The preview file allows the user to browse the objects without accessing any data from the low bandwidth tertiary storage devices. This helps to improve the user satisfaction on searching the objects for display.

Fourth, when the amount of disk space is insufficient to store the first slices of all segments, the preload data some cold objects may be loaded on demand from the tertiary storage devices. The preload data of the hotter objects still reside on disks and the preload data of the colder objects are loaded on demand from the tertiary storage devices. The actual number of objects with preload data resident on disks would depend on the storage space available on the disks. This allows flexibility in controlling the amount of usage of the disk space for resident data and the consumption of tertiary bandwidth in preloading. If the preload data of an object is loaded on demand from the tertiary storage devices, then they can be preloaded while the user is viewing the preview file. This leads to two outcomes. First, more tertiary bandwidth is consumed in preloading. Second, the start-up latency and response time of streams that access cold objects are increased. For both metrics, the system would perform better in selecting the cold objects as the objects that are loaded on demand.

The disadvantage of the segmented pipelining method is that more disk space is required. Apart from hiding the start-up latency, the disk space is used to support the stream continuity. Since we have split the objects into segments, more disk space is required since the total length for overlapping is reduced. Therefore, the pipelining efficiency is slightly lowered.

The staging method moves the entire object before using it. The entire object is available, but the start-up latency to start displaying the object is very long. When the start-up latency is tolerable and the staging disk space is available, the staging method is the most flexible that it supports any access patterns on the staged object.

The time slicing method moves only a fraction of the object before displaying it. The start-up latency is reduced but extra switching overheads are required. When the tertiary storage devices have high bandwidth and the tertiary storage devices are not too busy, the reduction in start-up latency gives better satisfactions to the waiting users.

The pipelining method moves only the sufficiently large part of the object prior to display. The start-up latency is minimized when only the retrieved portion needs to be consumed. This is particularly useful when the multimedia system only displays streams from the beginning to the end.

The space efficient pipelining method retrieves data at a rate lower than the data consumption rate. It keeps the front part of objects resident on disk to start a new stream at low latency. It uses the disk space efficiently to handle more streams. This method is desirable when the disk storage space is tight.

The segmented pipelining method supports efficient pipelining, supports interactive user requests, and provides object previews. When the multimedia system needs to provide some interactive VCR-like operations and object search function, the segmented pipelining is the most desirable data migration method.

Chapter Summary

The segmented pipelining method divides objects into segments and slices so that the object can be pipelined from the hierarchical storage system. We have analyzed the method on disk space requirement and the reposition latency.

The segmented pipelining method uses small extra disk space to support object previews and efficient interactive functions. It can offer extra flexibility in controlling the amount of disk space usage by adjusting the storage location of the preload data. Therefore, the segmented pipelining is an efficient and flexible data migration method for the multimedia objects on hierarchical storage systems.

References

Tse, P. K. C., & Leung, C. H. C. (1998). A low latency hierarchical storage organization for multimedia data retrieval. In *Proceedings of the IAPR International Workshop on Multimedia Information Analysis and Retrieval* (LNCS 1464, pp. 181-194). Springer-Verlag.

Summary to Section IV

Data Migration

In hierarchical storage systems, data migration is the process of moving data from tertiary storage devices to secondary storage devices. There are three approaches to migrate multimedia data objects across the storage levels. These methods are:

1. Staging,
2. Time slicing
3. Pipelining.

Three pipelining methods are used to reduce the start-up latency and staging buffer size. They include:

1. Normal pipelining
2. Space efficient pipelining
3. Segmented pipelining

The staging method is simple. Using the staging method, the entire object is available after staging. The program can freely access any part of the required object after waiting for the time required to migrate the object to the staging buffers. The staging method is also flexible. The access time from tertiary storage is completely separated. This is suitable for any type of data on any tertiary storage systems. Unfortunately, the time spent in waiting for the stage one to complete can be very long. This leads to a very slow response to even the simplest request. Since the entire object is stored on the staging buffers during the complete consumption time period, this wastes disk space for a considerably long time. In addition, the entire object is written to and read back from the disks, it may unnecessarily waste disk bandwidth in migrating unused data.

The time slicing method accesses objects at the unit of slices instead of objects. It reduces the start-up latency in accessing objects from the tertiary storage devices. Streams can start to respond at an earlier time. It also saves tape drive bandwidth if some streams are canceled when objects are canceled in the middle of consumption. Unfortunately, extra tape switching overheads are incurred unless all concurrent objects reside on the same tape. The service time in accessing objects is however increased.

The normal pipelining method has been explained in this chapter. The normal pipelining method finds the minimum fraction of the object before the stream can start to display it. It minimizes the start-up latency for the tertiary storage devices whose data transfer rate is lower than the data consumption rate of the objects. The formula to find minimum size of the first slices is explained in this chapter. We have also described the start-up latency in using the normal pipelining method.

The space efficient pipelining method is designed for pipelining objects from low bandwidth storage devices for display. It retrieves data at a rate lower than the data consumption rate. It keeps the front part of objects resident on disk cache to start a new stream at disk latency. It uses the disk space efficiently to handle more streams.

The basic policy reuses the circular buffer to store the later slices of the objects. Thus, the circular disk buffer only contains the second and the third slices.

The shrinking buffer policy reduces the circular buffer size after a slice is displayed. It is particularly useful when the circular disk buffer constraint is tight. The space stealing policy reuses the storage space containing the head of the object as part of the circular buffer. However, the head of the object should be restored after the object is displayed and this leads to increased workloads.

The segmented pipelining method divides objects into segments and slices so that the object can be pipelined from the hierarchical storage system. We have analysed the method on disk space requirement and the reposition latency. The segmented pipelining method uses small extra disk space to support object previews and efficient interactive functions. It can offer extra flexibility in controlling the amount of disk space usage by adjusting the storage location of the preload data. Therefore, the segmented pipelining is an efficient and flexible data migration method for the multimedia objects on hierarchical storage systems.

Section V

Cache Replacement Policy

Introduction

In the previous chapters of this book, we have focused on the efficient methods to store and retrieve multimedia objects. In the last part of this book, we describe how to deliver multimedia objects from the storage systems efficiently.

On the Internet, many multimedia objects are stored in the content servers. The clients are located over a wide area network far from the content server. When clients access multimedia objects from a content server, the content server must have sufficient disk and network to deliver the objects to the clients. Otherwise, it rejects the requests from the new clients. Thus, the popular content server can easily become the bottleneck in delivering multimedia objects. Therefore, server and network workloads are important concerns in designing multimedia storage systems over the Internet.

Multimedia objects, like other traditional data files and Web pages, may be transferred across networks, such as the Internet. In order to provide efficient delivery of data across the networks, some data can be stored in the middle of the network. When requests for the same object have been received, these data can be used to satisfy the requests at the middle of the network instead of forwarding the request any further. This method to satisfy requests with previously accessed data is called caching.

Since caching needs to consume a certain amount of storage space, the cache performance is affected by the size of the cache memory. If the storage space is large, more objects can be stored on the cache storage and the probability of finding an object in the cache is thus high. The cache performs better. If the storage space is limited, only a few objects can be stored in the cache storage, and the probability of finding an object in the cache is low. As a result, the cache performance becomes low. Therefore, the cache size influences the cache performance.

Since caching stores some previously fetched objects on the storage devices, the presence of an object exists on the storage devices significantly affects the efficiency of the caching. When a new object is being accessed, the cache admission policy decides whether an accessed object should be stored onto the cache devices.

Since the cache performance increases monotonically with the number of objects in the cache, the cache storage space is often full in order to keep the most number of objects in the cache. When an accessed object needs to be stored and the cache space is full, the cache replacement policy decides which object should be deleted from the cache storage to release space. The choice of whether an object is kept in the cache is determined by the cache replacement policy. Thus, the cache replacement policy significantly affects the efficiency of caching.

The cache replacement policy can be divided into memory caching and stream dependent caching. Memory caching uses the memory storage as cache of the multimedia objects. We shall describe the memory caching policies in Chapter XXII. Since multimedia objects are accessed as streams, it is useful to use the cache as a temporary storage for buffering data among streams that access the same object with a small difference in accessing time. In Chapter XXIII, we shall present the stream dependent caching policies. When multiple proxy servers are available, they may cooperate to work as a large cache storage space for multimedia objects. Cooperative Web caching is described in Chapter XXIV.

Chapter XXII

Memory Caching Methods

Introduction

The objective of data caching and object caching is to improve the performance in accessing multimedia objects from their storage. An efficient cache storage method can have many benefits:

First, caching can increase server capacity in serving more streams. Since the cache may satisfy some requests before they arrive at the server, the server will receive fewer requests to its data. Thus, the workload on the data server can be reduced. As a result, the server can serve more streams.

Second, it can reduce access latency when a recently accessed object is being accessed again. When an object is accessed again, the first copy of the accessed object in the cache can already satisfy the request. Since the cache can often access objects with smaller delay, the latency on accessing the objects is thus smaller.

Figure 22.1. Memory caching is achieved by two copies of storage levels

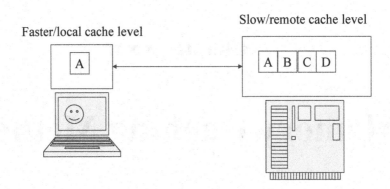

Third, caching can also reduce network bandwidth need when a request can be served locally by the local cache. If the cache is on the hard disk within local area network, the request may be served without sending the requests outside the local area network. Thus, the network traffic may be reduced.

Fourth, caching may be used to balance the workload among cache devices by directing the request to different cache devices evenly. If the cache servers containing the same cache copies have different workloads, the request can be directed to the server with the lightest workload. Therefore, the workload among the cache devices can be balanced.

In order to achieve memory caching, there must be at least two or more different storage levels. Each storage level consists of storage devices that can store data for later retrievals. The local cache storage level is closer to the client or the source of request. The data at this cache level can be accessed faster or with lower delay. The remote cache storage level is closer to the destination or the source of data objects. It takes longer time to access data from this storage level than the local cache level.

When a request for data is being served, the local cache is first searched to find if a copy of the required data object exists. If such a data copy can be found, the validity of the data copy is then checked. If the data copy is valid, then the condition is considered a hit. The data copy in the local cache level is then delivered to satisfy the request.

If the data copy cannot be found or the data copy in the local cache is invalid, then a cache miss occurs. The request is then forwarded to the remote storage level to be served. The request is then served at the remote level and a data copy is returned; the data copy is then stored onto the local cache level according to the cache admission policy.

There are two types of cache misses. The compulsory miss occurs for the first retrieval of objects. The compulsory misses occur independently of the cache replacement policy. The capacity miss occurs when an object is replaced from the cache before it is accessed again. Efficient cache replacement methods attempt to minimize the capacity misses.

When more requests are served at the local cache level, the storage system can serve requests at a faster rate. As a result, the performance of the storage system is higher. If fewer requests are served at the local cache level, the storage system serves requests slowly and the storage system performs poorly. In addition, more requests will go through the network to the remote storage level. This results in an increase in workload at the network and the remote storage servers.

When there are more than two storage levels and each storage level performs differently, the remote cache level can be further divided into another pair of cache level and storage level. In this way, the remote storage level is called the parent of the local cache level. A tree of parent and child cache hierarchy can thus be built.

To compare the efficiency of different cache replacement policies, the performance of caching is usually measured using the metrics called hit ratio or byte hit ratio. The hit ratio is defined as

$$= \frac{\text{the number of requests being served at the cache level}}{\text{the number of requests being served}}$$

Similarly, the byte hit ratio is defined as

$$= \frac{\text{the number of bytes being accessed at the cache level}}{\text{the number of bytes being accessed}}$$

At the local cache, the cache replacement policy decides which object should be deleted to release space for the newly accessed objects. The objective of an efficient cache replacement policy is to achieve the highest byte hit ratio or hit ratio for the local cache.

Although different cache replacement methods may have different ways to achieve its highest efficiency (Hosseini-Khayat, 1998), a general algorithm to achieve an efficient cache replacement method using different priority value is described below. Each cache object/block is assigned a cache value to indicate its priority to be kept in the cache. This cache value can often be specified as the result of a cache replacement function on the object/block.

When space is needed, the cache replacement algorithm (Tse & So, 2003) will perform the following:

1.   Find the objects/data blocks with the lowest cache priority value.
2.   Delete the found object with the lowest priority value.
3.   Repeat step 1 and step 2 until enough space is released.
4.   Insert the new object into the cache.
5.   Update the cache values of all the objects in the cache.

We shall describe different cache replacement methods in the following sections according to the criteria for priority value. The least recently used (LRU) method section considers the period of time when the object is previously accessed. The object access pattern and the least frequently used (LFU) method are then described. Afterwards, the LRU-min section considers the size of objects. The size and access latency are then considered in the greedy dual-size (GD-size) method and the least unified value (LUV) method sections, respectively. Last, all the characteristics are considered by the mix method section.

The Least Recently Used Method

It has been commonly known that after a data object or a stored program is accessed, the probability that the same object or the same program is being accessed again within a short time is high. Therefore, the period of time that an object has been accessed is being considered to increase the efficiency of the cache performance.

The recency of an object is defined as the period of time from which an object has been accessed to the present time. When an object has been recently accessed, its recency is said to be high. When an object has not been accessed for a long time, its recency is then low.

The least recently used method removes the least recently accessed object from the cache first. It stores a timestamp for each data object. The timestamp shows the time when the object was last accessed. Thus, it uses the recency history of the object as the cache value.

A simple cache replacement function for LRU is

$$\text{CV}_{\text{LRU}} = \frac{1}{(T - T_i)},$$

where T is the current time and T_i is the timestamp of object i (Aggarwal & Yu, 1997).

The oldest object, the least recently used one, will have the lowest value and will be deleted by the cache replacement method to release space. The LRU policy achieves good performance for the cache replacement algorithm. The achieved hit ratio is good for caching memory blocks containing programs files and data object files.

The LRU method is also simple. It only needs to store and compare the timestamps of the accessed objects in the cache. The time complexity to calculate the cache values of all objects in the cache is $O(n)$. That is, the amount of time to find calculate the cache values of objects increases linearly with the number of objects, n. Therefore, the LRU method is commonly used traditional cache replacement functions to calculate the cache value of objects and stored programs. However, the LRU method only considers the recency history. Since the least recently accessed hot object may not be the most unlikely to be accessed, the LRU method may not be able to perform well when the cache size is small. Also, the LRU method does not consider other characteristics in accessing the objects. The latency time to recover the deleted objects, the past access frequency, and the size of objects should be considered for multimedia objects in order to achieve efficient cache storage system. We shall describe how other cache replacement methods can improve the efficiency of cache storage for multimedia objects in the following sections.

Object Access Patterns

Since the access patterns of requests can significantly affect the probability of which object will be accessed. In order to achieve higher cache efficiency, we should investigate the access pattern of multimedia objects.

Traditional data files are more often being read than being modified. Multimedia objects are even more often read than modified. Thus, the number of requests reading multimedia objects is much more than the number of requests writing or updating multimedia objects.

Each multimedia object has a certain probability of being accessed. When an object is popular, it is frequently accessed. Its access temperature is high. It is called a hot object. When an object is unpopular, it is rarely accessed. Its access temperature is low. It is called a cold object.

The user access patterns of video rental stores have been investigated. It was found that most of the accesses are on a few hot objects. The access pattern of video tapes in the rental stores can be described using a Zipf-like distribution. In the Zipf-like distribution, the objects are arranged in the order of their access popularity. The probability that the ith popular object is accessed can be modeled as:

$$\text{Prob}(i\text{th popular object is accessed}) = \frac{c}{i^\alpha}, \text{ where } 0 \leq \alpha \leq 1.$$

The Zipf-like distribution is a family of probability distributions (Figure 22.2). The parameter α determines the characteristics of each distribution. The parameter c can be found using $\sum\text{Prob}(\ ) = 1$.

When $\alpha = 0$, the access probability of all the objects are the same. The access probabilities are evenly distributed.

When $\alpha = 1$, the distribution becomes a Zipf distribution. The access probability of the ith object is

$$\text{Prob}(i\text{th popular object is accessed}) = \frac{c}{i}.$$

From observations on the video rental store, it is found that the access pattern follows a Zipf-like distribution where $\alpha = 0.729$. In addition, objects popularity varies over time. Variations in the request rate can be observed

Figure 22.2. Access pattern of multimedia objects follows a Zipf-like distribution

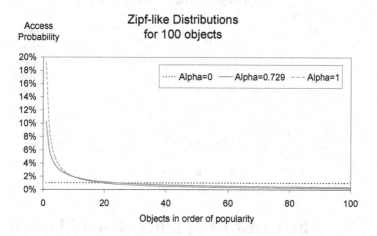

on a daily basis and weekly basis. A simple time distribution model may be used to find the arrival rate of the *m*th object as

$$\lambda_m(t) = p_m \lambda_0 + p_m A \sin(\gamma t)$$

where λ_0 is the daily average arrival rate, p_m is the popularity of *m*th object, and A is the amplitude, and $\gamma = 2\pi/T$. The access pattern of 10 objects over a seven-day period is shown in Figure 22.3.

In addition, different types of multimedia objects have different prime time. This is due to the fact that customers access different objects at different time of the day. For example, daily prime time is 7 pm to 10 pm for movies on demand. The daily prime time for cartoon series is between 11am to 5pm.

In addition, the popularity of multimedia objects changes over time. The popularity of multimedia objects may increase rapidly at first and then it drops slowly over time. Some new objects may become the hottest object in two weeks and then its temperature reduces in the following weeks.

When all the above characteristics of multimedia object accesses are considered, the long term behaviour of accessing an object follows an exponential curve plus a random effect.

Figure 22.3. Arrival rates of 10 objects over a seven-day period

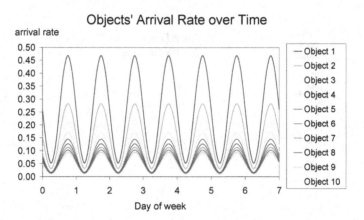

The Least Frequently Used Method

As described in the previous section, multimedia objects are accessed with different popularity at different times. Since the access temperature of objects varies slowly over time, the object temperature can be used to raise the efficiency of the cache replacement methods. Thus, it is reasonable to assume that the past access frequency provides a good prediction for future accesses.

The least frequently used method uses the frequency of past object accesses to predict the future accesses. The objective of the method is to keep the hot objects in the local cache and remove the coldest objects when space is needed.

Thus, the LFU method uses the access frequency of the data objects as the cache value of the object. The cache value of an object can be defined as equal to the access frequency of the object. The cache value of an object i is defined in the LFU method as

$$CV_{LFU} = N_i,$$

where N_i is the number of past accesses on the object i. Thus, hot objects have higher cache value than the cold objects. The coldest objects which is accessed the least number of times will be deleted from the cache to release space.

Application Note: *In order to find the access frequency of the objects in the cache, the LFU method needs to keep the number of times that each object is being accessed. To calculate the number of past accesses, the number of accesses of all the objects needs to be kept.*

The LFU method is also simple. It only needs to keep and compare the number of past accesses for the objects. The time complexity of the search algorithm is rather low. To find the least accessed object among n objects, the time complexity of the algorithm is $O(\log_2 n)$.

The main benefit of the LFU method is that it achieves the best performance when the access frequencies of the objects are stable and they change only slowly over time. However, the LFU method needs to keep the number of reference of all accessed objects even when the objects are not in the cache.

The LFU method that keeps the number of accesses on all the objects is also called the perfect-LFU method. Alternatively, if the storage system only stores the access frequencies of the objects that are in the cache, this method is called the in-cache-LFU method.

The in-cache-LFU method removes the number of past accesses on the object when the object is deleted from the cache. It may reduce the access overheads and the amount of data being stored in order to find the coldest object. However, this approach has two disadvantages. First, it does not accurately reflect the number of past accesses on the objects. Second, it performs worse than the LRU method since the access frequencies of the objects are incorrectly counted. The access frequencies of the uncached objects are counted incorrectly. Thus, the in-cache-LFU method does not adjust the cache content according to changes in access frequencies.

The LRU-Min Method

The LRU method is very simple to implement. Multimedia objects are however very large in size when compared with traditional data files. Only a few large multimedia objects, or even only one object, may completely occupy the entire cache space. Thus, it is reasonable to consider the object size in the cache replacement policy.

Consider the situation that three objects have exactly the same access pattern and the size of the large object is equal to the sum of the sizes of the two smaller objects. If the cache stores the large object only, only the requests for the large object can be served at the cache. The requests for the two smaller objects will become cache misses.

However, if the cache stores the two smaller objects, the cache will be able to serve more requests at the cache. Thus, the cache hit ratio is higher by storing the smaller objects instead of the large objects. Therefore, it is desirable for the cache replacement function to reduce the cache value of large objects. Although the cache hit ratio is higher when the cache stores the smaller objects, the request on the large object will deliver more bytes from the cache. Thus, the byte hit ratios of the cache are roughly the same even though the large objects are not served.

The LRU-min method is a cache replacement method that considers the object sizes. It is similar to the traditional LRU method. Same as the LRU method, the LRU method uses the recency history as the cache value. The cache value of an object is defined as

$$CV_{LRUmin} = \frac{1}{(T - T_i)},$$

where T is the current time and T_i is the timestamp of object i (Hoisseini-Khayat, 2001). The LRU-min method however has a different algorithm to find the victim object to be deleted. The algorithm is described below:

1.   It sets s equal to the size of the desired free space.
2.   Find the least recently accessed object whose size is larger than s.
3.   If such an object is found, then delete this object.
4.   Repeat Steps 2 to 3 for all the objects whose size is larger than s until enough space is released.
5.   If enough space is not freed, sets s to s/2 and repeat the procedure until enough space has been freed.

Considering the size of objects, the LRU-min method increases the cache hit ratio by removing large objects from the cache. Among the objects whose sizes are larger than the required space, the objects with low access recency are still chosen to be deleted.

The LRU-min method keeps many small objects in the cache. This increase in the number of objects in the cache however has some disadvantages. First, the cache storage space becomes fragmented over time. As the objects kept in the cache are small, the space occupied for each object is small. It is inefficient to store or retrieve objects from a fragmented storage system.

Second, the time complexity of the cache replacement algorithm becomes high. As the algorithm repeats the process at half size to find the victim objects, the time complexity of the algorithm is $O(n)$, where n is the number of objects in the cache. When the number of objects in the cache increases, the performance of the algorithm in searching for victim objects deteriorates.

The Greedy Dual Size Method

Similar to the LRU-min method, the greedy dual-size method also considers the size of objects in the cache replacement policy. In addition, it considers the latency cost in accessing the object from the remote storage level.

Since the objects in the same local cache level may come from different remote storage device, the latency cost in accessing the objects from the remote storage varies. The latency cost in accessing the object from the remote storage level directly determines the access time of the object. Thus, the cache performs better if it stores the objects with high access latency instead of storing the objects with low access latency.

The greedy dual-size method considers the access latency as the cost and the size of object in its cache value function. It also uses the recency information to maintain the list of objects in the cache (Breslau, Cao, Fan, Phillips, & Shenker, 1999).

In the GD-size method, the cache value of an object i is defined as

$$CV_{GDSize} = \frac{L_i}{S_i},$$

where L_i is the network latency cost of object i and S_i is the size of object i. The network latency cost is the delay time in accessing the object i from the remote storage level.

Instead of setting the recency information in the cache value, the GD-size method reduces the cache value when an object is deleted from cache and it resets the cache value of accessed objects. Thus, the cache value of an object achieves its highest value when it is accessed. This value gradually reduces after the objects on the cache are modified.

When space is needed, the GD-size performs the following steps to release space:

1. Remove the object with the smallest cache value.

2. Reduce every cached object's value by the removed object's value.

3. Repeat step 1 and step 2 until enough space is released.

When an object in the cache is accessed or referenced, the GD-size method resets the object's cache value back to its initial value, that is $= \dfrac{L_i}{S_i}$. The advantage of the greedy dual-size method is that it maintains good cache efficiency. It keeps many small and hot objects that are stored remotely with high latency. It has similar disadvantage as the LRU-min method. As it updates the cache value of all the objects in the cache when an object is removed, the time complexity of its algorithm is $O(n)$, where n is the number of objects kept in the cache.

The Least Unified Value Method

Similar to the GD-size method, the least unified value method considers the latency cost and the object size in the cache replacement function. In addition, it considers the complete access history for the objects. The cache value of an object i is defined in the LUV method (Bahn et al., 2002) as

$$CV_{LUV} = \frac{P_i L_i}{S_i},$$

where L_i is the network latency cost of object i, S_i is the size of object i, and P_i is the estimated reference potential of object i. The estimated reference potential, P_i, is found as

$$P_i = \sum_j F(\alpha(T - T_j))$$

and

$$F(x) = 0.5^x$$

where $0 \le \alpha \le 1$, T is the current time, and T_j is the times when the object was accessed. When space is needed, LUV removes the object with the smallest cache value from the cache.

The main technical advantage of the LUV method is that it uses the complete history of all the accesses. The trade-off is that it needs to keep the history of all the accesses. The second advantage is that the LUV method can optimize the performance measure according to the expected access pattern of the objects. However, it relies on the user to tune the parameter, α, for the best performance suitable for the realistic environment. In order to recalculate the cache value of all the objects in cache, the time complexity of the cache replacement algorithm using the LUV method is $O(n)$.

The Mix Method

Similar to the LUV method, the mix method considers all the characteristics of the object access patterns. It includes all the access history as parameters in the cache value function. The cache value of an object i in the mix method (Bahn et al., 2002) is defined as

$$CV_{mix} = \frac{(L_i)^l (N_i)^n}{(T_i)^t (S_i)^s}$$

where L_i is the network latency cost of object i, T_i is the last access time, and S_i is the size of object i. The parameter N_i is the number of cache hits of object i is accessed since it has been brought into the cache. The parameters l, n, t, and s are constants with default values $l=0.1$ and $n = t = s = 1$.

An advantage of the mix method is that it considers all the characteristics of the object access pattern as parameters in the cache value formula. Thus, the cache values of the objects can easily be compared to find the victim object.

Application Note: *In order to recalculate the cache value of the objects in cache, the time complexity of the cache replacement algorithm in the mix method is O(n). Since the cache values of the objects changes only when new requests are served, the cache value needs to be updated only when requests are being served.*

Chapter Summary

Memory cache replacement policies assign a cache value to each object in the cache. This cache value decides the priority of keeping the object in the cache. When space is needed to store a new object in cache, the cache replacement function will choose the object with the lowest cache value and delete it to release space. As a result, the objects with high cache values will remain in the cache.

Different cache replacement policies will assign different cache values to the objects. The traditional LRU method keeps the objects that are accessed most recently. It is simple and easy to implement and the time complexity is very low. All methods except the LFU method also keep the objects that are accessed recently.

The pattern in accessing multimedia objects has been described. The access pattern of video tapes in the rental stores can be described with a Zipf-like distribution. The long term behaviour of accesses for an individual object follows an exponential curve plus a random effect. The LFU, LUV, and mix methods keep track of the object temperature and remove the coldest objects from the cache first.

Due to the large size of multimedia objects, the cache may completely be occupied by a few objects. To maintain a good cache hit ratio, the priority of keeping large objects in the cache is reduced. Thus, the LRU-min, GD-size, LUV, and mix methods keep the small and recently accessed objects in the cache.

Since multimedia objects in the same local cache level may come from remote storage level at different distances, the latency cost in accessing the remote storage level varies. When cache misses occur, the objects in the remote storage level will be retrieved. Thus, the cache system would perform better if it keeps more objects that take longer to access. The GD-size, LUV, and mix methods include latency cost of objects in the cache to lower the priority of objects that can be easily replaced.

Several cache replacement methods have been described. The methods are simple to implement but may not perform optimally. The optimal methods have high time complexity and they are more difficult to implement. The trade-offs between simplicity and efficiency will remain until new cache replacement methods are designed.

References

Aggarwal, C. (1997). On disk caching of Web objects in proxy servers. In *Proceedings of ACM CIKM* (pp. 238-245).

Bahn, et. al. (2002). Efficient replacement of nonuniform objects in Web caches. *IEEE Computer, 35*(6), 65-73.

Breslau, L., Cao, P., Fan, L., Phillips, G., & Shenker, S. (1999). Web caching and Zipf-like distributions: Evidence and implications. In *Proceedings of IEEE INFOCOM* (pp. 126-134).

Hosseini-Khayat, S. (1998). Replacement algorithms for object caching. In *Proceedings of the ACM Symposium on Applied Computing* (pp. 90-97).

Tse, P. K. C., & So, S. (2003). An overview of multimedia proxy servers. In *Proceedings of the 7th World Multiconference on Systemics, Cybernetics and Informatics* (Vol. 3, pp. 289-293).

Exercises

1. **LFU method:** A list of objects A, B, C, D, and E are referenced for 25, 40, 32, 16, 20 times respectively. The cache now contains A, B, and C. A request for object E arrives; which object will be replaced from cache?

2. **LRU-min method:** A list of objects A(2GB), B(4GB), C(6GB), and D(8GB) have been requested at times = 10, 12, 15, 20 seconds, respectively. A request for object E(3GB) arrives at T=30 seconds.

   a.   Which object will be replaced from cache?

   b.   If object E is 10GB, which objects will be replaced from cache?

3. **GD size method:** A list of objects A(2GB), B(4GB), C(6GB), and D(8GB) have been requested at latency costs of 4, 4, 6, 6 seconds, respectively. A request for object E(5GB) with latency = 4 seconds arrives.

   a.   Which object will be replaced from the cache?

   b.   What are the new cache values after replacement?

4. **Mix method:** A list of objects A, B, C, D in the cache have been requested according to Table 22.1 below. A request for object E (1GB) arrives. Which object will be replaced from cache according to the mix method using r1=r2=r3=r4=1?

Table 22.1. List of requests

Object	Size	No. of references	Last reference time	Access latency
A	2 GB	10	10 seconds	4 seconds
B	4 GB	6	25 seconds	4 seconds
C	6 GB	5	30 seconds	6 seconds
D	8 GB	4	20 seconds	6 seconds

Chapter XXIII

Stream Dependent Caching

Introduction

Caching has been successfully implemented on the Internet to reduce work-load on the content server and the Internet. We have seen in the last chapter how the cache replacement methods are adapted for multimedia objects in memory caching. In this chapter, we shall show how the caching is tailored to provide better performance for continuous request streams.

Even though caching reduces the access latency when there are cache hits, there are chances that cache misses occur. When cache misses occur, the request stream is sent through the network to the remote storage devices. The requests are then served at the remote storage devices. The requested multimedia objects are retrieved from the storage devices, delivered through the network to the client. The cache content will also be modified to store the accessed object.

Multimedia data requests are continuously sent to the remote storage devices. Each request may ask for only a small part of data. The union of all the requested data is the entire object. In order to provide continuous display of media object for a period of time, the storage system needs to provide a guarantee on the continuous delivery of data (Chae et al., 2002; Chang & Hock, 2000).

Although caching increases the service rate of data requests, it is inevitable that some misses occur. When the cache hit ratios are low, the workload on the remote storage devices becomes heavy. When the workload on the storage device is too heavy, response time and access delay of the requests could increase indefinitely. As a result, the data cannot be retrieved within the guarantee time. This results in violations of the continuous display guarantee.

In order to provide continuous display guarantee of multimedia information, the requested multimedia data must be delivered continuously. However, this cannot be easily achieved on today's Internet. Congestions in the network could also hinder the smooth delivery of data. Unfortunately, the Internet is designed and implemented in a way that congestions cannot be completely avoided. It may be a fact that congestions persistently occur when the stream is running for a long enough time.

Many methods to provide continuous multimedia streams have been proposed and investigated. However, the implementation of these techniques on the Internet still has some difficulties due to the presence of legacy routers.

As multimedia objects are large in size, the limited memory cache space can only store a few objects. If all the accessed objects are of the same size, the size aware cache replacement methods would not increase the number of objects being cached. In this situation, the cache hit ratio is still constrained by the size of the local cache.

As the multimedia objects are so large, it becomes necessary to create the cache level on local disks, instead of the random access memory. With a bigger cache space, the cache level on disks can reduce more capacity misses. However, the cache level on the disks must be created carefully. As the service time of disk requests is rather long, the disk throughput is limited. Thus, the disk throughput should be higher than the data rate of the objects so that the objects on the cache are accessible.

If the workload is too high for an individual disk, multiple disks or disk array may be used. In such condition, the workload of the disks should be well balanced. Balanced disk load can avoid bottlenecks to build up and overload individual disk.

The storage techniques on stream dependent caching include resident leader, variable length segmentation (VLS), video staging, hotspot caching, and interval caching. They will divide each multimedia object into smaller segments and store selected segments on the cache level. We will first describe the resident leader in the next section. Then we will show the variable length segmentation. After that, the video staging technique uses the cache space to reduce the maximum network bandwidth required. The hotspot caching technique that provides a preview on objects is described. Last, the interval caching will provide better caching for concurrent streams. In each of these sections, we shall explain the objectives, details, and the analysis of the methods.

The Resident Leader Method

Objectives

Multimedia systems transfer and consume data in a way that is different from traditional computer systems. In traditional systems, the data file or data object is completely accessed from the storage system before it is being used.

In multimedia systems, the multimedia stream begins with getting some data from the storage system. These data are kept in the memory buffer for consumption. When sufficient data are ready, it starts to display and consume data. While at the same time, it continues to retrieve the remaining data for consumption so that the consumption may continue for an indefinite amount of time.

In essence, the start-up delay of the stream is the time to prepare for the start-up of the multimedia stream. Thus, the start-up delay of a stream depends on the access time it takes to fill up the memory buffer with the beginning portion of the multimedia object.

In addition, the start-up delay of the multimedia streams depends on the size of the memory buffer. If the memory buffer is large, more data needed to be accessed. The buffer can maintain continuity of the stream against a bigger variation in the data access time. However, the time to fill up the memory buffer and the start-up delay of the multimedia streams are longer.

If the memory buffer is small, the time to fill up the memory buffer and the start-up delay of the multimedia streams are short. However, the buffer can maintain continuity of the multimedia stream for a small variation in the data access time.

Details of the Method

The resident leader method assumes that the object is consumed from the beginning to the end. This assumption is valid for most systems such as video-on-demand systems and near video-on-demand systems.

The resident leader method divides the multimedia data object into two main parts: the head and the tail (Figure 23.1). The head part, or the leader, is the beginning portion of the object, and the tail part is the remaining part of the object except the beginning portion. The size of the head part is large enough to fill the memory buffer (Tse & So, 2003).

In the resident leader method, the storage system reserves some space in the local cache level to store the head part of all the objects permanently. Thus, the requests for the head part are always served as cache hits. As the local cache level is always accessed with shorter latency than the remote storage, the head part is accessed at the latency of the cache.

The tail part of the object is stored on the remote storage level. Apart from the reserved area for the head part, the remaining space in the cache level is used as cache storage for the tail part of the objects. The cache replacement methods for memory caching can be used to choose the tail part of the appropriate objects.

It should be noted that the tail part should be retrieved from the remote storage within a certain time limit. As the head part from the cache already allows the multimedia stream and data consumption to begin, the tail part should be retrieved in time before the memory buffer is empty. If the tail part cannot be accessed before the memory buffer is empty, the consumption of data will stop due to shortage of data called starvation.

Figure 23.1. Resident leader

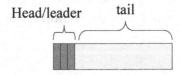

In addition, the tail part should be continuously accessed to fill the memory buffer. If the delivery of data is too slow, the memory buffer may also starve and the display or consumption of data would be suspended. This will result in violation of the continuous display guarantee requirement on multimedia streams. If the delivery of data is too fast, the memory buffer becomes full. The retrieval of data should suspend momentarily to allow for the data consumption.

Analysis

Without the resident leader method, the cache replacement methods in memory caching store the most likely accessed objects in the cache to serve future request. When an object is cached, the service times of all requests on the object are reduced. The cache replacement methods minimize the average response time of requests on the objects. As a result, the start-up delay of the streams is short if a valid copy of the object is stored on the cache.

However, the objects that are less likely to be accessed are deleted from the cache when cache space is needed. The head part of these objects is accessed from the remote storage level when needed. The start-up delay of the streams on these objects is thus long. The long start-up delay of these streams has a direct observable impact on the users. It would be nice if the maximum start-up delay of the streams can be kept to an acceptable level.

Using the resident leader method, the multimedia stream begins after the head part is retrieved. Thus, the start-up delay of the stream is reduced. In order to keep the head part resident on the local storage, some storage space in the cache is reserved and the storage space used to cache the tail part of the object is reduced. Fewer objects can be stored on the cache, resulting in an increase in the capacity misses and the average response time. Therefore, the savings in the start-up delay come with a price. The resident leader method trades off the maximum start-up delay of streams with the average response time of requests.

When sufficient cache space is available, the resident leader method is simple to implement. It reduces the maximum start-up delay of streams so that the user will observe a short start-up delay for all the streams being requested.

However, the resident leader method increases the average response time of requests. This reduction in cache efficiency leads to heavier workload on the remote storage level and the communication network in-between. The cache efficiency and performance is thus low.

In addition, the tail part of most objects is not cached. It is accessed from the remote storage level when needed. As the network delays are unpredictable and unbounded, it is very difficult, if not impossible, to guarantee the stream continuity.

Variable Length Segmentation

Objectives

When multimedia objects are stored in the cache, objects with large sizes require a lot of space when they are brought into the cache. The cache storage space may store only a few objects. The cache hit ratio is thus low and capacity misses are high.

Users may not view the entire object from the beginning to the end. It wastes cache space to keep the entire object in the cache if only the beginning segments are consumed. By breaking down the objects into segments, the beginning segments of many cold objects can be stored. The cache space may be more efficiently used by storing the initial segments of more objects. Also, the start-up latency of more streams is reduced similar to the resident leader method.

A simple method is to divide objects into fixed length. If the segments are short, many segments will be created. Many segments need to be deleted for any incoming object. The cache space will be divided into many small fragments and it takes a long time to find enough segments to cache a new object. If the segments are long, it takes a long time to access the first segment before a new stream is started. The start-up latency to initiate a new stream is high. The storage system also needs to reserve bigger cache space for each segment. In the next section, we shall describe a method to divide an object into increasing length so that the large segments may be deleted to release space more efficiently.

Details of the Method

The variable length segmentation divides an object i into segments (Aggarwal & Yu, 1997; Wu, Yu, & Wolf, 2001). For an object i of n blocks, the jth segment contains media blocks

$$2^{j-1}, 2^{j-1}+1, \ldots, 2^{j}-1, \text{ for } j >= 1.$$

The first segment contains block 0 only. In general, the $j+1$th segment is twice as large as the jth segment. It divides the objects into segments of exponentially increasing length. The number of segments for an object of n blocks is

$$= \lfloor \log_2(n) \rfloor + 1$$

The cache value of a segment depends on the recency of the object and the segment distance. The segment distance is defined as the distance of the segment from the beginning of the object. The cache value of the jth segment of an object i is defined as

$$CV_{VLS} = \frac{1}{(T - T_i) \times j}$$

where j is the segment number, T is the current time, and T_i is the timestamp of object i. When space is needed, the VLS removes the segment with the smallest cache value from the cache.

Analysis

The variable length segmentation method has several technical advantages. It divides an object into large and small objects. The beginning segments are small and they have higher cache value. The latter segments are longer and they have lower cache values. It allows the storage system to remove the later segments before they remove the beginning segments. Thus, the beginning segments of many objects can be kept in the cache. This helps to reduce the start-up latency of many streams.

If all the streams are consumed from the beginning of the objects, the later segments will only be used after the earlier segments are used. When the user stops displaying and the stream is terminated in the middle, the storage system would not need to access the later segments. Thus, the cache storage space is used efficiently.

Also, the storage system removes the larger segments before they remove the smaller segments of the same object. Thus, it may release sufficient space for the incoming object by removing only a few segments. Thus, the cache replacement algorithm performs efficiently.

Since the size of latter segments is large, the number of segment for each object is not many. Thus, it is fast to find a segment from $N*\log(n)$ where N is the number of objects in cache and n is the number of blocks in each object. Thus, the cache replacement algorithm performs fast.

The present variable length segmentation method is simple by using the recency of the objects as the cache value. The cache system only needs to keep the recent access time of each object in the cache. The current variable length segmentation method is also flexible. It may be possible to adapt the cache value function to include more access characteristics of the streams, such as access frequency and access latency. Thus, the advantages of the segmentation method remains while cache efficiency increases.

Also, the earlier segments of an object are smaller than the later segments. These smaller segments have higher cache value than the large segments of the same object. The larger segments would be deleted to release space before the smaller segments. Thus, it helps to reduce the number of segments being deleted and increase the average size of deleted segments. Therefore, the fragmentation problem can be avoided.

Application Note: *A disadvantage of this method is that the streams must be displayed from the beginning to the end. When a stream starts to display from the middle of the multimedia object, the cache system needs to access the later segments before the stream can continue.*

The Video Staging Method

Objectives

In order to deliver multimedia objects across the Internet, the network bandwidth should be high enough to support the continuous display requirement. However, this is not always achievable for these reasons:

1. The network bandwidth is limited by the link that has the smallest bandwidth. Thus, a video stream cannot be continuously delivered over a network with smaller bandwidth than its data rate requirement.

2. In addition, different network segments have different bandwidths. A stream over the Internet may traverse through different networks, including local area networks (LANs) and wide area networks (WANs). The WAN bandwidth for a stream is not high enough for the video stream.

3. The TCP protocol is using the best effort approach to deliver the most data in the shortest period of time. It uses a sliding window to limit the number of packets being sent before the acknowledgment packets are received. To achieve the highest network throughput, TCP increases the number of packets in the sliding window until some packets are lost and acknowledgment packets are not received. When packets are lost, the size of the sliding window is halved. Thus, network bandwidth that is made available to a stream fluctuates a lot.

4. The network bandwidth needs to be continuously high enough for the entire duration of the stream. If the network bandwidth is low for a short time, the continuous display requirement cannot be met.

Figure 23.2. Video staging keeps the high bandwidth segments in local cache

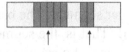

High bandwidth segments

Instead of increasing the WAN bandwidth to support the continuous display requirement, the video staging method reduces the maximum bandwidth requirement on the network. Thus, the objective of the video staging method is to reduce the maximum WAN bandwidth to retrieve video continuously from remote storage.

Details of the Method

Instead of increasing the WAN bandwidth to support the continuous display requirement, the video staging method reduces the maximum requirement on the network (Zhang, Wang, Du, & Su, 2000). When the objects are stored to the server, the objects are analyzed. The data rate requirements of the objects are found out. The data rate requirements will be used in the preloading stage.

Before the delivery of the object, the WAN network condition between the server and the client is first analyzed. This step finds out an estimated network bandwidth between the server and client. This estimated network bandwidth will be used as the WAN network bandwidth threshold in the delivery. The ranges of time of the object that has a data rate higher than the estimated bandwidth threshold are found out.

The video-on-demand system divides the delivery of a multimedia object into two stages. In the first stage, the system preloads the high bandwidth segments that exceed the estimated WAN bandwidth threshold to the local cache (Figure 23.2). In the second stage, it loads the remaining segments of the object while displaying object. As data rates of all the remaining segments of the object are lower than the WAN bandwidth requirement, the continuous display requirements of the object stream can be met.

Since the objective of the preloading stage is to reduce the bandwidth requirement, only the portion of these segments above the threshold needs to be loaded in the preloading stage. The portion of the high bandwidth segments but below the threshold can be loaded in the second stage as other segments.

For instance, the estimated WAN bandwidth is 2 Mbps and a one-hour object is divided into 1 minute per segment. The bandwidth threshold of each segment is 120MB or 15MB. That is, the segments that are larger than 15MB are high bandwidth segments. If a segment is 20 MB, the system needs to transfer 5MB (20MB - 15MB) in the preloading stage.

Discussion

The method is flexible that it is suitable for other low bandwidth conditions. It can be applied to the hierarchical storage systems, where the throughput of the tertiary storage is used as the bandwidth threshold. The video staging may be used together with optimal smoothing. The smoothing can be applied on the lower and/or upper portion of the video.

Unfortunately, the estimation of network bandwidth should be good enough. If the estimated network bandwidth is too low, many segments are larger than the threshold. A large amount of data needs to be transferred in the preloading stage, resulting in very long start-up latency. If the estimated network bandwidth is too high, only a small amount of data needs to be transferred in the preloading stage. However, the average network condition may not meet the estimated bandwidth threshold. Insufficient data are delivered to the client and the display quality becomes low.

Application Note: *The most difficult part is that the actual network condition fluctuates a lot. The network can suddenly become congested and the bandwidth drops below an accurate network bandwidth estimated that is made at an earlier time. Luckily, the video staging method only needs to use the average bandwidth estimation for a period of time. A short congestion would not cause a problem if the average bandwidth is only gradually lowered.*

It can be applied to stored video streams, but it cannot be applied to real-time streams where the data cannot be delivered in advance.

The video staging method transfers the data of the high bandwidth segments in the preloading stage. When the streams are delivered from the beginning, the actual data being transferred in the preloading stage can be modified. The same network bandwidth is required as long as the data being transferred in the preloading stage are within the range of segments from the beginning of the video to the high bandwidth segment. Thus, the head of the video can be included in the preloaded portion to reduce the start-up latency.

New network protocols, such as RSVP and DiffServ, reserve some bandwidths for a stream but they are unfair to the TCP protocol. These methods also have an implementation difficulty that existing network routers do not support these protocols. The video staging method can be applied only if the new protocol can be implemented on today's Internet with new and legacy routers.

The Hotspot Caching Method

Objectives

Multimedia objects are normally displayed from the beginning to the end. Apart from the normal display of data, there are other usage patterns.

For instance, when a user searches the storage system for the appropriate object, the user may not be able to find the desired object by looking at the object name, object description, creation date/time, and other metadata of the object.

Other methods may be used to search an object, including matching colour, shape, and texture. These methods still need more time and effort to research. At the current publishing time of this book, the matching of objects based on low level details is still not accurate enough. In addition, users may wish to match the objects according to their semantic meaning. User feedbacks are often required to provide good matching of multimedia objects.

The system may not be able to understand and capture the exact need of the user. The user may not be able to express what the user wants for the system to search. When there are not too many objects to search, an effective method is to browse the objects. Browsing of video objects involves looking at some segments of the video. It is time-consuming to browse video and audio objects at their normal display speed. It would be nice if the system can provide fast browsing of the objects.

To provide fast browsing of objects, the system should retrieve only low resolution objects for display. Otherwise, the workload of the system and network may become heavy. Apart from browsing of objects, the system may provide fast browsing option to advertise new objects to many potential buyers or viewers. Therefore, the hotspot caching technique is designed to provide efficient previews of objects.

Details of the Method

When proxy servers cache parts of an object, each proxy server may cache a portion of the object to reduce repeated accesses to the object (Fahmi, Latif, Sedigh-Ali, Ghafoor, Liu, & Hsu, 2001). As multimedia streams may retrieve the following data blocks while they are consuming the current data blocks,

Figure 23.3. Hotspot caching

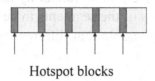

Hotspot blocks

a stream may start to respond when the first few leader blocks are available. These leader blocks are cached in the local proxy server to reduce the response time of the stream as shown in the resident leader method.

Apart from the leader blocks, the object is divided into a number of segments. Each segment should be independent of the previous segments. The beginning part of each segment is defined as the preview hotspot of the segment. Hotspot segments do not need to be distributed at uniform interval or be of equal size. It may be defined by the creator of the media object or the creator of the hotspot segments.

The storage system then keeps these preview hotspots together in its local cache. Apart from the preview hotspots, the other parts of the temporal segments are retrieved from the remote storage. These data blocks can be cached according to the chosen cache value function. For example, a segment should begin with an I-frame in MPEG coding. A hotspot is composed of data segments that are separated at equal temporal distance. A proxy server could provide a preview of the object using only the segments inside the hotspots.

Discussion

The hotspot caching method provides a fast preview of the object. The user may browse the hotspot to know the content of the object. It helps to provide relevance feedback when the user searches for a desired object from a database of multimedia objects. When only the hotspot is viewed, the storage system only accesses data from the cache level. Thus, objects can be previewed efficiently and quickly.

The hotspot method also provides caching when the user jumps to the later segments. If each segment is 10 minutes long and the first minute of each segment is included in the hotspot, the start-up latency is reduced when the user jumps to the first minute of every 10 minutes. Thus, the stream responds quickly when users move their displaying position on the object. Therefore, the hotspot method improves quality of service to the user when the object is being searched, previewed, or randomly accessed. The hotspot caching method allows the sizes of the segments to be determined by the creator of the segments. This is flexible that different segment sizes can be used in different systems.

Application Note: *The size of the hotspots in each segment is determined by the latency in accessing the object from remote storage. Longer hotspots should be created on objects that are accessed with long latency. Shorter hotspots can be created on objects that are accessed with short latency. The shortest display time of the hotspot should be longer than the access latency of the segment from remote storage.*

Interval Caching

Objectives

The principle contribution of caching is to reduce repeated access of the same piece of data from the remote storage. It would be better to store an object or a segment if we can be sure that it will be accessed again after it is stored on the cache. The choice of object depends very much on the length of time elapsed before it will be accessed again.

The durations of streams are long, in the order of minutes to hours. There is much overlapping time among streams on the same object. In true video-on-demand systems, these streams are initiated at different times. They access the object via the same proxy server at different times. Since the concurrent streams are accessing the same object, it is almost for sure that the object will be accessed again if it is stored to the cache. Thus, it is beneficial to keep in cache the objects for concurrent streams.

As it is beneficial to keep in cache the objects for concurrent streams, the storage system needs to compare the benefits of storing an object of concurrent stream with another object that may be accessed with a probability less than one. Thus, the objects of concurrent streams should have higher cache value than another object that is not concurrently accessed by multiple streams. When the cache storage space is scarce, the cache space may not be large enough to accommodate the objects for all the concurrent streams. Therefore, the time interval between the starting times of concurrent streams is used.

When the cache storage space is scarce, the cache space may not be large enough to accommodate the entire object. It is more efficient to store an object with a short interval than another object with a long interval. Therefore, the time interval between the starting times of concurrent streams on the same object is considered.

Details of the Method

The interval caching method uses the time separation between streams that access the same object to determine the priority of keeping the segments of the object in the cache. The streams that are close together will have high priority to be kept in the cache. The streams that are far apart have low priority (Sitaram & Dan, 2000).

When a new stream arrives at the cache, it finds if this object is being accessed by another stream. If the object is already accessed by another stream, then the time interval of the two streams is the difference of the two display times of the two streams. The interval size is the amount of data to be accessed for the time interval. The exact interval size would increase or decrease depending on the amount of data per unit time. The estimated size of an interval is the time to re-access all the blocks in that time interval.

Figure 23.4. Interval caching caches the shortest interval

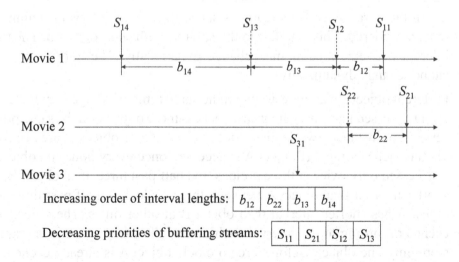

For instance, two streams access object A at 11:40 a.m. and 12:20 p.m. The time interval between the two streams is 20 minutes. The estimated size of the interval is the time to re-access all the blocks in 20 minutes. An estimated size is the average number of bytes over a 20-minute range.

The storage system then compares the interval sizes among the streams and chooses the data segments of the shortest intervals to be cached. Once an interval is chosen to be cached, its preceding stream places all blocks in the cache upon consumption. The following stream reads the block from the cache and places them in the free pool. Thus, the interval between the two streams is placed in the cache. The cached interval is immediately removed from the cache after display. For instance, three movies are accessed by seven streams in Figure 23.4.

Discussion

Since the following stream would display the interval after it is kept in the cache, the probability of being accessed again before it is replaced is close to one.

Application Note: *A limitation of the interval caching is that it can only be applied on several streams access the same object via the same cache level. When each stream accesses a different object, the cache values of the objects are unknown.*

When the duration of the streams is short, there is an interval caching has to be considered. This is unfair to the streams with short duration. The time interval between streams may change dynamically. The interval caching cannot change dynamically.

Different objects that are residing on the same remote storage may have different accessed patterns. Clients may access these objects via the same proxy server. For instance, two 1-hour objects, object A and object B, are accessed via the cache storage. If object A is accessed once every hour and object B is accessed only twice at three o'clock and half past three, then object B has shorter interval than object A between three o'clock to half past three and object A has shorter interval than object B at other times. The objects are cached according to the interval caching and the cache space is enough to store only one object. Before three o'clock, object A is already cached. At half past three, the storage system will start to cache object B. After half past four, the storage system will start to remove object B and cache object A. Depending on other access characteristics, the storage system should store the object with higher latency and smaller size. If the storage system replaces object A with object B, then the storage system will need to access the object B once and write the cache storage twice, once for replacing object A and once for replacing object B. The storage system will also access object A from remote storage once. Otherwise, the storage system only read object B from remote storage twice. Therefore, the storage system may perform better by keeping the object A in the cache.

Layered Based Caching

Objectives

Multimedia objects are different from textual data and programs. One main difference is that they are often kept in a compressed format. The original objects always have the lowest compression ratio but the highest quality. After the multimedia objects are compressed heavily, they occupy fewer bits but the compressed objects have lower quality. Very often the objects are compressed to a level that appears visually indifferent to the original object.

When the original object is accessed, the server and the network will need to transfer the amount of data that is equal to the size of the original object. If this is lower than the network bandwidth or the throughput capacity of the server, the object cannot be delivered by streaming. Instead of providing the highest quality version of the multimedia object, fewer bits are stored on the cache by lowering the quality of the cached object. Thus, more objects can be cached on the same amount of storage space. The storage system can thus deliver more objects of lower resolution.

One of the main difficulties to deliver multimedia objects over the Internet is that the network bandwidth fluctuates a lot. Although the average network may be considered, the network bandwidth may drop to zero when congestions happen. When network congestions occur, the server is almost disconnected from the proxy server and the client. The proxy server could only use its cached content and the buffered data to wait till the congestion period is over. Thus, the cache content should be tailored to maintain the continuity in streaming for the period of time when network bandwidth is insufficient.

Details of the Method

The layer based approach compressed each media object into several layers such that upper layers contain refinements of the lower layers (Paknikar, Kankanhalli, Ramakrishnan, Srinivasan, & Ngoh, 2000, Rejaie, Yu, Handley, & Estrin, 2000). Each layer is further divided into equal-sized segments. The lowest layer, layer 0, is called the base layer. The base layer consists of the elementary information and the data for the coarse information. The layer one contains data for the finer details of the media object that are not described in the base layer. Each layer contains refinement details of the media object that are not described in the lower layers.

For instance, a value of 43,892 is described. For simplicity, we use the number of base 10 digits. In reality, the value is described with base 2 digits. It may take too many digits to describe the exact value. The value is instead described by data in five layers. The data in the base layer may contain the most significant figure of 40000. The layer 1 may contain 4000. The detail values -100, -10, and 2 can be described in the layers 2, 3, and 4, respectively. If only the base layer is known, the estimate value is 40000. If both layer 0 and 1 are known, the value is estimated to be 44000. Similarly, the value is estimated to be 44900, 44890, and 44892 when layer 0 to layer 2, layer 3, and layer 4 are known, respectively.

When more layers are available from the base layer, the system can restore the media object that looks more like the original object. Since the upper layers only contain the less refinement details such as the less significant values, the upper layer information are useless without the lower layers.

Figure 23.5. Layer based caching

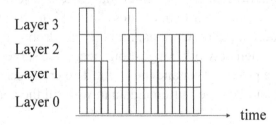

Figure 23.6. Prefetching priorities in the sliding window

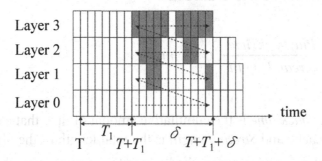

Without the base layer, all the upper layers cannot be used to reproduce the object. Thus, a layer can only be consumed when all the layers below it are available. Therefore, only the base layer is independent of other layers. All the upper layers depend on the lower layers below.

When a proxy first accesses an object for a client, the proxy always caches the missing stream. If cache space is exhausted, the replacement algorithm flushes enough segments from the cache to make room for the new stream. Thus, the proxy accumulates more objects in its cache for subsequent accesses until the cache is full.

The proxy uses a sliding window mechanism to prefetch segments (Rejaie et al., 2000). At playout time T and a fixed T_1, it examines the interval $[T+T_1, T + T_1 + \delta]$ and identifies the missing segments in this interval. It sends a new prefetch request that contains an ordered list of all the missing segments according to their priorities. The priority of a segment is defined as a combination of the layer number and the time of the segment. Segments of lower layers always have higher priority than the upper layers. The segments in the same layer are delivered according to their time. When the server receives a prefetching request, it stops the previous requests from the same client. It then sends the requested segments according to their priorities.

The proxy organizes the cache values of objects at the granularity of a layer, but it deletes at the granularity of segments. The cache value of a layer at time t is defined as

$$CV_{layer} = \sum_{x=t-\Delta}^{t} whit(x)$$

where Δ is the width of the popularity window. The *whit(x)* is the weighted hit of the layer and it is defined as

$$whit(x) = \frac{PlaybackTime}{StreamLength}, 0 \leq whit \leq 1,$$

where *PlaybackTime* is the cumulative amount of time that a layer is played from the cache and *StreamLength* is the total length of the object.

When cache space is needed, the layer with the smallest cache value is chosen as the victim layer. The cached segments of the victim layer are then deleted from the last to the first until enough space is released. In order to hide start-up latency, the first few segments of the base layer are kept in the cache for a longer period.

The performance of the method is measured by completeness and continuity. Completeness measures the percentage of a stream residing in the cache. When a layer has larger portion in the cache, the completeness of the layer is higher. The completeness of layer l in cached object s is defined as the percentage of the layer's size in cache and it is found as

$$Cp(s,l) = \frac{\sum_{\forall i \in Chunks(l)} L_{l,i}}{RL_l}$$

where *Chunks(l)* is the set of all chunks of layer l. A chunk is defined as a continuous group of segments of a single layer of a cached object. $L_{l,i}$ is the length in segments of the ith cached chunk of layer l. RL_l is the length in segments of layer l. If every byte of a layer is cached, the completeness of the layer is equal to 1. Obviously, the range of the completeness is [0, 1].

Continuity measures the level of smoothness of a cached stream. It counts the number of breaks in a cached stream. A long continuous stream has a high number of bytes between breaks. The continuity of a layer is defined as the mean number of bytes between two consecutive layer breaks. Thus, the layer l in cached stream s is found as

$$Ct(s,l) = \frac{\sum_{\forall i \in Chunks(l)} L_{l,i}}{LayerBreaks + 1},$$

where *LayerBreaks* is the number of layer breaks in the layer and *Chunks(l)* is the set of all chunks of layer *l*. A layer break occurs when there is a missing segment in the layer. The continuity counts the average chunk size. When the entire layer is cached, the continuity is equal to the length of the layer.

Discussion

This method changes the quality of a stream with the popularity of the layer of the object. More layers are cached for more popular objects. Fewer layers are cached for less popular objects. Thus, the more popular objects are cached to achieve higher cache efficiency. When the user is not satisfied with the quality of a stream, the user may repeatedly access the same stream and the quality of the stream may increase after each subsequent access.

It uses a sliding window mechanism to prefetch segments from the server. The size of the sliding window may affect the smoothness of the streams. When the sliding window is small, only a few segments are delivered in each layer. When the sliding window is large, many segments of a layer are transmitted. If the sliding window only includes one segment from each layer, one segment of each layer is delivered within the window. When traffic congestion occurs, the server may not be able to deliver any segments within the sliding window. Thus, a layer break occurs in every layer.

The proxy organizes the cache values of objects at the granularity of a layer, but it deletes at the granularity of segments. This method helps the cache replacement algorithm to find the victim layer quickly at the granularity of layers. It maximizes the cache efficiency and avoids space fragmentation by deleting the victim layer at the granularity of a segment.

Application Note: *This method is applicable to varying client bandwidth and stream popularity environments. When the server to proxy bandwidth is higher than the client to proxy bandwidth, stream popularity is dominant. When the server to proxy bandwidth is lower than the client to proxy bandwidth, the client bandwidth overshadows stream popularity.*

The cache values of the segments depend on the cache content. The cache content in term depends on the cache values. This recursive definition of the cache value is not flexible. Convergence needs to be guaranteed and proven. Some studies have shown that the cache content converges. However, it may not be true for another system with different access patterns. Thus, the method may not be applicable in very stringent and volatile environments.

The less popular objects may be completely flushed out from the cache. It may not be suitable to reduce the quality of less popular objects. The cache space is provided to increase the quality of cached streams. When more cache space is available, the quality of more streams is improved. This method trades off the caching of the less popular layers for that of the more popular layers. In addition, it may be more desirable to keep the base layer of a less popular stream in the cache instead of the uppermost layer of a popular stream. Thus, it is more flexible to define the cache values of layers based on the completeness and continuity of the layers so that the cache efficiency can be optimized.

The Cost Based Method for Wireless Networks

Objective

The cost based method for wireless networks has three objectives (Xiang, Zhang, Zhu, & Zhong, 2001). First, it caches the popular media to reduce network resource cost in transmitting media objects from server to proxy. Second, it improves media quality for wireless clients by calculating and caching the redundant data in the computation cache. Third, it decreases start-up latency by caching the leaders of media objects.

Details of the Method

The media objects are divided into two types of segments, data segment and redundant data segments. The data segments are segments that are composed of the media object. The redundant data segments are redundant data created to recover the transmission errors over the wireless network. The data segments are cached in the data cache. The redundant data segments are cached in the computation cache. The media distortion cost of data segments and redundant data segments are calculated differently.

The cache value is composed of three costs: network cost, start-up latency cost, and media distortion cost. The network cost of segment j in object i is defined as

$$NC_{ij} = S_{ij} \times H_i \times F_{ij}$$

where S_{ij} is the size of segment, H_i is the network distance between server and proxy, and F_{ij} is request frequency of segment.

Long segments consume more network bandwidth to deliver. Thus, it increases the network cost as well. The network distance between server and proxy is a function of the round trip time. When the round trip time is longer, the network distance becomes longer. The request frequency of the segments takes into account the early termination of streams. When a stream is often terminated before it ends, the request frequency of the last segments would be lower than its earlier segments.

The start-up latency cost of segment j in object i is defined as

$$LC_{ij} = \begin{cases} L_i \times F_{ij}, & \text{if } j < J_{threshold} \\ 0, & \text{otherwise} \end{cases}$$

where L_i is the network latency cost in accessing the leader of object i, F_{ij} is request frequency of segment j, and $J_{threshold}$ is the size of the leader in number of segments. The network latency cost is the delay for accessing the leader from server to proxy and it is a function of the round trip time (RTT) between the remote storage and the local cache.

When a segment is part of the leader of an object, the request frequency of the segment and the network latency cost will be used to increase the start-up latency cost of the segment. Otherwise, the start-up latency cost is zero.

For data segments, the media distortion cost for the segment j of object i is defined as

$$QC_{ij} = X_{ij} \times F_{ij}$$

where X_{ij} is the measured distortion in PSNR, and F_{ij} is request frequency of the segment.

The values of the above three costs all contributes to the cache value function. The cache value of data segment j of an object i is defined as

$$CV_{wireless} = \frac{n \times NC_{ij} + l \times LC_{ij} \times F_i + q \times QC_{ij}}{S_i}$$

where $NC_{ij}, LC_{ij}, QC_{ij}$ are respectively the network cost, start-up latency cost, and the media distortion cost of the segment j of object i, and S_i is the size of object i. The parameters n, l, and q are constants whose values depend on the real world demand.

For redundant data segments, the cache value only depends on the media distortion cost of the redundant data segment. The cache value of a redundant data segment j of an object i is defined as

$$CV_{wireless} = \frac{q \times X_{ij} \times F_{ij} \times \lambda_{wireless}}{S_i}$$

where X_{ij} is the measured distortion in PSNR, F_{ij} is the request frequency of the segment j of object i, $\lambda_{wireless}$ is the proportion of the wireless clients to all clients, S_i is the size of object i, and q is a constant.

The cache replacement algorithm is similar to traditional cache replacement policy. When cache space is needed, the segment with the lowest cost is deleted to release space until enough space is released.

Analysis

This cost based method for wireless clients takes care of wireless clients by considering the quality distortion over wireless networks. It caches the redundant data segments separately from the data segments so that the quality of the media streams can be maintained over the error-prone wireless networks. This method is simple; it can be applied on the legacy cache replacement algorithm. It uses a cost that is different from the traditional recency value for each segment in the cache. The storage system however needs to keep some information about each cached segments, including the request frequency, network distance, network latency cost, and the quality distortion.

The cache performance of this cost based wireless method is flexible. The parameters can be adjusted to modify the relative importance of the network cost, start-up latency, and media quality. Unless the users are well-experienced, it is difficult to find the most appropriate values for the parameters, n, l, and q. After the network conditions change, it may also be necessary to adjust the parameter $J_{threshold}$ which is the size of the leader in number of segments. Apart from keeping the information for each segment, this method also needs to calculate the cost for each segment. This involves expensive computation cost in addition to the amount of data stored.

Application Note: *The computation and data cost may be reduced by considering only the last cached segment of each object for comparison. When the last cached segment is compared to other segments of the same object, it should have the lowest request frequency. This is because a segment is usually accessed after its previous segments are accessed. The last cached segment should have the lowest request frequency among segments of the same object. The request frequency is an important multiplying factor in the calculation of the network cost, start-up latency cost, and media distortion cost.*

Chapter Summary

The stream dependent caching methods were designed to guarantee continuous delivery for multimedia streams.

The resident leader method stores the beginning segment to hide the latency in accessing the object from the user. It trades off the average response time of requests to reduce the maximum response time of streams.

The variable length segmentation method divides the objects into segments of increasing length. The earlier segments are shorter and have higher cache value. The later segments are longer and have smaller cache value. First, the earlier segments have higher priority to be kept in the cache than the later segments of the same object. The beginning of many streams may be stored in the cache to reduce the start-up latency. Second, the large segments are deleted before the small segments are deleted. The number of segments to be deleted is reduced and the cache replacement algorithm becomes more efficient. Third, the large segments are deleted and it avoids the fragmentation problems.

The video staging method retrieves high bandwidth segments to reduce the necessary WAN bandwidth for streaming. Unfortunately, network congestions happen at any time and the network bandwidth fluctuates a lot. The WAN bandwidth threshold cannot be guaranteed before the reservation based protocols are implemented on today's Internet.

Hotspot caching creates the hotspot segments of objects and these hotspots are stored as preview segments to provide fast object previews from local cache.

Interval caching keeps the shortest intervals of video to maintain the continuity of streams from the local cache content.

Layer based caching adapts the quality of streams to the cache efficiency. It fetches segments in the prefetching window to control the congestion of networks. It finds the victim layer and deletes unpopular segments to achieve fine granularity replacement. It uses the continuity and completeness as metrics to measure the suitability of the caching method for multimedia streams.

The cost based method for wireless clients reduces the quality distortion over the error-prone wireless networks with the help of the cache content. The cache value of the segments is composed of network cost, start-up latency cost, and quality distortion costs. The cache replacement algorithm finds the victim segment and deletes at the granularity of segments.

References

Chae, Y., et al. (2002). Silo, rainbow, and caching token: Schemes for scalable, fault tolerant stream caching. *IEEE Journal on Selected Areas in Communications, 20*(7), 1328-1344.

Chang, Y., & Hock, N. C. (2000). Providing quality of service guarantee in Internet by a proxy method. In *Proceedings of IEEE TENCON* (Vol. 3, pp. 51-54).

Fahmi, H., Latif, M., Sedigh-Ali, S., Ghafoor, A., Liu, P., & Hsu, L. H. (2001). Proxy servers for scalable interactive video support. *IEEE Computer*, *34*(9), 54-60.

Paknikar, S., Kankanhalli, M., Ramakrishnan, K. R., Srinivasan, S. H., & Ngoh, L. H. (2000). A caching and streaming framework for multimedia. In *Proceedings of ACM Multimedia* (pp. 13-20).

Rejaie, R., Yu, H., Handley, M., & Estrin, D. (2000). Multimedia proxy caching mechanism for quality adaptive streaming. In *Proceedings of IEEE INFOCOM* (pp. 980-989).

Sitaram, D., & Dan, A. (2000). *Multimedia servers: Applications, environments, and design*. Morgan Kaufmann Publishers.

Tse, P. K. C., & So, S. (2003). An overview of multimedia proxy servers. *In Proceedings of the 7th World Multiconference on Systemics, Cybernetics and Informatics* (Vol. 3, pp. 289-293).

Wu, K.-L., Yu, P., & Wolf, J. L. (2001). Segment-based proxy caching of multimedia streams. In *Proceedings of the ACM WWW10 Conference* (pp. 36-44).

Xiang, Z., Zhang, Q., Zhu, W., & Zhong, Y. (2001). Cost-based replacement policy for multimedia proxy across wireless Internet. In *Proceedings of IEEE* (pp. 2009-2013).

Zhang, Z., Wang, Y., Du, D. H. C., & Su, D. (2000). Video staging: A proxy-server-based approach to end-to-end video delivery over wide-area networks. *IEEE/ACM Transactions on Networking, 8*(4), 429-442.

Chapter XXIV

Cooperative Web Caching

Introduction

Most clients are placed behind the proxy servers on the Internet. Proxy servers have the disk cache space, network bandwidth, and availability to cache part of the objects for clients. In addition, the number of proxy servers can be increased or decreased dynamically according to the anticipated server workload, making them good candidates to alleviate the bottleneck problem. We have described in the last two chapters how the caching methods provide better performance for continuous request streams in individual proxy servers. In this chapter, we show how the proxy servers may work together to improve the overall performance in delivering objects.

At present, large multimedia objects are not cached or only partially cached in current proxy servers mainly for two reasons. First, the owner of the multimedia objects needs to ensure security and control of access of the objects before they are willing to let any proxy servers cache their objects. Thus, any new methods need to allow the content owner have complete control over the objects' security. Second, the owner of the proxy server wishes to have full autonomy control over its own cache content so that the proxy server may maximize the cache efficiency for its own clients.

One of the main contributions of proxy servers to the clients is their cache storage. The content of the cache storage depends on the cost function in the cache replacement policy that determines the cache performance. The cache replacement policy is often optimized to achieve the highest cache hit ratio and byte hit ratio. When many clients access multimedia objects via proxy servers, some of them may access the same objects. Several proxy servers which are in the network neighbourhood of each other may access the popular objects for their clients. If these proxy servers can cooperate with each other by sharing their cache contents, the congestion on the network and content server can be reduced (Dykes & Robbins, 2001; Wolman, Voelker, Sharma, Cardwell, Karlin, & Levy, 1999). It is effective when the objects are accessed by many requests in a period of time (Lee, Amiri, Sahu, & Venkatramani, 2002).

If each proxy server caches a different fraction of a popular object, the union of these parts may form a large fraction of the entire object. Only the missing parts are then requested from the content server. Therefore, the cooperative object partitioning methods thus help to reduce the amount of data that must be delivered from the content server.

As the cooperation of Web caches assist the clients in delivery of multimedia streams, the efficiency of the cooperation is measured with additional metrics. Local hit ratio and local byte hit ratio measures the efficiency of the local cache level. The hit ratio and byte hit ratio measures the overall efficiency of all the cooperative caches. The stream response time and the stream service time indicate how the cache performance would affect the user. The number of server streams is used to measure the capacity of the content servers and proxy servers.

We shall describe the recursive leader method in the next section. Then, hierarchical Web cache is shown. After that, the array of Web caches is presented. Afterwards, the multiple hotspot caching method is described.

Hierarchical Web Caches

Objectives

The multimedia objects are large in size and the proxy servers may run out of cache space by storing a few objects. For an object stored in the cache, it would be more efficient if the cached object is accessed by more clients. Thus, a proxy server may share its cached objects with other proxy servers in the neighbourhood to reduce the capacity misses.

One method to share the cached contents is to build the caches into a hierarchy of cache storage as illustrated in Figure 24.1. The cache storage that is closest to the clients is the local cache level. The proxy servers at this local cache level do not directly access the objects from the content server. Instead, they access objects from the content server via the parent proxy server. A parent proxy server may have several child proxy servers. Each child proxy server has only one parent proxy server.

Details of the Method

On the Internet, many proxy servers are present. A proxy server may access an object from the server via another proxy server in the local area network (LAN). The later proxy server is called the parent of the child proxy server. Repeatedly, these proxy servers can be built into a large tree. Beginning from the root of this cache tree, each proxy server is a node in the tree and the clients are the leaves of the tree (Park, Baek, & Chung, 2000).

When an object is accessed from the content server, the client requests are forwarded through the child and parent proxy servers before they reach the content server. The child proxy server which is closest to the client checks if the object has been cached or not. If it is not being cached, then the child proxy server forwards the request to the parent proxy server.

The parent proxy server checks if the object has been cached or not. If it is not on the cache, then it forwards the request to its parent proxy server. If the object is already on the cache, it returns the object to the child proxy server.

When an object is initially accessed, the root parent proxy server accesses the object from the content server. When data of the object are delivered from the

Figure 24.1. Parent proxy server, P, and child proxy servers, C, build into a hierarchical Web cache

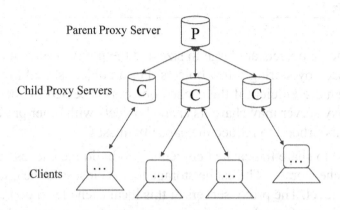

content server, it passes the received segments to the requesting child proxy server. In addition, it caches the object for other child proxy servers which have not requested the object. When a child proxy server receives the object from its parent proxy server, it caches the object and delivers the object to the client requesting it.

Analysis

The parent proxy server keeps on its cache the objects requested by its child proxy servers. The network traffic is reduced when the object is accessed by any other clients via any child proxy servers. More clients are connected to this proxy server and more object accesses are directed to this proxy server. The cached object can be accessed by more clients. This helps to reduce the capacity misses. Thus, the cache performs more efficiently.

Since the parent proxy server caches the objects, it helps to reduce the network latency in accessing the object by other child proxy servers. As the parent proxy server in the LAN is closer to the client than the content server, the network latency is shorter. It helps to reduce the start-up latency of the streams.

Since the parent proxy server caches all objects that are requested by its child proxy servers, the parent proxy server needs to be very large in order to cache the large number of objects. The parent proxy server becomes a bottleneck as too many objects are accessed from it.

Front and Rear Partitioning

Objectives

The multimedia objects are large in size and the proxy servers may run out of cache space by storing a few objects. For an object stored in the cache, it would be more efficient if the cached object is accessed by more clients. Thus, a proxy server may share its cached objects with other proxy servers in the neighbourhood to reduce the capacity misses.

One method to share the cached contents is to build the caches into a hierarchy of cache storage. The cache storage that is closest to the clients is the local cache level. The proxy servers at this local cache level do not directly access the objects from the content server. Instead, they access objects from the content server via the parent proxy server. A parent proxy server may have several child proxy servers. Each child proxy server has only one parent proxy server.

The objective of the resident leader method is to completely hide the start-up latency of the streams by keeping the leaders resident in the cache close to the client. The objective of the front and rear segments method is similar. It keeps the leaders in the local proxy server that is closest to the clients to hide the start-up latency. In addition, it stores the rest of the object in the parent cache so that the cached object is shared by more clients.

Details of the Method

On the Internet, many proxy servers are present. A proxy server on the sub-LAN may access an object from the server via another proxy server in the LAN. The later proxy server is called the parent of the child proxy server. Repeatedly, these proxy servers can be built into a large tree. Beginning from the root of this cache tree, each proxy server is a node in the tree and the clients are the leaves of the tree.

Similar to the resident leader method, the recursive leader method divides an object into two contiguous parts: the front segment and the rear segment (as illustrated in Figure 24.2). The front segment is the same as the leader in the resident leader method. The rear segment is same as the rest of the object in the resident leader method (Park, Park, & Son, 2001).

Figure 24.2. Front and rear segments

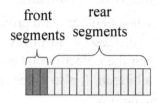

When an object is accessed from the content server, the client requests are forwarded through the child and parent proxy servers before they reach the content server. The child proxy server, which is closest to the client, checks if the front segment has been cached or not. If it is not being cached, then the child proxy server forwards the request to the parent proxy server.

When an object is initially accessed, the parent proxy server accesses the object from the content server. When data of the object are delivered from the content server, it will perform three operations on the object stream. First, it passes the received segments to the requesting child proxy server. Second, it caches the rear segment. Third, it pushes the front segment to other child proxy servers which are not requesting the object.

When the child proxy server receives the front segment from its parent proxy server, it caches the front segment and delivers the rear segment to the client without caching it.

Analysis

Similar to the resident leader method, the child proxy server caches the front segment and hides the start-up latency from the user.

The parent proxy server keeps the rear segment in its cache. The network traffic is reduced when the object is accessed by any other clients via any child proxy servers. More clients are connected to this proxy server and more object accesses are directed to this proxy server. The cached object can be accessed by more clients. This helps to reduce the capacity misses. Thus, the cache performs more efficiently.

Since the parent proxy server caches the rear segments, it helps to reduce the network latency in accessing the object. As the parent proxy server in the LAN is closer to the client than the content server, the network latency is shorter and the network traffic can be better predicted. It helps to provide a guarantee on the continuity of the streams.

The front segment is pushed to other child proxy servers. Before the cached front segment is removed, these child proxy servers can thus serve their clients immediately when the object is first accessed. The start-up latency of more streams is then hidden. It also helps to reduce compulsory misses which were not possible before.

Since the addition of another proxy server as a parent proxy server, each request will be routed through more network links. Each request will travel through more proxy server and there is a small increase in the average delay. In addition, the parent proxy server could become a bottleneck when too many objects are delivered from it.

Similar to the resident leader method, this method also assumes that the object is consumed from the beginning to the end. Similar to the resident leader method, the caching of the front segment is a trade-off between the maximum start up delay of streams and the average response time of requests. It helps the problems in the resident leader method by caching the rear segment. The network delays become more predictable and the stream continuity can be guaranteed. The workload on the remote storage level becomes light and the cache efficiency is maintained.

Directory Based Cooperation

Objectives

The main objective of the directory based cooperation is to reduce the network latency in accessing the objects. The proxy server in the neighbourhood is closer to the remote content server. When an object is delivered from one of the proxy servers in the neighbourhood, the network distance is shorter.

When the parent proxy server caches the requested objects, it needs to store all the objects that are accessed by its child proxy servers. This would increase the number of objects being cached at the parent proxy server. The parent proxy server can become overloaded.

Instead of delivering the objects from the parent's own cache, the requested object may be delivered from other child proxy servers that have the requested object. The group of proxy servers thus serve more requests on the objects in their cache. The cache efficiency is thus increased.

Details of the Method

The parent proxy server and child proxy servers form a tree of proxy servers similar to the hierarchical Web caching. A proxy server has only one parent and it may have more than one child. Only the root parent proxy server does not have any parent. Each proxy server is identified with its location. Each object is identified by its universal resource locator (URL). The proxy servers use the Internet caching protocol (ICP) to communicate with each other.

In order to know which proxy servers in the neighbourhood have the accessed object, all the proxy servers keep track of the request objects being cached in all its child proxy servers. A global resource index (GRI) table is built and kept in the proxy servers. The GRI table is created similarly to the inverted index. Each entry in the GRI table contains two parts: the URL of an object and the proxy servers the have cached this object (Wu & Liao, 1997).

When an object is accessed, the client requests are routed through the proxy server tree upwards before they can reach the content server. When a proxy server receives a request from its client or its child proxy servers, it processes the request using an object look-up algorithm.

In the object look-up algorithm, the proxy server may returns the object if it exists in its local cache. Otherwise, it finds the location of the object. If the location is not found, then it passes the requests to its parent for processing. If the location is not found at the root, then the location is the URL of the object. If it needs a copy of the object, then it gets the location of the object, cache a copy, and returns the object to the requesting child. Otherwise, it returns the redirection message containing the location of the object. The child proxy server receiving the redirection message will retrieve the object from the content server.

Details of the object look-up algorithm in the proxy servers are below:

1   Check if the requested object is kept in its local cache.

2   If the requested object is in the local cache, then return the objects from its local cache.

3	Check if the object exists in the GRI table.
4	If the object exists in the GRI table, then get the location of object from GRI entry.
5	If the object does not exist in the GRI table, then
5.1	If this proxy server is not the root, then
5.1.1	Forward the request to its parent.
5.1.2	If response is redirection, then get object location from the redirection message.
5.1.3	If response is success, then get the location of parent.
5.2	Otherwise, get the location of the content server.
6	If it is not the last child in the requesting chain, then
6.1	If it needs to cache this object, then
6.1.1	Get the object from the location.
6.1.2	Cache a copy of the object.
6.1.3	Return the object to the requesting child or client.
6.2	Otherwise, return a redirection message with the location to the requesting child.
7	Otherwise,
7.1	Get the object from the location.
7.2	If it needs to cache this object, then cache a copy of the object.
7.3	Return the object to the requesting client.

When a proxy receives a request for an object which has just been removed from the cache, the request cannot be forwarded to the parent proxy server. Otherwise, infinite loop of requesting may occur. The proxy server needs to get the object directly from the content server.

When several child proxy servers have the same object being requested, the parent proxy server may decide which proxy server's location will be included in the redirection message. This decision depends on the distance from the requesting child to the other child proxy servers.

Analysis

This directory based cooperation method does not store many objects in the parents. The parents may provide directory look-up functions only. Thus, there is little contention on the parent proxy servers.

There are two types of overheads involved in this method: the storage overheads and the update overhead. The parent proxy server needs to store the GRI table. It also needs to modify the GRI table when new requests are processed.

One of the main difficulties is on the political issue. The owners of proxy server may wish their proxy server to serve requests of clients within the organization only. When cooperation among owners of proxy servers is not established, it is unlikely that their proxy servers may cooperate to achieve better performance.

Hash Based Cooperation

Objectives

Instead of keeping the directory of object, the object locations are defined by their object ID. Based on the object ID, the object is cached on only one of the cooperative proxy servers. In addition, the overheads in updating the directory entries are avoided.

Details of the Method

In the hash based cooperation approach, the cooperative proxy servers are organized into an array. Each proxy server is assigned a unique proxy number. The proxy servers communicate with each other using the cache array routing protocol (CARP).

Each object is assigned an object ID. The proxy server that can cache the object is defined by a hashing function of the object ID. The proxy server number is defined as

$= \mathrm{Hash}(ObjectID),$

where Hash(.) is a hashing function that returns a random number within the range of proxy servers.

Analysis

Proxy cooperation is achieved without any directories to be updated. The list of locations of the proxy array is small and the update overheads are low. Each object is cached in only one proxy server. Other proxy servers within the array do not cache a second copy of the object. Thus, only one copy of the object can be found in the cache array. Thus, the entire space of the cache array will be used like a single cache. No duplications of objects are found. Thus, the storage space of the cache array is used efficiently to minimize the capacity misses.

Since the array of proxy servers is fixed, the objects have their destination proxy server determined by the hashing function. The hashing function depends on the total number of proxy servers. After new proxy server joins the array or old proxy server leaves the array, the hashing function returns different proxy server numbers. Thus, the cached objects need to be relocated to the new proxy servers. This reorganization overhead is expensive.

The Multiple Hotspot Caching Method

Objectives

Clients access multimedia objects from the content servers. These clients may reside behind the same or different proxy servers. When the clients access an object via the same proxy server, the proxy server may store the entire object in its cache to serve multiple clients. The proxy server can access the object from the remote storage only once and store it on the cache. It can then server other clients from the object in the cache. Thus, the proxy server reduces the server load, network load, and start-up latency of streams.

When the clients access an object via different proxy servers, each proxy server accesses the object from remote storage. The network load, server load, and start-up latency of streams are high. The multiple hotspots caching method reduces the amount of data being accessed from the remote storage.

In order to provide fast previews, the hotspot caching method stores hotspot segments of media objects in the local cache level (Fahmi, Latif, Sedigh-Ali, Ghafoor, Liu, & Hsu, 2001). When the hotspots on different proxy servers are the same, each proxy server still accesses the other segments besides the hotspots from the remote storage. A better mechanism to share hotspots would be able to reduce the amount of data being delivered from the remote storage while providing fast previews.

When users access multimedia objects from the Internet, the multimedia objects may traverse through several different networks in the delivery. The networks, in particular the wide area network (WAN), are often unstable and sometimes congested. It would be nice to reduce the amount of data being delivered over the network. The streams can become more stable by reducing the amount of data being accessed from the remote storage.

Details of the Method

The server mechanically partitions an object into multiple segments for distribution (Tse, Leung, So, & Lau, 2003). Each object is divided into a number of low temporal resolution segments (Figure 24.3). Each segment is a small fixed number of group of pictures (GOP). A segment is a short continuous object by itself.

Instead of creating a single hotspot by the media creator, the multiple hotspots method creates hotspots automatically by grouping segments that are

Figure 24.3. Multiple hotspots caching

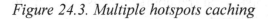
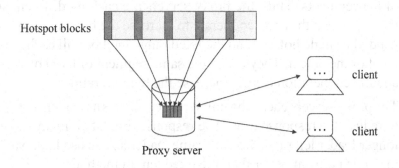

separated from each other at a fixed time intervals (Tse & Lau, 2004). Each single hotspot can thus provide a preview of the object to its clients.

Each proxy server will cache one of these hotspots so that it may provide a preview of the object to its clients from its local cache. The cached hotspots may also improve the performance of the searching algorithm by letting users give feedback quickly.

In the multiple hotspots partitioning method, each segment belongs to one of the hotspots and all the hotspots together form a large fraction of the object. When enough hotspots are accessed from neighbouring proxy servers, the entire object can be restored. Thus, the media object can be displayed without any requests being sent to the remote storage server.

Discussion

The multiple hotspots method increases the sharing of data among neighbouring proxy servers. Thus, it affects the cache performance in terms of local hit ratio, local byte hit ratio, byte hit ratio, and response time.

For the local hit ratio, the methods using the variable length segments perform better than the methods using fixed length segments. This is because the local proxy cache is more efficient when longer segments of hot objects and shorter segments of cold objects are cached.

The local byte hit ratio of the methods using variable length segments perform similarly to the fixed length methods at small cache sizes. The variable length methods perform better than the fixed length methods when the cache size is sufficiently large.

The byte hit ratio is similar to the local hit ratio. The better performing group are the methods using multiple hotspots and random segments. These methods partition the object into several different segments and the proxy caches one of the segments. Thus, the proxy servers are caching different segments of the object and they can cooperate to increase the byte hit ratio. On the other hand, the single hotspot and the fixed range methods all cache the same segment of the object. They cache the same segment of fixed or variable length and the cooperation cannot increase the byte hit ratio.

The proxy servers cache the initial part of objects as leaders in the local cache to reduce the response time. The response time of all methods reduces with longer leader length. When the same leader size is used, the variable length methods perform better than the fixed length methods.

In summary, the methods creating multiple segments perform better than the methods creating only single segment. Among all methods, the random multiple hotspot fixed size performs the best.

Chapter Summary

Research on the large scale operations of Web caches have shown that the benefits on caching Web documents do not increase beyond the capability of a single proxy server. Hierarchical Web caching reduces network latency on requests. Front and rear partitioning reduces the start-up latency of streams. Directory based cooperation avoids the contention on the parent proxy server. Hash based cooperation achieves low storage overheads and update overheads. Multiple hotspot caching keeps the hotspot blocks to provide fast local previews.

The performances of various object partitioning methods in cooperative multimedia proxy servers are compared. The performance of cooperative proxy caching is significantly affected by the chosen partitioning method. The partitioning methods creating variable length segments perform better than the methods creating fixed length segments in local metrics. The methods creating multiple segments perform better than the methods creating single segment when cooperative caching is used. Among all methods being investigated, the random multiple hotspot fixed size uses the shortest service time.

References

Dykes, S. G., & Robbins, K. A. (2001). A viability analysis of cooperative proxy caching. In *Proceedings of IEEE INFOCOM* (Vol. 3, pp. 1205-1214).

Fahmi, H., Latif, M., Sedigh-Ali, S., Ghafoor, A., Liu, P., & Hsu, L. H. (2001). Proxy servers for scalable interactive video support. *IEEE Computer, 34*(9), 54-60.

Lee, K. W., Amiri, K., Sahu, S., & Venkatramani, C. (2002). On the sensitivity of cooperative caching performance to workload and network characteristics. *ACM SIGMETRICS, 30*(1), 268-269.

Park, Y. W., Baek, K. H., & Chung, K. D. (2000). Reducing network traffic using two-layered cache servers for continuous media data on the Internet. In *Proceedings of the IEEE Computer Software and Applications Conference* (pp. 389-394).

Park, S. C., Park, Y. W., & Son, Y. E. (2001). A proxy server management scheme for continuous media objects based on object partitioning. In *Proceedings of IEEE ICPADS* (pp. 757-762).

Tse, P. K. C., & Lau, G. K. M. (2004). *Performance analysis of multiple layers object partitioning methods in cooperative multimedia proxy servers* (Tech. Rep.). University of Hong Kong, Hong Kong SAR, China.

Tse, P. K. C., Leung, C. H. C., So, S. W. W., & Lau, G. K. M. (2003). Cooperative multimedia proxy servers. In *Proceedings of the International Conference on Computer, Communication and Control Technologies (CCCT'03) and the 9th International Conference on Information Systems Analysis and Synthesis (ISAS'03)* (Vol. 1, pp. 244-249).

Wolman, A., Voelker, G. M., Sharma, N., Cardwell, N., Karlin, A., & Levy, H. M. (1999). On the scale and performance of cooperative Web proxy caching. *Proceedings of the ACM Symposium on Operating Systems Principles, 34*(5), 16-31.

Wu, S., & Liao, C. C. (1997). Virtual proxy servers for WWW and intelligent agents on the Internet. In *Proceedings of the Hawaii International Conference on System Sciences* (Vol. 4, pp. 200-209).

Summary to Section V

Cache Replacement Policy

On the Internet, many multimedia objects are stored in the content servers. The clients are located over a wide area network far from the content server. When clients access multimedia objects from a content server, the content server must have sufficient disk and network to deliver the objects to the clients. Otherwise, it rejects the requests from the new clients. Thus, the popular content server can easily become the bottleneck in delivering multimedia objects. Therefore, server and network workloads are important concerns in designing multimedia storage systems over the Internet.

Multimedia objects, like other traditional data files and Web pages, may be transferred across networks, such as the Internet. In order to provide efficient delivery of data across the networks, some data can be stored in the middle of the network. When requests for the same object have been received, these data can be used to satisfy the requests at the middle of the network instead of forwarding the request any further. This method to satisfy requests with previously accessed data is called caching.

Since caching needs to consume a certain amount of storage space, the cache performance is affected by the size of the cache memory. If the storage space is large, more objects can be stored on the cache storage and the probability of finding an object in the cache is thus high. The cache performs better. If the storage space is limited, only a few objects can be stored in the cache storage and the probability of finding an object in the cache is low. As a result, the cache performance becomes low. Therefore, the cache size influences the cache performance.

Since caching stores some previously fetched objects on the storage devices, the presence of an object exists on the storage devices significantly affects the efficiency of the caching. When a new object is being accessed, the cache admission policy decides whether an accessed object should be stored onto the cache devices.

Since the cache performance increases monotonically with the number of objects in the cache, the cache storage space is often full in order to keep the most number of objects in the cache. When an accessed object needs to be stored and the cache space is full, the cache replacement policy decides which object should be deleted from the cache storage to release space. The choice of whether an object is kept in the cache is determined by the cache replacement policy. Thus, the cache replacement policy significantly affects the efficiency of caching.

Memory cache replacement policies assign a cache value to each object in the cache. This cache value decides the priority of keeping the object in the cache. When space is needed to store a new object in cache, the cache replacement function will choose the object with the lowest cache value and delete it to release space. As a result, the objects with high cache values will remain in the cache.

Different cache replacement policies will assign different cache value to the objects. The traditional LRU method keeps the objects that are accessed most recently. It is simple and easy to implement and the time complexity is very low. All other methods except the LFU method also keep the objects that are accessed recently.

The pattern in accessing multimedia objects has been described. The access pattern of video tapes in the rental stores can be described with a Zipf-like distribution. The long term behaviour of accesses for an individual object follows an exponential curve plus a random effect. The LFU, LUV, and mix methods keep track of the object temperature and remove the coldest objects from the cache first.

Due to the large size of multimedia objects, the cache may completely be occupied by a few objects. To maintain a good cache hit ratio, the priority of keeping large objects in the cache is reduced. Thus, the LRU-min, GD-size, LUV, and mix methods keep the small and recently accessed objects in the cache.

Since multimedia objects in the same local cache level may come from remote storage level at different distances, the latency cost in accessing the remote storage level varies. When cache misses occur, the objects in the remote storage level will be retrieved. Thus, the cache system would perform better if it keeps more objects that take longer to access. The GD-size, LUV, and mix methods include latency cost of objects in the cache to lower the priority of objects that can be easily replaced.

Several cache replacement methods have been described. The methods are either simple to implement but they may not perform optimally. The optimal methods have high time complexity and they are more difficult to implement. The trade-offs between simplicity and efficiency will remain until new cache replacement methods are designed.

The stream dependent caching methods were designed to guarantee continuous delivery for multimedia streams.

The resident leader method stores the beginning segment to hide the latency in accessing the object from the user. It trades off the average response time of requests to reduce the maximum response time of streams.

The variable length segmentation method divides the objects into segments of increasing length. The earlier segments are shorter and have higher cache value. The later segments are longer and have smaller cache value. First, the earlier segments have higher priority to be kept in the cache than the later segments of the same object. The beginning of many streams may be stored in the cache to reduce the start-up latency. Second, the large segments are deleted before the small segments are deleted. The number of segments to be deleted is reduced and the cache replacement algorithm becomes more efficient. Third, the large segments are deleted and it avoids the fragmentation problems.

The video staging method retrieves high bandwidth segments to reduce the necessary WAN bandwidth for streaming. Unfortunately, network congestions happen at any time and the network bandwidth fluctuates a lot. The WAN bandwidth threshold cannot be guaranteed before the reservation based protocols are implemented on today's Internet.

Hotspot caching creates the hotspot segments of objects and these hotspots are stored as preview segments to provide fast object previews from local cache.

Interval caching keeps the shortest intervals of video to maintain the continuity of streams from the local cache content.

Layer based caching adapts the quality of streams to the cache efficiency. It fetches segments in the prefetching window to control the congestion of networks. It finds the victim layer and deletes unpopular segments to achieve fine granularity replacement. It uses the continuity and completeness as metrics to measure the suitability of the caching method for multimedia streams.

The cost based method for wireless clients reduces the quality distortion over the error-prone wireless networks with the help of the cache content. The cache values of the segments are composed of network costs, start-up latency costs, and quality distortion costs. The cache replacement algorithm finds the victim segment and deletes at the granularity of segments.

Research on the large scale operations of Web caches have shown that the benefits on caching Web documents do not increase beyond the capability of a single proxy server. Hierarchical Web caching reduces network latency on requests. Front and rear partitioning reduces the start-up latency of streams. Directory based cooperation avoids the contention on parent proxy server. Hash based cooperation achieves low storage overheads and update overheads. Multiple hotspot caching keeps the hotspot blocks to provide fast local previews.

The performances of various object partitioning methods in cooperative multimedia proxy servers are compared. The performance of cooperative proxy caching is significantly affected by the chosen partitioning method. The partitioning methods creating variable length segments perform better than the methods creating fixed length segments in local metrics. The methods creating multiple segments perform better than the methods creating single segment when cooperative caching is used. Among all methods being investigated, the random multiple hotspot fixed size uses the shortest service time.

About the Author

Philip Kwok Chung Tse is now with the Department of Electrical and Electronic Engineering of the University of Hong Kong. He received the bachelor of science (Computing Studies) from the University of Hong Kong (1983) and the doctor of philosophy (Computer Science) from the Victoria University of Technology (2002). He has taught computer science and information technology subjects in the University of Hong Kong, the Chinese University of Hong Kong, and the Macquarie University, Sydney. He had worked for more than 12 years in the industry prior to joining the academic sector. His research interests include multimedia information storage and visual information systems.

Index